D1621250

# The
# FAMILY NATURALIST'S COMPANION

## MIKE TOWNS

HAMLYN

Published 1985 by
Hamlyn Publishing
A division of The Hamlyn Publishing Group Ltd,
Bridge House, London Road,
Twickenham, Middlesex TW1 3SB

Copyright © Charles Herridge Ltd 1985

All rights reserved. No part of this publication may
be reproduced, stored in a retrieval system or
transmitted, in any form or by any means, electronic,
mechanical, photocopying, recording or otherwise
without the prior permission of Hamlyn Publishing
and the copyright holder.

Produced by Charles Herridge Ltd,
Woodacott, Northam, Devon EX39 1NB
Typesetting by P & M Typesetting, Exeter, Devon EX1 1LG
Printed in Italy by New Interlitho SpA, Milan
ISBN 0 600 30611 9

Line illustrations by Ethan Danielson
Half tone illustrations by David Webb, by courtesy of Linden
Artists Ltd, London

Colour illustrations by Graham Allen, Trevor Boyer, Jim
Channell, John Francis, Tim Hayward,
Stuart Lafford, Alan Male, Colin
Newman, Eric Rowe, Rod Sutterby, by
courtesy of Linden Artists Ltd, London

# INTRODUCTION

Watching and learning about wildlife are very rewarding and a great deal of fun but, perhaps more importantly, they can lead to a deeper understanding and appreciation of the natural world. There are more threats to wildlife and the environment today than ever before. By the year 2000AD most of the world's tropical rainforest will have been destroyed; as many as 25,000 species of plants and animals are threatened with extinction, and even in Britain much of our most fascinating and remarkable wildlife is dangerously reduced in numbers. British bats, for instance, have declined so rapidly and unexpectedly that now all species have been given protection by law, otters have disappeared from most of England's rivers and the large blue butterfly, an insect with a wonderfully complex life history, became extinct in Britain in 1983. Only through an understanding of the natural world can we hope to conserve it, and through understanding anyone who cares about wildlife can make an important contribution to its survival — even in their own backyards. However, to gain understanding you must first find out about wildlife, and it can be difficult to know where to begin.

Despite the enormous numbers of books about wildlife, books on the identification of species and books on particular fields of wildlife study, I am still constantly asked by schoolchildren and adults, 'How do I go about studying wildlife?' My job requires me to have a broad knowledge of the countryside and the things that live in it, and most people want to acquire a similar background rather than study one narrow branch of natural history. Most wildlife books give little help to the beginner who wants to learn the techniques of studying wildlife, so in writing this book I have tried to bridge the gap between the budding specialist and the enthusiastic beginner. In fact, I have tried to write the book that I would have liked to have had when I was just starting to learn about wildlife. The book is not only a guide to species but is also an introduction to the biology and life histories of our common (and sometimes not so common) plants and animals. It is also a practical guide, with advice on what clothing to wear, what equipment to use and where to get it, and methods of study. It also suggests places to visit where you can see some of Britain's most outstanding scenery and wildlife. Above all, though, I intend the book to be a family book that will bring the pleasure of shared experience to everyone, young or old. To this end I have included a series of projects that can be carried out by all the family in the countryside or in the reader's own garden. These are intended both to help wildlife and to give pleasure and information.

## ACKNOWLEDGEMENTS

I wish to thank Guinness Superlatives Ltd for permission to use extracts from the *Guinness Book of Records*, the Henry Doubleday Research Association for allowing the reproduction of details of their hedgehog hibernation box and the author of *Experiments with your Microscope* by Henry Darlington (© Henry Darlington published by Corgi Books 1977) for the Feather Windmill and Feather Glider projects. I am also indebted to my wife Elaine who typed my manuscript and was a patient source of help and advice. Thanks too for the forebearance of Anthony and Georgia.

# CONTENTS

# BIRDS

Of all the creatures in the animal kingdom that can fly, only birds have truly mastered the air. Buzzards soar for hours on rising air currents with hardly a wingbeat, while the peregrine falcon can swoop out of the sky at over 100 mph in pursuit of its prey. Some birds, such as the albatross, stay in the air constantly, coming to the ground only to nest. Others, however, have lost their power of flight altogether. The penguins, for instance, use their wings as flippers to propel them through water.

## FEATHERS and FLIGHT

The key to the success of birds is feathers. When the fossil remains of the first primitive bird, the Archaeopteryx, were discovered, scientists were amazed to see the feathers. Without feathers, they would have said that the Archaeopteryx was just another reptile. Even today, birds are still remarkably similar to their dinosaur ancestors, and their closest living relatives are crocodiles, another ancient group which also belonged to the dinosaur order.

Feathers are, in fact, just modified reptile scales. Many reptiles have scales extended into sharp points or odd-shaped spines but in birds these have become more complex. Scientists think that originally the cold-blooded ancestors of birds evolved feathers to keep themselves warm. With only slight changes in feather length they were soon able to glide from tree to tree and eventually to fly.

There are two main types of feather: flight feathers and contour feathers. Flight feathers are found on the wings, are long and have a series of hooked barbules that link together to make a solid barrier to air, providing the lift needed for flight when the bird flaps its wings. Contour feathers are smaller than flight feathers and have hooked barbules along only part of their length. Nearest the body they are quite fluffy. These feathers not only keep the bird warm but also streamline the body, making flight easier.

To keep the barbules hooked together, birds constantly have to comb their feathers with their beaks. This is known as 'preening'. When birds preen they also rub their beaks over a special oil gland on

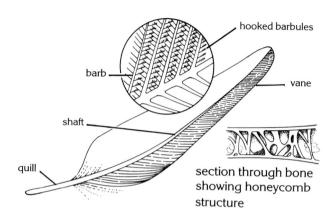

a typical flight feather

the rump. The oil is spread over the feathers and helps keep them waterproof and in good condition. Waterproofing is especially important for birds which live on water or dive under water for their food.

Bird bones are interesting, too. Unlike reptilian or mammalian bones, they have a honeycomb structure, which makes them very light and surprisingly strong. This reduction in weight enables birds to fly at speed for great distances.

The body shape of birds is very important for flight and therefore all birds are very similar in form. Birds don't spend all their lives in the air, though, and they have evolved a startling variety of bill shapes and foot shapes, each precisely adapted for the habitat the birds came to live in. Long bills are used to probe for food in mud-flats or tree and rock crevices, and stout, powerful bills are used to crush seeds and nuts. Lots of fish-eating birds have backward-pointing teeth in their bills to prevent the fish escaping once they have been caught, and birds of prey have strong, hooked beaks ideal for tearing the flesh of their victims. The four-toed perching feet of early birds have also undergone many changes. Swimming birds have evolved webbed feet or fringed toes to paddle with, swamp-living species have elongated toes to help spread their weight over mud and floating vegetation, preventing them from sinking, and birds of prey have enormously powerful talons to grasp their prey.

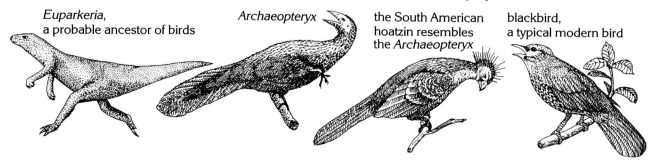

*Euparkeria*, a probable ancestor of birds

*Archaeopteryx*

the South American hoatzin resembles the *Archaeopteryx*

blackbird, a typical modern bird

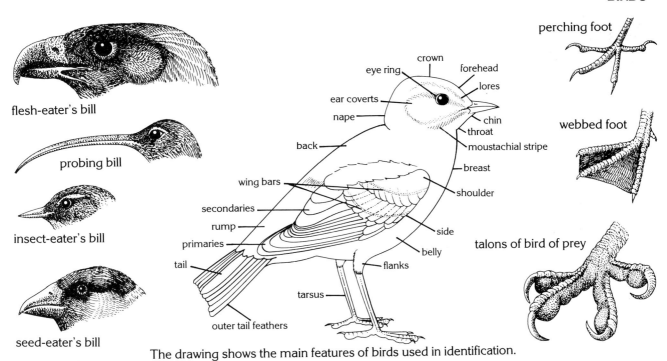

flesh-eater's bill

probing bill

insect-eater's bill

seed-eater's bill

perching foot

webbed foot

talons of bird of prey

crown
eye ring
forehead
lores
ear coverts
nape
chin
throat
back
moustachial stripe
breast
wing bars
secondaries
shoulder
rump
primaries
side
belly
tail
flanks
tarsus
outer tail feathers

The drawing shows the main features of birds used in identification.

# COURTSHIP and NEST-BUILDING

Feathers and beaks also have a different purpose: they are important for courtship and nest-building. Cock birds often have gaudy plumages or bright splashes of colour to attract the attention of hen birds during courtship and mating. The feathers of hen birds are usually drab to provide camouflage on the nest. This is particularly true of ground-nesting birds, which are very vulnerable to predators.

Birds' nests are enormously varied. The guillemot has no nest at all and lays its eggs directly on to bare rock ledges. At the other extreme, the golden eagle builds a massive stick nest which can weigh over a ton. Nests can be grouped into four types: the familiar cup nests of the blackbird and chaffinch, the domed nests of long-tailed tits and goldcrests, the hole nests excavated by woodpeckers or the natural crevices in rocks and trees used by jackdaws and tits, and the simple ground nests of the waders. Beaks are skilfully used to collect and weave sticks, cobwebs and hair. Mud is collected to plaster the inside of the nest, or in the case of the house martin, to build a complete nest. Swifts collect floating material while on the wing and glue it together with saliva.

Throughout the nesting period the cock bird sings vigorously to establish his territory. Singing is a bird's way of saying 'Keep out, Private property'. When two cock birds meet at the boundaries of their territories, they will sing loudly against one another and possibly fight until one gives way. Usually, the stronger and more determined bird will have a bigger territory. The size of the territory and its defence is important because that is where the parent birds will gather food for themselves and their chicks. If the territory is too small they will be unable to feed and raise their families. Birds such as gannets which feed in the open sea and have nesting sites crowded close together also have territories. The gannet's territory is only a small space around the nest, yet the sitting bird will kill any intruder if it enters its nest space.

Young chicks grow rapidly and soon have to fend for themselves, although their parents sometimes teach them how to catch their food. Learning to fly can be difficult for some and the parent birds have to push them out of the nest! How incredible then that in many species the young birds, only weeks out of the nest, have to fly hundreds, possibly thousands, of miles on migration.

## BIRD FACTS AND FEATS

**LARGEST BIRD**

| | |
|---|---|
| *Great Britain* | Mute swan, weighing up to 18kg (40lb). |
| *World* | North African ostrich, weighing 156.5kg (345lb) and standing up to 2.74m (9ft) high. |

**SMALLEST BIRD**

| | |
|---|---|
| *Great Britain* | Goldcrest 90mm (3½in) long and weighing between 3.8g and 4.5g (0.108–0.127oz). |
| *World* | Bee hummingbird 5.7cm (2.24 in) in length, half of it bill and tail, and weighing 1.6g (0.056oz), less than a privet hawk moth. |

**MOST AIRBORNE LAND BIRD**

| | |
|---|---|
| *World* | The swift remains airborne for 2-3 years after leaving the nest before it lands to breed. |

**LARGEST NEST**

| | |
|---|---|
| *Great Britain* | The golden eagle's. One nest in Scotland was 4.51m (15ft) deep and had been used for 45 years. |

**MOST FEATHERS**

| | |
|---|---|
| *World* | The whistling swan – 25,216 feathers. |

11

# BIRDS of TOWN and CITY

*Swifts fly directly into small crevices under roof tiles, and house martins build cup nests of mud under the eaves. Sparrows nest in the most unlikely places, including street lamp housings.*

To us a city is an alien form on a natural landscape, a monster of glass and concrete that swallows up the land and devours the countryside. Surprisingly, to many birds there is little difference between a windy, high-rise apartment block or a town house and a natural cliff-face with its rock ledges and deep crevices. Kestrels nest on window ledges, seagulls on chimney pots and swifts find their way into tiny gaps under the eaves to build their nests. Winter brings thousands of birds to city centres, where they roost on ledges at night, benefiting from the warmth of heated buildings and the generally higher temperature. Overhanging eaves are colonised by house martins which build cup nests of mud; previously they were confined to a few cliff-faces or overhanging rock ledges. Swallows find the cross-beams of a garden shed a marvellous substitute for a ledge in a cave entrance. Towns and cities have become a major habitat for both these birds and without buildings to nest in their populations would be very much reduced.

New habitats are quickly exploited by adaptable birds. During medieval times city streets were populated by ravens and kites scavenging for refuse thrown into gutters. Modern refuse tips also attract their birds, black-headed gulls in particular, which now spend most of their lives scavenging amongst rubbish and rarely, if ever, visit the sea, even to nest. Many quite shy birds now live happily alongside us in our cities and gradually decreasing levels of pollution mean that many more species are able to move into built-up areas and to survive in neglected corners and overgrown wastelands.

Overgrown railway sidings, thick with shrubs and tussocky grassland, and undeveloped wasteland beside rivers and canals run into the heart of most of our major cities. Along these green corridors come the bolder birds of the countryside and migrant birds too, often unseen, use them as they prepare to leave on their long journeys. The sprawling buildings of large industrial complexes and abandoned derelict buildings are adopted by sparrows and pigeons for roosting and nesting, and also, surprisingly, by tawny owls which are quite often found in cities.

12

The **pigeon** is probably the best-known and most photographed bird in the world. Every town square, city park and monument has its share of pigeons, sometimes in flocks of thousands. The birds become very tame and are fed by well-wishers and by people who want to be photographed covered in birds – and bird droppings! Town pigeons are descendants of the stock dove which was tamed and bred in the Middle Ages as a source of food, and since the nineteenth century as a fancy pet. Wild stock doves live on rocky sea coasts, nesting on cliffs; city buildings with their vertical faces and jutting ledges are probably not too different from their ancestral home.

**House sparrows,** although far more abundant than the pigeon, are often overlooked. Chirpy and cheeky, they are present in all built-up areas and around farm buildings. They feed on a variety of weed seeds and grains, gathering in flocks in late summer to feed on the ripening corn of the countryside. They build large, untidy nests of fibre, straw, hair and feathers in buildings or behind ivy.

Well-known but unloved, the **starling** breeds in a great variety of habitats and is highly successful in towns and cities, where it nests in buildings or holes in trees. It is a greedy, noisy, aggressive bird that chases off smaller birds from garden bird tables, bringing down on it the anger of the house owner. Winter populations are swollen by immigrants from northern Europe, possibly doubling the total number of starlings present in Britain. Together they form huge flocks which roost in thousands on buildings in London and other major cities. Starlings eat enormous numbers of insects. One pair was found to feed its young as many as 27,000 insects, a quarter of them leatherjackets, from hatching to their leaving the nest.

Although superficially similar in appearance, swifts and house martins are not related. **Swifts** have independently evolved a way of life similar to that of the swallow family and can truly be said to be masters of the air. They remain airborne throughout their lives except for the brief period when they build their nests and incubate their young. Even nest material is collected on the wing. Their nests are built under the eaves of houses and the birds use their saliva to cement it together.

**House martins** also nest under eaves but they build cup nests of mud pellets stuck against the wall. They are colonial, several pairs building close to each other, and they often return to the same nest site year after year.

Rarest of the town-dwelling birds is the **black redstart.** It first started to breed regularly in Britain in the 1940s, in bombed buildings and on derelict sites. Rebuilding after the war reduced its numbers but it soon began to nest on power station buildings, factories, marshalling yards and old walls. Thirty or forty pairs now breed regularly in the south-east and on occasion as many as a hundred pairs may nest.

House sparrow
14.5cm, 5¾in

Pigeon 33cm, 13in

Black redstart
14cm, 5½in

Starling 21.5cm, 8½in

House martin
13cm, 5in

Swift 16.5cm, 6½in

# BIRDS of PARKS and GARDENS

*The robin is the friendliest garden bird and the wood pigeon one of the most destructive, causing damage to green vegetables. A bird table will attract many different species of birds to a garden.*

Running through every town and city there are ribbons of greenery bringing the countryside to the dusty streets. Large parks with wide open spaces and tall trees may be a haven for wildlife among the buildings and traffic. Surburban gardens are perhaps even better refuges – back to back, a cluster of gardens can equal the area of a town park and contain within it an astonishing variety of habitats.

Gardens resemble areas of wild scrubland — masses of small shrubs with an occasional tall tree and close mown lawns in between. In the wild these patches of grass would be cropped by grazing animals such as rabbits. Gardens differ from natural scrub in the greater variety of plants that they contain. Shrubs from all corners of the world provide birds with a succession of berries and fruit, and insect pests such as greenfly, which are the main prey of many birds, thrive in the unnatural conditions of cultivation. Smooth lawns provide an ideal catching ground for blackbirds and thrushes as unwary worms venture to the surface. Many people now provide bird feeding tables in their gardens and this has begun to attract some unusual birds such as woodpeckers and birds of prey. Regular feeding by householders can sometimes enable large numbers of birds to survive hard winters that would otherwise cause their deaths. Garden ponds are an important source of water for birds in hot, dry weather and they will travel long distances to drink from and bathe in them. The dense evergreen trees and hedges that are to be found in our gardens make excellent nesting cover and the thick growth provided by regular pruning of small trees and shrubs creates perfect nesting sites for small song-birds.

Ancient royal hunting parks are often situated close to or inside the boundaries of our large cities. For centuries they were protected for the sport of kings and now their ancient stag-headed trees and herds of semi-wild grazing deer are preserved for our recreation. Here we can see not only the common garden birds but also the more unusual woodland species that are usually confined to more rural areas.

The melodious song of the **blackbird** is one of the first bird songs of the morning. From high on a prominent perch the male's song carries across the rooftops. There are thought to be as many as ten million blackbirds in Britain, making it one of our commonest birds, and the densest populations are found in parks and gardens. They are mostly ground feeders, taking worms and snails and also soft fruit and berries. The male blackbird with his black feathers and orange bill is quite unmistakable but the dark-brown female can easily be mistaken for a song thrush.

The **song thrush** has a more speckled breast than the female blackbird. Like the blackbird it uses a high perch to deliver its beautiful song, with many repeated phrases. These birds are often seen on lawns, standing upright with their heads cocked to one side, listening for worms. Snails, insects and

especially is a garden favourite, often put through its paces by the use of intelligence-testing containers where the bird has to solve the puzzle to get the reward of a peanut. It feeds more commonly on the ground than do other tits and has a large bill with which it can hammer open hazel-nuts, which it collects and wedges into the bark of trees. As well as nest boxes and old woodpecker holes in trees, great tits are known to nest in a variety of odd sites such as letter-boxes and lamp-posts.

**Blue tits** also use lamp-posts, but as a roost rather than as a place to nest. A number of birds will huddle into the lamp housing to get the benefit of the heat from the lamp and may even extend their feeding time by snapping up the moths attracted to the light of the lamp. It is the most attractive of the tits, delighting us with its acrobatic antics as it breaks open peanuts on a string, or feeds upside-down on

Song thrush 23cm, 9in

Great tit 14cm, 5½in

Blue tit 11.5cm, 4½in

Hedge sparrow 14.5cm, 5¾in

Blackbird 25.5cm, 10in

berries also make up a large part of their diet. Snails are carried to a stone – an 'anvil' – and dashed against it until their shells are broken.

Since more people have started to provide food for birds at bird tables, particularly in winter, the tits have become regular visitors to gardens. Blue tits and great tits are by far the commonest tits and take readily to nest boxes provided for them. The **great tit**

suspended kitchen scraps. In woodlands they perform in exactly the same way, hanging on the ends of branches as they search for insects.

In contrast to the lively tits the **hedge sparrow,** or **dunnock,** is a secretive bird. It is often overlooked but is really quite common in gardens. The long, slender bill distinguishes it at once from the true sparrows. It feeds on the ground, picking up insects and seeds.

Robin 14cm, 5½in

Greenfinch 14.5cm, 5¾in

Tawny owl 38cm, 15in

Chaffinch 15cm, 6in

The **robin** is regarded as the typical British garden bird. Friendly, easily tamed, and adopted as the nation's national bird, it follows gardeners about their work, picking up worms and small insects disturbed by their digging and hoeing. Despite their tameness robins are very aggressive towards each other. The bright red breast is used as a signal to tell other birds to keep away, but fights are frequent. Robins are very much at home with man, nesting in such strange places as old kettles, hats and under the bonnets and wheel arches of cars. They have a pleasant, almost sad, warbling song which may become lost in the general chorus of bird song in the spring, but in autumn, freed from the competition of the migrant birds, the carrying song, delivered from a roof top or tall tree, is a herald of winter. In built-up areas robins often sing at night because of the extra light from the street lamps, and are regularly mistaken for nightingales. This leads to letters and stories in the press every year.

At the other extreme, the **tawny owl** is a bird most people would never associate with built-up areas but it is quite common in parks and gardens, even in the centre of our biggest cities, where they feed mainly on sparrows. Mostly a woodland bird, the tawny owl hunts small mammals and birds at night, using sensitive ears and large eyes which have the ability to gather in even the faintest glimmerings of light to help it search out its prey. Owls' feathers have 'frills' along the edges to deaden the sound of their flight so that their unlucky victim has no warning of their approach. The indigestible remains of their prey — bones, fur and feather — are regurgitated as compact pellets, usually at a favourite roosting site. Examination of these remains is a valuable aid to discovering what owls eat. Tawny owls make the familiar 'to-whit-to-whoo' call but they also make a sharp 'kee-vik' sound.

The **chaffinch** is not only a common garden bird, it is also one of the most abundant of British birds. In winter their numbers are boosted by arrivals from the Continent and they descend in large flocks on farmland where they search for grain and weed seeds or gather under beech trees to eat beech mast. They are regular visitors to bird tables, nesting in bushes and thick hedges around the garden.

**Greenfinches** prefer evergreen trees or tall, dense hedges to nest in, picking a high point from which to deliver their rattling song. Their large bills are used to crush seeds and grain but are also well adapted to breaking up peanuts which they take avidly from bird tables and nut-bags. It seems likely that the survival of greenfinches during hard winters may now depend on garden peanuts.

The charming and minute **wren** is a common garden bird but because of its secretive habits it is not often noticed. It is most likely to bring attention to itself by its very loud song, quite out of proportion to its small size. Wrens are present wherever there are bushes and shrubs and their spherical nests are built behind bark and ivy or in holes in walls. The male builds several nests for his mate to choose from and where the food supply is plentiful may have more than one mate. Being such small birds, wrens suffer greatly during severe winters and many die. Populations recover fast, however, and they also try to beat the cold by roosting communally, huddling close together for warmth. Forty or fifty wrens have been found packed together in a single nest box.

The **pied wagtail,** usually seen as a solitary bird on garden lawns or town streets, is also a communal rooster. In winter thousands of them gather at night in trees and on buildings in city squares and they have also learnt how to enter heated greenhouses through the air vents. Small flying insects are the mainstay of their diet, which they catch with short, fast runs or a hopping flight into the air, using their tails to manoeuvre.

Two recent colonists of parks and gardens are wood pigeons and black-headed gulls. **Wood pigeons** are rather shy birds of woodland and scrub but in town parks they have become quite tame, even feeding from the hand like the familiar town pigeon. On farmland they feed on grain, clover and green vegetables, often forming large flocks. In gardens too they can become troublesome pests, eating cabbages and other greens, particularly in dry weather or in areas by the sea. Their nests, just flimsy platforms of twigs, are built in trees or tall bushes and occasionally on buildings. The young are fed on a cheesy, protein-rich milk produced in the bird's crop.

The aggressive and noisy **black-headed gull** almost became extinct in Britain in the eighteenth century. By the nineteenth century, however, benefiting from waste food and scraps poured on to city rubbish dumps, its numbers had soared and it had penetrated most of our major towns and cities. The resident population in Britain numbers around 100,000 individuals but in winter thousands of birds arrive from Europe and there may be over 200,000 black-headed gulls in London alone. Each evening these gulls fly out to roost on reservoirs and lakes, sometimes in flocks tens of thousands strong. Although named the black-headed gull, the summer hood is chocolate rather than black and in winter this is reduced to a dark smudge behind each eye.

Pied wagtail 18cm, 7in

Wren 9.5cm, 3¾in

Wood pigeon 40.5cm, 16in

Black-headed gull 38cm, 15in

# BIRDS of WOOD and SCRUB

*Sparrowhawks chase small birds through the tree tops, jays collect and bury acorns, and woodpeckers probe in rotten wood for grubs. Long-tailed tits flit in small parties amongst the scrub and the woodland edge.*

Before man began to clear the ancient woodlands for agriculture, broadleaved forest was the natural vegetation over most of Britain. Where trees died or decayed, or freak winds felled whole groves of trees, light would penetrate the forest floor and shrubs and saplings would soon grow. Berry-bearing shrubs and small trees, which had been denied a place in the dense forest, would flourish for a time, relying on woodland birds to disperse their seeds. If our land was left untended, most of it would very soon return to its natural state. Shrubs and briar would form dense scrub through which trees would eventually grow and spread to form closed, shady woodlands.

It is not surprising, therefore, that the majority of our common birds are dependent on woodland or scrub for feeding and nesting. The agile and acrobatic tits are at home in the high canopy of the trees where they search the swinging twigs and branches for food; woodpeckers hammer away bark from dead and dying branches to expose the insects beneath, while below blackbirds and robins sieve

through the leaf litter in search of worms and snails. Holes excavated in rotten wood by woodpeckers are later used by many woodland birds for their nests, and the strong, upright branches of trees support the large stick nests of birds of prey, or birds such as herons which forage outside the wood for food.

Scrubland shrubs carry heavy crops of berries in the autumn which feed huge flocks of winter immigrants as well as sustaining resident birds. Soft berries such as hawthorn are taken by thrushes, fieldfares and redwings, while hard seeds such as those of the spindle are eaten by finches with their powerful crushing beaks.

Dense young thickets provide night-time shelter and protection for roosting birds that sometimes descend in their thousands on suitable habitats. Starlings, magpies, jays and thrushes all use scrub and woodland for roosting. Where there is a thick ground-cover of bramble and herbage, warblers build small dome- and cup-shaped nests near the ground and skulk unseen among the bushes.

Nightingale 16.5cm, 6½in

Mistle thrush 27cm, 10½in

Redstart 14cm, 5½in

Jay 34.5cm, 13½in

In the popular imagination the most magical and mysterious of all British birds must be the **nightingale.** Its beautiful liquid song, delivered during the day or night, is thought to be one of the most perfect of bird songs. Once it was so common that its song was a familiar sound in town squares but now, due to changes in countryside management and the loss of much of its preferred habitats, its numbers have declined. Broadleaved woodland with a good shrub layer and ground flora are favoured, especially where coppicing is still being carried out. They are migrant birds. The male nightingales arrive early in the spring and sing to establish their territories before the arrival of the females. The females build their nests low down in dark places among a tangle of vegetation. Like thrushes, their close relatives, they feed on the ground, searching for worms, beetles and moth larvae, although they also eat berries in the autumn.

The **mistle thrush** is also a fruit eater and is named after its great liking for the berries of the mistletoe. It is a pugnacious bird, particularly in defence of its young or a chosen food supply. Cats and humans are regularly 'dive-bombed' and even struck by mistle thrushes if they approach too close to the birds' young. In winter, they also fight off other birds that approach berry-laden holly bushes in their territory, thereby preserving the berries for themselves until late winter when food is scarce. Mistle thrushes can easily be confused with song thrushes but they are larger, have bolder spots and a greyish-brown back. These birds can be found in large gardens as well as in woods and their habit of singing from a very high perch in the middle of a storm has given them the name of 'storm cocks'.

Another relative of the thrushes is the **redstart,** a fairly abundant summer visitor to Britain distinguished by its striking reddish-brown tail. The male, with reddish-brown breast, black throat and grey back is an extraordinarily handsome creature, and he uses his colours to great advantage during courtship with display flights and beautiful tail-fanning rituals. Redstarts are most common in the west in open oakwoods, especially where there are areas of open grassland with old stone walls nearby. It nests in holes in trees and walls.

Equally exotic but far more secretive is the **jay.** It is a woodland bird but can also be common in parks and large gardens where, surprisingly, it may become quite tame. More often heard than seen, its call is a harsh screech as it hunts among treetops for eggs, nestling birds and acorns. Usually only its white rump is seen as it flees from the presence of an intruder. During years of peak populations in Europe our native jays may be joined by large numbers of continental immigrants.

Birds of the tit family are probably the most noticeable species in woodlands and scrub. In winter they travel in mixed flocks, drawing attention to themselves by their constant twittering. The tiny **long-tailed tit** is often regarded as the most endearing of the tits and has been aptly described as 'a ball of wool on the end of a knitting needle'. Parties from eight to twenty or more in number move among the trees and hang upside-down on the ends of the flimsiest twigs in search of small insects. Being such small birds they are susceptible to cold and numbers fluctuate according to the severity of the winter. They roost communally during the winter, packing tightly together in the middle of thick shrubs. In the breeding season a pair build an enclosed purse nest from moss, cobwebs and hair. This is built against a tree trunk and covered with lichen for camouflage.

Of the larger tits the shy **marsh tit** is very much a bird of dense deciduous woodland. These tits remain in pairs over the winter, rarely wandering from their chosen territory and joining tit flocks only briefly as they pass. It is difficult to distinguish the marsh tit from the willow tit by their looks alone but the nasal, 'churring' call of the marsh tit is distinctive. Marsh tits eat mainly insects in summer but in winter they eat seeds, some of which are stored in bark crevices or in hiding places on the ground.

The **coal tit** is found throughout Britain in all types of woodland but it prefers conifer woods and has benefited from recent widespread conifer planting. The coal tit is easily distinguished from other tits by a white patch on the back of the head. Unlike other tits, the coal tit has a long, thin beak useful for probing among pine needles for insect prey. Coal tits are hole nesters like other tits but in the absence of holes in trees they will nest in old mouse holes on the ground. Like marsh tits they store food in bark crevices.

**Goldcrests** are regular companions of tits in their winter feeding flocks, when their numbers may be swollen by immigrants from Scandinavia. They are the smallest of British birds, weighing only 5g; the wren, their nearest rival in size, weighs 9g. They are common in deciduous woods but like the coal tit have a preference for conifers. Their nests, made of cobwebs, wool, moss and feathers, and covered in lichen, are suspended beneath branches.

The long, curved bill of the **treecreeper** is ideal for extracting insects from crevices in bark. A small, secretive, mouse-like bird, it climbs trees in a jerky spiral, moving up the trunk and then flying down to the base of the next tree, using its short, stiff tail as a prop as it climbs the tree trunks. It nests behind loose bark or ivy and can often be seen with tits in winter flocks.

Long-tailed tit 14cm, 5½in; tail 7.5cm, 3in

Marsh tit 11.5cm, 4½in

Goldcrest 9cm, 3½in

Coal tit 11.5cm, 4½in

Treecreeper 13cm, 5in

The warblers are a large group of birds well represented in Britain. They are migrants, coming to Britain in the summer from Africa, and their beautiful, varied songs liven the woods and hedgerows. All the warblers have pointed, insect-eating bills and build their nests on or near the ground, usually in dense vegetation.

closed canopy and it has a fondness for beech woods. The song is a distinctive trill preceded by a quiet, plaintive call. Like the other 'leaf warblers' – so called because they search for prey among the canopy of leaves – the wood warbler's nest is a domed structure built on the ground, usually in a hollow.

Willow warbler 11cm, 4¼in

Blackcap 14cm, 5½in

Crossbill 16.5cm, 6½in

Wood warbler 12.5cm, 4¾in

Pied flycatcher 13cm, 5in

The **willow warbler** is our commonest warbler, with a total population of over one million birds. It arrives in Britain in March or April after a continuous flight at a steady 24 mph that brings it across the Sahara desert to our shores. Its quiet, melodious song, a twittering warble that gently fades away, can be heard from every woodland, hedgerow and thicket where there is some ground cover of bramble and dense, low vegetation.

The **blackcap** is a warbler chiefly of woodland, though it also inhabits scrub where there are scattered trees. Its rich, beautiful song is thought by many to rival that of the nightingale. An insect eater, in winter it also takes berries and fruit. In recent years this bird has begun to overwinter and comes to bird tables to feed on kitchen scraps. The male has a black-capped head and the females and juveniles have brown caps. The nest is built several feet above the ground in a thicket and some of the nest material is woven around plant stems for extra support.

The **wood warbler** is a bird of woodlands and is found over most of Britain especially in the north and west. It prefers tall-grown, fairly open forest with a

Another bird of the north and west is the **pied flycatcher** and it too migrates from Africa in the spring. It is very selective in its choice of habitat, preferring open oak woodlands with a relatively high rainfall. Sites near water are preferred for nesting and these birds often nest socially, two or three pairs living close to each other. Pied flycatchers have an upright stance and flutter from twig to twig in search of caterpillars on oaks. The male is black and white, his mate brown and cream.

The strangely-crossed bill of the **crossbill** is ideal for twisting seeds out of pine cones. It is a bird of Scotland and East Anglia where there are extensive pine forests but it is a mobile bird, making regular migrations to new areas in search of abundant cone crops. In bad seed years the British population is augmented by arrivals from the Continent and at this time the birds can be found far from their usual haunts. Crossbills climb branches with their beaks and feet, parrot-fashion, and often hang upside-down at the ends of branches to get at the pine cones. They nest very early, in January or February, so that the young are fledged as the new cones ripen.

The **turtle dove** is another summer migrant from Africa. It is quite common in central, southern and eastern England but largely absent from Scotland and scarce in the west of England and Wales. This patchy distribution is linked to some extent with arable farming. Where this is practised, it provides plenty of weed seeds for the birds to feed on. They also need scrub and woods in which to build their nests – thin platforms of twigs with a skimpy lining of grass, built low down in trees or shrubs.

The **great spotted woodpecker** is the commonest of our woodpeckers. It feeds up in the crowns of trees, extracting insects from rotten wood and beneath loose bark. Nuts are also collected, wedged into bark crevices and hammered open to get at the kernels. Nestling birds are another regular item in its diet. Recently, it has taken to visiting garden bird tables and has learnt, like the tits, to hammer open milk bottle tops to get at the cream on top of the milk. The male sports a crimson patch on the back of his head and drums out his territorial 'song' on a hollow branch. The great spotted woodpecker excavates its nest in a rotten tree or branch. Its old, abandoned nest holes are later used by many other hole-nesting birds.

The **sparrowhawk** can now be found throughout Britain but in the early 1960s it almost became extinct. Before 1963 certain agricultural seed dressings were poisoning the birds that the sparrowhawks fed on and they in turn succumbed, dying in large numbers. Seed dressings are now more tightly controlled and the sparrowhawk has recovered well. It is a true woodland bird, nesting in trees – with a preference for conifers – and flying with great agility through treetops and along woodland edges in pursuit of small song-birds. The female is a dull brown and larger than the male, which has a slate-grey back.

The **long-eared owl** is also a bird of woodland and in Britain particularly prefers coniferous forests. It has large ear tufts from which it derives its common name but its true ears are placed much lower down on the sides of the head. The true ears are lop-sided, one being situated lower on the head than the other. This creates a time lag between incoming sound waves and makes it easier for the bird to pinpoint accurately the positon of its prey. Long-eared owls are nocturnal and are only likely to be seen during the day at a roost. Communal roosts are formed in winter when immigrants also arrive from Scandinavia. If they are disturbed these birds will stretch themselves upwards, to look even longer and thinner than they are. Abandoned squirrel dreys and old crows' nests are taken over for nesting. The female stays with the young and feeds them with small mammals and birds – brought by the male.

Turtle dove 28cm, 11in

Great spotted woodpecker 23cm, 9in

Sparrowhawk
28–38cm, 11–15in

Long-eared owl 35.5cm, 14in

# BIRDS of FARMLAND and HEDGEROW

*Lapwings and skylarks fly above their territories to stake their claim while yellowhammers sit atop a hedge to deliver their song. Partridges gather their broods into the cover of hedges and dense grass.*

Modern 'prairie' farms have enormous fields which are regularly ploughed and reseeded and contain few if any hedges to break the monotony of the landscape. They can support very few birds. Although ground-nesters such as skylarks may nest in ploughed fields, the majority of species on farmland need hedgerows for feeding and nesting. Where hedges have been removed bird populations have drastically declined. Nest sites are lost not only in the hedgerow itself but also in the weedy, grassy border alongside it, and weed seeds, berries and insects — vital foods for farmland birds — are no longer available.

Where farms do retain a pattern of arable field and permanent pasture, criss-crossed by well-grown hedgerows, bird life is abundant. In good farmland country most bird species which prefer scrub and the woodland edge are present, especially where tall trees are allowed to grow in the hedge. Songbirds of open countryside might use a lone hedgerow as a song post. Overgrown hawthorn hedges, thick with berries in autumn, are visited by chattering flocks of wintering fieldfares and redwings that rapidly strip the bushes of their red fruits.

In lowland river valleys most of the fields are turned over to permanent pasture. Here the soil is rich and damp, teeming with worms, leatherjackets and beetles, all avidly taken by foraging flocks of lapwings and rooks. In summer these fields ring to the call of a variety of ground-nesting birds, while in winter huge mixed flocks gather to feed in favoured river meadows. Black-headed gulls keep a close watch on lapwing flocks on pasture, flying in to harass them and rob them of any large prey that they cannot swallow immediately.

Old or disused farm buildings and decaying trees provide roosts and nesting places for owls, the farmer's rat-catching friends. Sadly, increasing modernisation and mechanisation on farms is rapidly reducing the numbers of the most spectacular owl of them all — the barn owl. Dutch elm disease has also hit this bird hard by destroying many of the old trees that it once used for roosting and nesting.

The finches are a colourful group of birds with sturdy bills used for crushing seeds, which are their staple diet. Mixed flocks of finches, sometimes over a thousand strong, roam the winter countryside in search of food. Prettiest of the finches, decked in scarlet and gold, is the **goldfinch.** It is so attractive that during Victorian times it was a popular cage bird, caught by the thousand and sold from market stalls. Their twittering flocks were known, appropriately, as 'charms'. Thistle seeds are their main food and their bills have a fine point which enables them to pluck the seeds from thistle heads, and so avail themselves of a food that other species are unable to exploit. During feeding forays goldfinches travel long distances, often on a regular 'beat', frequently arriving at food sources at roughly the same time each day. They have become increasingly common recently in towns and gardens.

**Bullfinches**, once very much woodland birds, are also invading town parks and gardens. Normally they are shy, secretive birds keeping to the cover of hedgerow and scrub and calling quietly to one another. They are sedentary birds which rarely move far from their home range. They prefer to eat the seeds of trees such as ash but in poor seed years these birds will attack the buds of fruit trees,

systematically stripping the branches and taking as many as thirty buds a minute. In bad years the damage done can reduce a potential fruit crop from several tons to just a few pounds. A unique feature of bullfinches is the development of pouches to carry food for the young during the breeding season.

The commonest bunting found in farmland, on commons and in country lanes is the **yellowhammer**. The female is a dull yellow-brown but the male sports a bright lemon-yellow head and sits atop an exposed perch in a hedgerow to deliver his song.

**Corn buntings** are much less common, preferring open, arable farmland. Their distinctive trilling song has been likened to 'the jangling of a bunch of keys'. These are migrant birds, the males establishing their territory early in the year and before the females arrive. Their territorial song posts command a view of the nest, or nests, for the corn bunting may be polygamous, the male often tending several females. The nests, cups of grass lined with roots and hair, are built late in the year, in May or June, mostly by the female. They also incubate and rear the young, generally without any assistance from the male. The young leave the nest after only nine to twelve days, before they can fly.

Goldfinch 12cm, 4¾in

Bullfinch 14.5cm, 5¾in

Corn bunting 18cm, 7in

Yellowhammer 16.5cm, 6½in

Recent agricultural changes have brought about a decline in the numbers of **skylarks** but they are still a widespread and abundant bird. There are three to four million nesting pairs in Britain and the winter population is swollen by the immigration of continental birds seeking a milder climate. Skylarks are birds of open country, nesting in shallow depressions in the ground, often under tufts of grass. The male hangs high in the sky above the nest singing his beautiful trilling song so characteristic of summer meadows. They do, in fact, sing for much of the year and only deep cold will silence them.

**Lapwings** or **peewits** also make themselves conspicuous by their call as well as their dramatic

mixed arable and pastoral farmland. The female lays her eggs (8–20, sometimes more) in a shallow hollow lined with grass. Eggs are laid at intervals of one or two days and covered with nest material until all the eggs have been laid and are ready for incubation. Partridge young may leave the nest within a day. They grow quickly and can fly at sixteen days, but remain with the parents in a family party until the spring. Delayed incubation means that many eggs are lost to predators but the birds seem able to cope with this. Unfortunately, they have not coped so well with the changes in the countryside. Pesticides, stubble burning and hedgerow removal have reduced their numbers.

Red-legged partridge 35cm, 13¾in

Skylark 18cm, 7in

Pheasant 76–89cm, 30–35in

Lapwing 30.5cm, 12in

Partridge 30cm, 11¾in

and acrobatic courtship flights. Their slow, flapping flight on broad, rounded wings gives them the name lapwing and their call 'pee-wit' gives them their other common name. In some places lapwings were thought to be birds of ill omen because their call sounded like 'be-witched'. Lapwings frequent arable land and pasture and in winter they form very large flocks, often several thousand strong, on lowland marshes. They nest on the ground in shallow depressions. Their young are hatched fully feathered and mobile, leaving the nest within a day or two of hatching to follow their mother in search of food.

The **partridge** is another ground-nesting bird on

The **red-legged partridge**, common in some areas, was introduced from southern Europe in 1770. It is now well established and spreading, preferring open, sandy heaths and stony ground similar to its native habitat. Unlike the partridge it runs rather than flies when disturbed.

The **pheasant** is another bird introduced to Britain, probably by the Normans. Originally a woodland species it is now found on farmland as well as in woods, and in winter may shelter in waterside reed beds. Its flight is strong but it rarely flies more than a few hundred yards, preferring to run, with its long tail streaming behind.

In winter the hedgerows resound with the rattling 'chack-chack-chack' call of the **fieldfare**, a winter visitor from Scandinavia. It is a large thrush which shows a bright white underwing and grey rump in flight. Each year fieldfares, usually in the company of redwings, another winter visitor from Scandinavia, strip berries from hedgerow bushes or search the ground beneath them for insects. The **redwing**, smallest of the thrushes, has a conspicuous eyestripe and red underwings. It succumbs easily to cold and will visit gardens in hard weather, becoming relatively tame in its search for food.

At the other end of the year, the **cuckoo** is regarded as the harbinger of summer in Britain. Every spring newspapers carry the claims of those who think they have heard the earliest cuckoo. It is a large, hawk-like bird with swept-back wings and a long tail, resembling a sparrowhawk not only in shape but also in colour. Early to arrive, cuckoos are also early to leave, the adults returning to Africa in July or August after their eggs are laid. They have no need to rear their young as the eggs are laid in the nests of song-birds. Dunnocks, meadow pipits and reed warblers are favourite hosts, and these foster parents rear the young cuckoos. Cuckoo nestlings eject the eggs and nestlings of the host bird from the nest to ensure that all the food their foster parents collect goes to fuel their own fast-growing bodies.

Among the birds of prey that hunt over farmland the **kestrel** is the commonest. It hovers over fields and rough grassland, flapping its wings to remain stationary in even strongly-blowing wind. Voles, mice, beetles and birds are the main prey, captured by a swift swoop with perhaps a momentary pause just above the ground before the final plunge.

**Buzzards** use a different hunting technique, flying low along the ground to pounce on prey located from a post or low branch or by circling lazily in the sky watching for signs of a potential meal below. The buzzard is mainly a bird of the north and west but since persecution by gamekeepers has been reduced its range is slowly expanding once again. Rabbits were the buzzard's main prey but after myxomatosis reduced the rabbit population they turned to small mammals, beetles and ground-dwelling creatures. Buzzards build large nests made of sticks in the branches of trees or on rock ledges.

Fieldfare 25.5cm, 10in

Buzzard 51–56cm, 20–22in

Redwing 21cm, 8¼in

Kestrel 34.5cm, 13½in

Cuckoo 33cm, 13in

Barn owl 34.5cm, 13½in

Little owl 21.5cm, 8½

Carrion crow 47cm, 18½in

Rook 45.5cm, 18in

The **barn owl** is the typical farmyard owl, nesting and roosting in old barns and buildings, lofts and church towers. It builds no nest, simply depositing its eggs on a ledge, though it will sometimes line a suitable hollow with regurgitated pellets. Strictly nocturnal, barn owls feed on mice, voles and other ground-living night animals. Their flight is silent and their white faces and undersides give them a ghostly appearance. Strange too is their varied repertoire of calls: snorts, hisses, snores and a terrifying screech. In all likelihood barn owls have been responsible for quite a number of ghost stories, especially when they have emerged from their nest sites coated in the luminous bacteria that grows on rotten wood!

The smallest owl in Britain, often seen by day, is the **little owl**. Native to southern Europe and the Mediterranean it was introduced into England in the late nineteenth century and has since spread to most parts of the country. No bigger than a starling it is a bird of open farmland, hunting principally for insects and other invertebrates. Small mammals and birds make up the rest of its diet. Little owls nest in holes in trees and farm buildings or in a burrow in the ground.

Insects, particularly wireworms and leatherjackets provide regular food for **rooks**. In permanent pasture they dig into the ground to find insects and prolonged dry weather can cause the birds great hardship. Grain and fruit are also taken, habits which upset farmers, resulting in regular rook 'shoots' in arable areas during the winter. Rooks are social birds, feeding in flocks and building their nests in colonies in tall trees, copses and small woodlands. These 'rookeries' may be very large, housing several thousand birds and hundreds of nests, but most are quite small with perhaps only twenty or thirty nests to a colony.

Rooks can be distinguished from **carrion crows** by their whitish faces and the loose, baggy feathers ('trousers') around their thighs. Also, carrion crows are solitary birds though they may gather in small parties in the winter. The bulky cup nest of the carrion crow is usually built high up in a tree with a commanding view of the surrounding countryside. During incubation of the eggs and in the first days after the young are hatched the female is fed by the male. The food taken by carrion crows is very varied, ranging from grains, vegetables and fruit to insects, birds' eggs, nestling birds and carrion.

# BIRDS of HEATH, MOOR and COMMON

*Stonechats watch for insects from a convenient perch and harriers fly low over the ground in search of prey. When disturbed, grouse 'explode' from cover with a loud whirring of wings.*

All over Britain there are areas of land which are unsuitable for intensive agriculture but which for centuries have been grazed or managed by fire. In the lowlands, impoverished sandy soils develop into heathland, thick with heather and gorse. On high, cold, wet uplands there develops a moorland of rough grass, thin and stony and usually grazed by hardy sheep. Commons, often sparsely grazed rough grassland, are traditional features of the British countryside.

All these habitats were created by man centuries ago when he cut down the forests to make pasture for his animals. Worsening climatic conditions in the centuries following and the deterioration of the soil have turned them into the habitats we see today. Despite their very different appearance, their very different flora and their extremes of wetness and dryness, heaths, moors and commons support very much the same species of birds, some of them rare and remarkable.

Open country is ideal for birds of prey. Birds such as the hen harrier lazily quarter the ground while the hobby speeds over the open terrain in pursuit of small birds and insects. Where populations of voles or mice build up to plague proportions in the neglected grassland the day-flying short-eared owl moves in. In winter hundreds arrive here from the Continent to fly with their low flapping flight over the commons.

Of the three types of country, heathland is the most threatened. Because it is the habitat most easily reclaimed for agriculture, its extent has been greatly reduced since the Second World War. Where there were once vast, unbroken tracts of heather and gorse there are now green fields and housing estates. Most heathland species, like those of the moorland, need very large areas of open ground over which to hunt and when that is lost they soon disappear. The Dartford warbler, at the edge of its range in Britain, is now very rare in the southern heaths and the mysterious nightjar has been lost from many of its former haunts because of the destruction of its habitat. Game birds too are suffering from the neglect of moor and heath. Over-burning is destroying the heather moors, robbing the birds of the young shoots and berries on which they feed.

Perched on a fence post or exposed branch the brightly-coloured male **stonechat** surveys his territory, constantly flicking his wings and tail and uttering a sharp call that sounds like two pebbles knocking together. From his perch he swoops down on insects, sometimes briefly hovering before dropping down on to his prey. Insects, particularly ants, are the stonechat's main diet but seed is often taken and the young are fed on caterpillars which are mashed up on a stone. They live and nest on heaths and commons, building their nests low down in gorse or bracken. At the end of the breeding season most British birds migrate to the Mediterranean. The ones that remain, joined by immigrants from

tips, sewage works and railway sidings.

**Meadow pipits** are common in grassy places around the coast, on upland moors and mountain grasslands. Inconspicuous and coloured a dull brown they are most likely to be noticed as they perform their territorial song flight, dropping from the sky with tail upturned and uttering a distinctive triple-noted 'pheet-pheet-pheet' call. Their nests are built in the shelter of a tuft of grass where the female lays 3–5 mottled grey-brown eggs. Meadow pipits are a favourite host species of the cuckoo, the cuckoo's egg blending remarkably well with the host bird's eggs. In winter most meadow pipits move south to the Mediterranean but some remain on

Stonechat 13cm, 5in

Whinchat 12.5cm, 4¾in

Meadow pipit 14.5cm, 5¾in

Linnet 13.5cm, 5¼in

northern Europe, tend to move to western coasts where the climate is milder and winter food more plentiful.

Closely related to the stonechat and similar to it in appearance is the **whinchat**, but it is easily distinguished by its clear eye stripe and the lack of a black hood in the male. It is a summer visitor to Britain, spending its winters in tropical Africa south of the Sahara Desert. The heathlands and rough grasslands of the north and west are the whinchat's strongholds but for successful breeding there must be low, projecting songposts in its habitat. Provided the habitat is right it will nest in newly-planted forestry plantations and in close proximity to man on rubbish

lowland pastures and coastal salt-marshes.

**Linnets** make most unusual winter migrations. By and large, all the British birds move south to the Mediterranean while all the Scandinavian birds move into Britain to replace them! These attractive birds form twittering flocks on scrub-covered commons, heaths, downs and dunes and they often nest socially, a number of pairs building nests in adjacent bushes. Linnets were popular cage birds in the nineteenth century and commercial bird-catching caused a marked fall in their population. They have recovered, however, and are now widespread throughout the countryside, feeding on a variety of weed seeds.

The **Dartford warbler** is a resident bird of warm, dry, southern lowland heaths and has only a precarious hold in Britain. Here, at the extreme edge of its range, it is vulnerable to hard weather and the gradual loss of heathland to agriculture. At times as many as a hundred pairs may be present and widely distributed in the southern counties but after severe winters numbers drop dramatically; only twelve pairs remained after the terrible winter of 1963. It builds its nest of moss, grass and cobweb low down in a bush. The male sings very briefly in March to establish his territory and apart from his harsh 'tchack' is seldom heard singing until the following year.

The **ptarmigan**, a member of the grouse family, is also a bird of extremes. It is very rare in Britain, occurring only on the stony, barren slopes of Scottish mountains. A hardy bird, it survives the winter cold by burrowing into snow with its powerful feathered legs and feet. In winter it becomes completely white, except for its black tail, the perfect camouflage in the wintry mountain wastes. Ptarmigan live permanently above the tree line, descending into the valleys only in the severest cold. They feed on mountain berries and green shoots.

Once considered a bird unique to Britain, the **red grouse** is now believed to be a sub-species of the very common willow grouse of northern Europe. It thrives in the moorlands of the north and west but is suffering from poor husbandry of the moors and their reclamation for agriculture. Red grouse feed on moorland berries and young heather shoots. Regular burning of the heather keeps the plants in good condition and ensures a continuous supply of fresh young growth. The red grouse keeps to cover whenever it can, relying on its brownish-red plumage to hide it, but if disturbed it 'explodes' into a low, whirring flight.

Another bird of the high moorland of the north and west is the **ring ouzel**. It is very similar to the blackbird but is distinguished by its white 'bib' and a silvery-grey sheen on its wings. Ring ouzels winter in the Mediterranean and in the cedar woods of the Atlas Mountains of North Africa, returning to Britain in March and April to nest, usually near mountain streams. Their diet is similar to that of the blackbird: insects, snails and worms, but they also eat large quantities of bilberries and rowan berries in the autumn.

Red grouse 38cm, 15in

Ptarmigan 35.5cm, 14in

Ring ouzel 24cm, 9½in

Dartford warbler 12.5cm, 4¾in

The **nightjar** is a bird of sandy heaths and like the Dartford warbler it is suffering from the widespread destruction of its habitat. Numbers have declined greatly in the past few decades and it is being lost from areas where it was once common. Oddly, planting of conifers on the nightjar's heathland habitat, while causing losses in the short term, may actually help in the long term. When large areas of these plantation trees are clear-felled nightjars are often attracted back, sometimes in good numbers, and the birds may actually prefer the 'edge' habitat of open space and woodland to the original open heath. Nightjars are strictly nocturnal. Hawk-like, they fly at night, catching moths and night-flying insects in their comparatively huge, gaping mouths. By day they roost on low branches or on the ground, relying on their dull, mottled colouring to hide them. The nightjar's song is an unmistakable, far-carrying 'churr' of extraordinary intensity. Delivered at dusk or during the night the sound seems to come and go as the bird slowly rotates its head.

The **hobby** breeds on downs, commons and moorland in southern England, choosing old nests in isolated trees or moorland woods in which to rear its young. Only 100–150 pairs of this beautiful bird of prey breed in England. A small falcon, it is readily recognised by the reddish feathers around its thighs. It is a fast, acrobatic bird with scythe-shaped wings that propel it so fast that it is one of the few raptors able to catch swifts or swallows in flight. Insects provide the major part of the hobby's diet and they usually catch birds only when they are feeding young.

Switching effortlessly from side to side in a low, slow, flapping flight, the **hen harrier** hunts over moorland and coastal marshes, often following banks and ditches in its search for small animals. The male is a striking bird with a slate-grey back and black wingtips. During the nesting season he brings food to his mate. She flies up from the nest, turning upside-down to snatch prey from his talons as he approaches. In winter they roost communally in favoured places, flying in one by one at dusk.

A grass tussock large enough to provide shelter from wind and rain is all the **short-eared owl** needs for a roost. Unlike most owls it flies regularly by day, quartering the ground with slow wingbeats in search of voles. Each winter our resident birds are joined by immigrants from Scandinavia and eastern Europe, large numbers of them gathering in places suffering from vole plagues. They are birds of open country, dunes, downs and marshes.

Nightjar 27cm, 10½in

Hen harrier 45cm, 17½in

Short-eared owl 38cm, 15in

Hobby 30.5–35.5cm, 12–14in

# BIRDS of PONDS, LAKES and RIVERS

*Herons and many other water birds skulk in dense vegetation and are hard to see. Grebes build their floating nests at the edges of reeds and sedge warblers sing from perches on the stems of rush.*

Water is one of the most fascinating and beautiful habitats and water birds are often more than equal to the beauty of their surroundings. Birds inhabit the water surface, dive for food in murky depths or skulk in reed-choked margins. Ducks sieve the flotsam of seeds and insects from the water's edge but some species dive to considerable depths for water weeds or aquatic invertebrates. Many water birds such as the great crested grebe are fish eaters, diving and swimming with great skill in pursuit of their prey, while the kingfisher plunges on fish from a convenient perch overhanging the water.

Diving birds prefer large stretches of open water but during the breeding season they need dense waterside vegetation in which to build their nests and shelter their young. Grebes and coots build large, floating nests using the stems of waterside plants. Vegetation on the water's edge varies from dense beds of reed and rush to close-grazed grass that reaches right down to the water. Thick stands of vegetation provide cover for shy, secretive birds like the water rail, while ducks and geese rest or feed on the short grass. Wigeon particularly are attracted to sheep-grazed pastures on the edges of lakes.

Most of the rivers in our lowland landscape have been tamed and channelled and are now regularly dredged. Dredging removes most of the water plants and with them go the aquatic insects. In consequence, water birds are much less common on our rivers today than they were in the past. Stretches choked with weed do persist, however, and here herons stand motionless watching for fish, or dabchicks dive when disturbed, to surface silently, hidden in bankside reeds. Upland rivers, rushing over giant boulders and gravel beds, still retain their wildness. Grey wagtails and dippers fly along these, loudly proclaiming their territories or searching for food among the sparsely-vegetated margins. Dippers even walk beneath the water to collect their food – a habit unique among British birds.

Nearly every body of water, from small ponds to large reservoirs, has its resident population of **mallards**, the most widespread duck in Britain. In town parks and village ponds they are so tame that some birds, overfed on bread and table scraps, are almost too heavy to fly. The dull-brown female mallards are well camouflaged on their nests, usually built on the ground. Our British population is joined by ducks from eastern Europe in the winter when the population swells to over 350,000 birds. Mallards are dabbling ducks, a name derived from their habit of dipping into shallow water, tail up, to sieve the water for their food of small insects, seeds and some water plants.

at home on open salt-pastures and salt-marshes. Teal are primarily seed eaters, dabbling for their food along the edge of the water where mud, seeds and debris have collected, or picking food from waterside vegetation.

Tufted ducks and pochard obtain their food by diving. The black and white **tufted duck** is the more common of the two, nowadays occurring in town parks as well as its more usual habitat of large lakes and reservoirs. Tufted ducks were once only winter visitors but the creation of new lakes in flooded gravel workings seems to have encouraged them to nest. Pike take many of the young ducklings but even so the resident population is steadily expanding.

Mallard 58.5cm, 23in

Shoveler 50cm, 19¾in

Teal 32cm, 12½in

Tufted duck 43cm, 17in

Pochard 45.5cm, 18in

The broad, spoon-shaped bill of the **shoveler**, another dabbling duck, is ideal for sieving food from the surface of the water. Plankton, small molluscs, insects and plant debris are all sifted from the water as the bird swims in tight circles with its neck outstretched. Often small parties of these birds circle frantically together to stir up food in the water or from the bottom of shallow lakes.

Smallest of the British ducks is the **teal**, a resident bird which breeds over much of Britain. In winter there is a general movement towards the south-west where it can be found on lakes and reservoirs or in shallow, flooded meadows. It prefers an area with some dense vegetation above the water but it is quite

Tufted ducks dive from the surface down to depths of 14m (46ft) in search of food. Insect larvae, mussels and freshwater shrimps are taken and swallowed under water. Plants are sometimes brought to the surface and eaten.

**Pochard** dive only to a depth of 2.5m (8ft) and so inhabit large, shallow waters with little floating vegetation but plenty of submerged weed on which they feed. They are mainly winter birds in Britain, only a few pairs nesting here and the greater part of the population moving off to the steppes of eastern Europe in the spring. One distinctive feature of the pochard is its habit of roosting on water in 'rafts' rather than roosting on land.

Grebes are among the most fascinating of British water birds. It is hard to believe that the beautiful **great crested grebe**, now so common, was once near to extinction in Britain. In the quest for bright feathers for women's hats this magnificent bird was reduced to just a few pairs by the nineteenth century. With the ban on shooting they have recovered and are now present everywhere except the Scottish Highlands and south-west England. They breed on large lakes, reservoirs and gravel pits, building nests of aquatic weed attached to bankside vegetation. Their courtship is very elaborate, involving a great deal of head-shaking with the brightly-coloured neck and head feathers spread wide in colourful display. Like other grebes, their main diet is fish.

The **dabchick** or **little grebe** is the smallest of the grebes. It is quite widespread on rivers, lakes and even in town parks but because of its secretive habits it often goes unnoticed. It prefers waters with well-vegetated margins where it can hide. Disturbance usually causes it to dive and swim under water to bankside cover but sometimes it will submerge with just the head showing above the water.

Most resplendent of all water birds must be the **kingfisher**. In flight it is a streak of fast-moving turquoise but perched on a post or branch from where it fishes it is an astonishing blend of blues and orange. Kingfishers plunge into the waters of slow-flowing rivers and streams to catch fish, sometimes hovering briefly before diving. Captured fish are taken back to the fishing perch and beaten before being swallowed head first. Both parent birds dig the nest hole in a river bank in which the eggs are laid. It rapidly becomes lined with regurgitated fish bones and is probably one of the most foul-smelling of birds' nests. Pollution is a serious threat to kingfishers and has caused some decline in their numbers.

Coots and moorhens are bolder representatives of the otherwise shy family of crakes and rails. Both birds are common on lakes and reservoirs although the **moorhen** haunts thick cover at the edges and is common on rivers and ditches. The constantly-flicking white tail of the moorhen gives it away immediately as it picks and probes along the water's edge.

**Coots** dive for their food, pulling up weeds from the bottom. They are aggressive, noisy, territorial birds, attacking rivals and intruders in a head-down charge with their wings raised. In flight, coots are clumsy birds yet they will undertake relatively long migrations to favourable waters, gathering in large flocks during the winter.

**Sedge warblers** arrive in Britain from tropical Africa in mid-April. They colonise dense vegetation in damp areas where there are rushes and reed beds. Sedge warblers are skulking and secretive but they can be seen perching on reed stems delivering a 'churring' song or flying up into the air and dropping down with tail upraised in a 'parachuting' song-flight.

Great crested grebe 48cm, 19in

Dabchick 27cm, 10½in

Kingfisher 16.5cm, 6½in

Sedge warbler 13cm 5in

Moorhen 33cm, 13in

Coot 38cm, 15in

So stately, majestic and exotic is the **mute swan** that it is hard to believe it is a truly wild bird. Most town parks have some swans on their lakes but they are also common on marshes, quite small ponds and even on the sea-shore. Mute swans were probably introduced from Holland many centuries ago. They quickly became the 'royal bird', the property of the Crown, and were eaten at banquets and feasts. Nowadays the only real threat to swans is the lead in fishing weights which they pick up as they fish for weed on lake bottoms. The lead weights are ground up in the swan's gizzard which releases the poisonous metal into its body, often with fatal results. Swans usually mate for life, the same pair often choosing a favoured nest site in successive years.

Two other swans occur in Britain, the **Bewick's swan** and the **whooper swan**. These are easy to distinguish from the mute swan as they have a rather straight-necked stance and have yellow bills instead of red. They are rarer, wintering in Britain away from the harsh Arctic cold of their breeding grounds. Bewick's swans are found in southern England. Small and noisy, they graze in flocks on low-lying pastures or fish for the roots and tubers of aquatic plants. Whooper swans are larger, with a more northerly distribution in Britain, although sizeable flocks gather on the flood plains of the Ouse Washes in East Anglia where they graze in the company of other swans.

The largest of the British geese, the **Canada goose**, was introduced from North America, as its name implies. The first recorded introduction of this now widespread bird was into the collection of Charles II in the late seventeenth century, but the first deliberate attempts to establish the bird in Britain were not undertaken until the nineteenth century. Grass, water plants and sprouting corn form the major part of the Canada goose's diet and flocks regularly move between lakes on feeding forays.

At first sight the large, long-necked grey heron and the short, squat bittern may not appear to be related but they have similar viciously sharp, pointed bills and long legs suitable for wading in shallow water. The **bittern** is a shy, skulking bird that haunts reed beds and other tall, dense vegetation. If alarmed it 'freezes' with its head stretched upwards to reveal a striped neck which camouflages it perfectly among the reeds. The bittern became extinct in Britain in 1850 but re-established itself in the early part of the twentieth century in the Norfolk Broads. Since then it has spread to other favourable habitats in Kent and the north-west, where its extraordinary, far-carrying, booming song can be heard echoing over the reed beds at dawn and dusk. The **heron** is a bolder bird, usually seen standing motionless over water waiting to stab at unwary eels and frogs. Despite their aquatic existence herons build huge stick nests in trees, occasionally at some distance from water. These heronries are used year after year and nests sometimes get so heavy that they break the bough on which they are built, bringing them crashing to the ground.

Bewick's swan 71cm, 28in

Whooper swan 152cm, 60in

Mute swan 152cm, 60in

Canada goose 91–101cm, 36–40in

Heron 91cm, 36in

Bittern 76cm, 30in

Very few terrestrial birds have become so at home in the water as the **dipper**, a large, dumpy, wren-like bird of the north and west. It inhabits fast-flowing upland streams and rivers which have stony or gravelly bottoms. In its search for small insects and other invertebrates the dipper deliberately slips into the water, walking against the current, completely submerged and shining silver with the bubble of air trapped around its body by its feathers. It probes among the stones for insect larvae or snaps up creatures dislodged by disturbance or the current. Emerging from the stream as effortlessly as it went in, it will sit on a rock bobbing (or dipping) constantly before flying fast and direct along its territory beside the watercourse.

Lowland marshes and reed beds, preferably where there are tall waterside trees, are the haunts of the shy, secretive **water rail**. This bird is more likely to be heard than seen, squealing like a pig from the cover of dense vegetation. It follows a regular 'beat' as it forages for food, often appearing at favourite feeding grounds at the same time each day. Insects, fish, worms, seeds, berries and even small birds and mice, which are killed by hammer blows of the sharp beak, are taken by water rails. In frosty weather when ice forms around the water's edge these birds are forced out of cover to find unfrozen patches where food is available and at this time they will become remarkably tame and tolerant of man. The water rail runs rather than flies and like the coot it has fringed toes that help it walk on soft mud without sinking. Food caught in muddy places is often taken to water and washed before it is swallowed.

The **bearded tit** is another elusive bird which inhabits only large stands of the common reed in East Anglia and other scattered localities across Britain. They were once much more common but their numbers have been reduced by drainage and hard winters. Bearded tits move jerkily among the reeds, often straddling two stems when perched. They are insectivorious, feeding mainly on insects which they pick off reed stems. They build a deep cup nest using dead leaves of reeds and sedges and lined with the flower heads of reeds. Not true tits, they are resplendent members of the babbler family, which are scrub-dwelling birds from Africa and the Middle East.

The **reed bunting** was until recently a bird of overgrown reed beds and tall herbage in damp places. Now it can be found in all types of rank growth with scattered shrubs, even wet hedgerows and tall crops. It builds a nest of grass and moss on, or a few feet above, the ground in tussocks of grass or rush, or in a bush. Intruders or predators near the nest are lured away by the parent bird feigning a wing injury which makes it appear vulnerable.

Dipper 18cm, 7in

Water rail 28cm, 11in

Reed bunting 15cm, 6in

Bearded tit 16.5cm, 6½in

Grey wagtail 18cm, 7in

Snipe 27cm, 10½in

Marsh harrier 48–56cm, 19–22in

Osprey 51–58.5cm, 20–23in

The **grey wagtail** can usually be found in company with the dipper on swift-flowing upland rivers where it flies with a low, bouncing flight, alighting on rocks and constantly flicking its very long tail. It is the most colourful of the wagtails and has the longest tail. In winter the upland rivers of the north and west, where it breeds, are forsaken for southern reservoirs and lowland flood meadows.

In the same meadows may be found **snipe**. Small parties of them gather together on the flooded ground, probing the soil for worms with their very long bills. The snipe's bill has a flexible tip that reacts instantly to the presence of a worm, nipping it tight so that it can be drawn out of its tunnel and swallowed. Snipe will wait until the very last moment before flying from an intruder, when they will 'explode' from the ground and fly off in a characteristic fast zig-zag flight, usually uttering a harsh call. In summer these same meadows may be used for breeding, especially where there are clumps of rushes or dense tussocks of grass to hide the nests. Snipe mark their territory by a unique 'drumming' display. The bird rises up into the air and dives with an outspread tail, allowing the wind to vibrate the stiff outer tail feathers and

produce a loud buzzing noise known as 'drumming'. When hatched, the young are divided between the two parents to reduce the risks of losses from predators.

Of the true wetland birds of prey the **marsh harrier** is probably the commonest species. There are only a handful of breeding pairs in Britain but it is a regular wintering bird in the south and east. It flies low over reed-beds, fens and marshes, searching for water birds but it also hunts away from marshland in open country, taking rabbits and game birds when the opportunity arises. Unlike the other harriers, the male has no white patch on the rump.

The marsh harrier may be the most common raptor seen on wetland but the **osprey** is the most famous. Lost as a British breeding bird in 1910 it recolonised in 1954, establishing a nest at Loch Garten in Scotland. Its return caused a sensation and hundreds of thousands of birdwatchers have flocked to the special viewing hide to watch this marvellous bird on the nest. The osprey is a handsome bird with a white head and underside. It catches fish, flying in circles or figures-of-eight above the water before diving and snatching the prey in its talons.

37

# BIRDS of ESTUARIES

*Dunlin and curlew feed on the ebbing tide while flocks of geese fly back and forth between their feeding grounds. Cormorants spread their wings to dry after a fishing expedition*

Where rivers meet the sea great expanses of apparently lifeless, sticky mud form on the flat lands drowned every day by the tide. Although this mud appears lifeless, it is actually teeming with largely unseen animal life. Britain's muddy estuaries are in fact crucial for the survival of many of Europe's wading birds. Every winter millions of migrants arrive at British estuaries, sometimes in small parties but often in large flocks, to feed on the countless creatures in the mud. In big estuaries huge flocks of wading birds fly over the mud-flats, twisting and turning like the smoke from a genie's bottle. Most waders have relatively long legs, useful for walking deep into the water, and long bills with which they probe for prey. They feed most avidly on the ebb tide while the mud is still wet or just covered in water and the prey still close to the surface.

In the higher reaches of estuaries the mud is colonised by algae and grass and divided by masses of shallow gulleys and deep drainage channels.

Plant-eating species of ducks and the marine Brent geese follow the rising tide, tearing at vegetation floated up by the water. Dabbling ducks follow the tide as it flows into the drainage gulleys and sieve the water surface for seeds and small creatures washed off the mud. Where the sward is closely grazed, sizeable flocks of geese gather to crop the grass. At high tide many waders seek the security of the open salt-marsh for their roosts, returning to the same roosts on every tide. Many different species gather at a roost, but each species has its own special place. By careful watching you can get to know where to find each species.

The ebbing and flowing of the tide also brings fish into estuaries and with them come the fish-eating birds. Most are primarily coastal species that follow the flooding tide to fish in the more sheltered waters. Others, such as the cormorant, are mainly estuarine birds that specialise in diving in deep estuary channels and are less often seen on the coast.

Probably the most regularly estuarine of the gulls is the **herring gull**. It nests on sea cliffs but flocks to the mud-flats of estuaries to scavenge among washed-up debris and prey on crabs and fishes.

On sandbanks in the mouths of estuaries **cormorants** sit with their wings spread out to dry. On some rivers parties of cormorants fly in each night to roost on favourite riverside trees. They can also be found on the coast but they are very much estuary birds, diving for flatfish on the flood tide. Their webbed feet make them strong swimmers and they will dive down to a depth of 10m (32ft). Captured fish are brought to the surface and swallowed, some with difficulty because of their large size. Adult breeding birds have white faces and thigh patches.

The commonest estuarine duck in Britain is the **wigeon**. They graze salt-marsh pastures but will also move inland to feed on meadows closely grazed by sheep. Like most ducks the male is a handsome creature but the female is a drab brown. Wigeon are now widespread throughout Britain yet the first recorded breeding success was in 1834. Winter numbers are swollen by continental immigrants escaping the cold of central Europe.

The striking, mostly black and white **shelduck** is half-way between a goose and a duck. It is almost entirely coastal, frequenting muddy estuaries where it sieves small molluscs from the mud with side-to-side sweeps of its bill. It is also somewhat unusual in that it nests in disused rabbit burrows, particularly in sand-dunes, or under hay ricks or in holes in buildings. On hatching the young are led down to the estuary where they gather together in small groups with other ducklings in sheltered, protected places. Most British shelduck fly to north Germany in July to moult, but a few remain to look after the young.

Of the true geese the **greylag goose** is the most abundant species likely to be encountered in estuaries or in sheltered Scottish lochs. It is the ancestor of the domestic goose and is a grazing bird that nests on moors, marshes and islands where it is safe from predators.

The **Brent goose** is the smallest and most truly marine of the geese. Once almost at the point of extinction because of shooting and also the loss of its major food plant through disease, it has now completely recovered and its populations are expanding. In estuaries it feeds on the green algae *Enteromorpha* but it will also move inland to graze on coastal pastures and young corn.

Cormorant 91.5cm, 36in
Herring gull 56cm, 22in
Wigeon 45cm, 17¾in
Brent goose 56–61cm, 22–24in
Shelduck 61cm, 24in
Greylag goose 76–89cm, 30–35in

Oystercatcher 43cm, 17in

Curlew 53.5–58.5cm, 21–23in

Redshank 28cm, 11in

Avocet 43cm, 17in

Common sandpiper 20cm, 7¾in

The **oystercatcher** is one of the most numerous and successful of estuarine waders. Unmistakable in its black and white plumage with bright red legs and bill, it gathers in flocks of thousands on estuaries all over Britain. They are noisy birds, restlessly flying from the advancing tide to roost on undisturbed salt-marsh. Two methods are employed in gathering food; the long bill is used to probe for worms, both marine and terrestrial, and shellfish are collected and hammered open with powerful blows from the sturdy bill. Despite their name, oystercatchers rarely eat oysters, preferring cockles and limpets instead.

The long, curved bill of the **curlew**, the largest of the waders, is used to extract worms, crabs and shellfish from the mud. Surprisingly, on their upland breeding grounds they use their enormous bills to pick berries delicately from moorland bushes, or grass seeds from their stems. They feed alone or in small parties, gathering together at favourite roosts as the rising tides push them off their feeding grounds. The name curlew is taken from their call, 'coor-li', usually followed by a bubbling trill, a particularly haunting sound at dusk.

The varied musical vocabulary of the ever-vigilant **redshank** makes it one of the best known shore birds. Because of its nervousness it tends to nest among lapwings where it gains further protection through their watchfulness and vocal warnings of danger. It nests in meadows, marshes and moorlands, moving to muddy estuaries in small flocks during the winter. There they eat enormous quantities of invertebrate prey, often feeding well into the night, sifting through mud with partly-opened bills. They also forage for earthworms and leatherjackets in flood meadows.

The **avocet** also sifts for prey, taking insects, crustaceans, worms and fish fry from the mud with sideways sweeps of its long, upward-tilted bill. Lost from Britain in 1825 due to land drainage and persecution, the avocet returned after the Second World War to Minsmere in Norfolk and Havergate Island in Suffolk. At first they came, probably from Holland, just to breed, but now wintering flocks have become established on the Tamar estuary in Devon and recently also in Suffolk.

Upland hill streams and the shores of lakes and reservoirs are the breeding sites of the **common sandpiper**. On estuaries it is a bird of passage, usually seen singly or in small parties on their way to tropical Africa, feeding on worms and snails picked from the surface, or flying up to catch small flies. It is easily recognised by its fast, direct flight — several rapid wingbeats followed by a short glide with wings held down.

Dunlin 18cm, 7in

Bar-tailed godwit 35cm, 13¾in

Grey plover 28cm, 11in

Greenshank 30cm, 11¾in

Turnstone 23cm, 9in

Grey phalarope 21cm, 8¼in

On any estuary around our coast huge flocks of **dunlin** acrobatically twist and turn, flashing light and dark as they wheel over the mud-flats. This is our commonest wader; the total population of British and Irish birds may exceed half a million. In breeding plumage this attractive small bird has a distinctive dark underbelly. It breeds on upland moors in the north, often nesting in loose groups, but a small breeding colony survives on Dartmoor in the south. As the tide ebbs they busily probe the wet mud for ragworms, crustaceans and small molluscs.

The **bar-tailed godwit**, a much larger wader than the dunlin, also follows the ebb tide, trotting along the shore to pick at prey on the surface or thrusting into the mud to reach a buried worm or shellfish. They prefer the sandier estuaries of the west coast, occurring mainly as passage or wintering birds. Resplendent in rich chestnut plumage in summer, winter birds become a dull grey-brown.

The striking black and white plumage of the **grey plover** also moults to a dull grey-brown in winter. As well as its characteristic upright stance and short, fast sprints, the grey plover is easily recognised in flight by its black axillaries, or 'unwashed armpits'. A migrant bird, it winters in muddy estuaries and harbours, forming small flocks. When feeding, the whole body tilts as it picks up small molluscs or ragworms.

One of the less common wintering waders is the **greenshank**. Although it breeds in Scotland, few birds remain for the winter and those that do move to the south and west. It can be seen as a migrant on all types of fresh water as well as on estuaries, usually issuing a ringing alarm call if it is disturbed. As it flies it reveals a conspicuous white rump between dark wings but in winter it is a much greyer bird.

The **grey phalarope** is a very uncommon passage migrant, seen only intermittently though it is quite a regular visitor in the south-west. It passes through Britain on its way to the South Atlantic and the waters off Chile. An oceanic bird, it settles on the open sea, even in stormy weather. On inland pools it swims well with its coot-like fringed feet, spinning round and round and picking insects off the water.

**Turnstones** are as much birds of shingly shores as they are of estuaries. With their short, upturned bills they turn over stones and seaweed to find small crabs, crustaceans and insects. They usually fly and forage in small parties, sometimes co-operating in turning over larger objects to search for food.

# BIRDS of COAST and SEA

*Razorbills, guillemots and fulmars nest on the cliff ledges. Gannets and terns soar above the rich inshore waters, plunging into the water to catch fish.*

The wildest and most dramatic of all habitats must be the coast. Huge waves pound and smash the shore while fierce winds sweep over headlands to stunt trees and blast cliff-side vegetation. Yet below the waves the rich inshore waters are little affected by storm and life is abundant. Out of the wind in sheltered bays and harbours the sea remains calm and untroubled. During winter storms sea birds may seek out these sheltered waters to rest and feed, but usually they are largely oblivious of the raging sea and are quite at home bobbing about on giant, storm-tossed waves. Most sea birds are fish and flesh eaters, diving from the surface or plunging into the sea from the air after their quarry. Others, particularly the gulls, take offal as well as fish and follow fishing boats to scavenge on the waste thrown overboard. Sea ducks dive in shallow off-shore waters to scrape molluscs and sea urchins off the rocks.

Although they may spend most of their time at sea all seabirds have to come ashore to breed, typically selecting islands or inaccessible cliff faces for nesting. Nearly all species breed colonially, sometimes gathering in huge numbers on rock ledges or grassy cliff tops where some nest in burrows which they excavate in the soil. Some seabirds nest contentedly side by side while others, such as gannets, although nesting close together, vigorously defend the areas around their nests with their viciously sharp bills.

Natural and man-made coastal structures attract coastal birds. Some species, like the delightful snow bunting, spend no time at sea, instead searching for weed seeds along shingle shores. The purple sandpiper, a dark, purplish coastal wader, picks among shoreline debris for insects and is a regular visitor to harbours and breakwaters.

Sadly, man's delight in the sea and coastal scenery has put serious pressure on our coastal birds. Development, ugly sea defence works and greater use by the public of previously inaccessible areas have become a threat to some breeding populations and special feeding sites. Beach-nesting birds such as the little tern are particularly vulnerable to disturbance.

Eider 59cm, 23¼in

Common scoter 45cm, 17¾in

Red-breasted merganser
58cm, 23in

Great northern diver 68–81cm, 27–32in

Largest and most numerous of the sea ducks, the **eider** is also the best known, not necessarily as a duck but for its feathers, collected from its nests and used in quilts and eiderdowns. The female, which is a drab brown, lines her nest with feathers plucked from her breast. Apart from nesting on land, eiders are entirely marine birds. They form small parties off-shore in shallow coastal waters or sheltered estuaries, diving for shellfish and sea anemones which they scrape from rocks with their rasping bills. They also take offal and seaweed and may gather around sewage outfall pipes. Eider nest in large colonies on the coast of northern Britain but disperse more widely in winter, occurring around most parts of the coast. Occasionally non-breeding immature birds will remain in sheltered sites in the south during the summer.

The **common scoter** is primarily a winter bird of sheltered coasts and estuaries, although non-breeders are present around our shores throughout the summer. Since the nineteenth century it has spread as a breeding bird across north-west Europe and now nests in small numbers in Scotland and Ireland. It makes its nest in a hollow, typically among heather and dense grass near freshwater margins, and lines it sparingly with grass, lichens, moss and down. Like the eider it dives for shellfish and crustaceans, usually at depths of 10-15m (32-48ft) but sometimes down to 20m (65ft). On its summer breeding grounds it dives for small crustaceans and

insect larvae. The all-black colouration of the male is relieved by the orange on the bill while the brown female has prominent pale cheeks and, in flight, contrasting pale underparts.

Of all the coastal birds the most highly adapted for an aquatic existence must be the divers. The **great northern diver** is the largest species to occur around British shores but only a few manage to breed here. The cylindrical, streamlined body shape and the webbed feet set far back on the body gives the diver great propulsive power and agility in the water. In pursuit of fish it may stay under water for up to a minute, emerging briefly only to dive again after its quarry. Fish form the bulk of the diet but they also take molluscs, crabs and marine worms.

Another diving bird, the **red-breasted merganser**, also eats fish, but in this colourful duck the bill has a series of 'teeth' along the edge to prevent the slippery fish from slithering out of its grasp. These 'teeth' have earned this and related species the name of 'sawbills'. They occur in small parties in estuaries and sheltered coasts, roosting on the open sea and moving in-shore to fish in shallow waters. Breeding takes place not only in marine bays and inlets but also on fresh and brackish rivers, where there must be woods or scrub for nesting. The nest is built at the end of a tunnel of dense vegetation, under rocks or in burrows. The females look after the young and occasionally several broods may be combined in a single flock.

Smaller than its relative the cormorant and without any white markings, the **shag** is a strictly marine bird, perching on low reefs off the shore or floating low in the water before flipping below in search of fish. Appearing black, the shag is in fact a rich bottle green and in its breeding plumage sports a small recurved crest. Shags dive deeper and remain submerged longer than cormorants and they also take a different range of fish. Sand eels are a major prey, with herring, whiting and other small fish making up the rest of the diet.

Until recently nearly all the western sea cliffs rang to the high-pitched call of the **chough**, a handsome member of the crow family. As a breeding bird it has now been lost from south-west England and parts of

where they nest.

Sea-parrot is one of the commonest folk names of the comical and quite endearing **puffin**. Its large, flattened, multi-coloured bill resembles that of a parrot and is used to carry as many as eleven sand eels or sprats back to the nest site. It may forage as much as 80km (50 miles) away from its nest on turf-covered cliff tops, returning at night on whirring, stubby wings. The nest is made in a disused rabbit burrow or in a hole dug in soft soil with its bright red webbed feet. Puffin breeding colonies may be huge and thousands of birds may assemble on the water at dusk. Great black-backed gulls are the puffins' greatest enemy, snatching many of the juvenile puffins from the tunnel mouths of their nest.

Shag 76cm, 30in

Chough 39.5cm, 15½in

Puffin 30.5cm, 12in

Razorbill 40.5cm, 16in

Guillemot 42cm, 16½in

Scotland; the rugged coast of Wales is now its only stronghold. The reasons for its decline are uncertain but the reclamation of cliff-top grasslands for arable crops and improved pasture have probably robbed it of good feeding grounds. Insectivorous rather than a scavenger like the other crows, it uses its bright red curved bill to dig for insects in the soil or to pick them out of dung. Choughs are very acrobatic birds, sweeping and diving around the cliffs and quarries

**Razorbills** and **guillemots** nest together in tight-packed cliff-face colonies and are similar in build and in habits. Guillemots are more numerous than razorbills and they dive deeper and remain below the water longer in pursuit of fish. Both birds lay a single, pear-shaped egg, so that if it is dislodged it rolls in a circle on the bare rock ledges rather than falling off. Razorbills prefer to nest on ledges where there is a little earth or vegetation.

Sanderling 20cm, 7¾in

Ringed plover 19cm, 7½in

Snow bunting 16.5cm, 6½in

Purple sandpiper 21cm, 8¼in

A true shore bird, the **sanderling** rushes back and forth like a clockwork toy, pecking here and there at small morsels of food left by the retreating waves. It is a winter visitor to our sandy beaches with many remaining here but many more passing through to the Mediterranean and North Africa. In winter plumage it is grey, relieved only by a dark smudge on the shoulder. Small parties may be quite confiding and can be watched as they snatch up sandhoppers, small snails and even bits of dead fish or seaweed.

The **ringed plover** frequents estuaries and mudflats but nests on shingle beaches. The eggs are laid in a hollow scrape and are so perfectly camouflaged as to be indistinguishable from the shingle that surrounds them; in some places where disturbance is great nests are unfortunately often crushed underfoot. Newly hatched young are also wonderfully camouflaged, freezing instantly when danger threatens, to blend completely with their pebbly background. They are also protected by the parent bird, who will try to distract predators by fluttering weakly along the ground pretending to have a broken wing. Extensive gravel pit workings have provided the ringed plover with artificial beaches and in recent years there has been an increasing tendency to nest inland. During the winter Britain's estuaries hold internationally important numbers of ringed plover.

On seaweed-covered shores as well as shingle beaches the **purple sandpiper** searches for small crustaceans, molluscs and shellfish. These birds arrive on British shores in October, spending the winter singly or in small parties. Their dark plumage blends with the seaweed and, despite their yellow legs and bills, hides them well. They are also rather tame and allow observers to approach quite closely before taking flight.

Another bird of shingle coasts is the **snow bunting**, but it can also be found on dunes and low-lying pasture. Although a confiding bird which often allows close approach, it is not often seen but is much sought after by the keen birdwatcher. A pretty bird, its plumage of black, brown and white is very striking. The snow bunting is an Arctic breeder but some do nest in the Scottish Highlands, where the male can be seen in its summer plumage of black and white. Their white patches, particularly noticeable as they flit along the shore, has earned them the name of 'snowflakes'. They eat the seeds of grasses and other low herbage.

Kittiwake 40.5cm, 16in

Arctic skua 45.5cm, 18in

Fulmar 47cm, 18½in

Common tern 35.5cm, 14in

Gannet 91.5cm, 36in

The fulmar and kittiwake are two successes of the bird world. The **fulmar** was until about the 1880s an uncommon bird confined to the island of St Kilda off the Outer Hebrides in Scotland. Since then it has undergone an enormous expansion in population and has colonised most of the suitable sea-cliff nesting habitats in Britain. The fulmar looks like a gull but is a relative of the petrels and albatrosses. With its wings held stiffly it glides on the up-currents of air from cliffs, briefly and rapidly beating its wings to maintain its speed. It can be found around the coast for most of the year except early winter when it moves out to the open sea. Offal thrown from ships and fishing vessels seems to be the key to the fulmar's success and the increasing availability of this food has also favoured the kittiwake. Both birds are scavengers at sea and offal provides easy pickings. **Kittiwakes** are almost entirely marine birds, coming to land only to breed. They nest in colonies on cliffs, often in company with razorbills and guillemots, building a cup nest of seaweed, debris and excrement stuck to a cliff ledge. The kittiwake population is increasing and they have now colonised the east coast of Britain. In some coastal towns the birds are so abundant that they even use window ledges as nest sites.

The **gannet** is the largest and probably the most spectacular sea bird around the British coast. The size of a goose, with a 2-metre (6ft) wing span, it wheels and dives into the sea from 30 metres (100ft) up in spectacular aerial displays. The gannet's skull is shaped to withstand the impact of hitting the water at great speed and an air sac under the skin further softens the blow. They are maritime breeders, gathering in very dense breeding colonies on a handful of islands around the coast. Britain holds three-quarters of the world's population of gannets. A curious habit of the gannet is that it incubates its eggs under its large webbed feet.

Terns have been given the country name of 'sea-swallows', perhaps because of their forked tails, and the **common tern** is one of the commonest species occurring in Britain. Summer visitors and passage migrants, they nest on sand and shingle in dunes and on islands. They have a light, dancing flight and hover over the water before diving in to catch sand eels and other small fish.

The rarest of British seabirds is the **Arctic skua**, an aggressive, dark-coloured relative of the gulls that comes to the Highlands and islands of Scotland to breed. Skuas can fish for themselves but prefer to rob gulls and terns of their catches, harassing and mobbing them in fast, acrobatic flight until they drop or disgorge their prey. The pirated food is often caught in flight and two birds may co-operate in a chase, taking it in turns to catch the booty.

# BIRDWATCHING EQUIPMENT

Birdwatching is one of the easiest of all natural history hobbies to pursue. Birds are abundant, often quite confiding and are not difficult to study. All the birdwatcher needs is sturdy weatherproof clothing, an enthusiasm for the outdoors and a good pair of binoculars.

## CHOOSING BINOCULARS

Binoculars are indispensable to the birdwatcher, quickly becoming like a second, more powerful pair of eyes. They are, however, expensive and choosing a pair from among the bewildering variety of makes and magnifications can seem a very daunting task. By shopping around carefully you will soon find a range you can afford, and then there are only two things to consider: the magnification and the weight.

All binoculars have their magnification and lens diameter marked on them. For example they may be 8 x 30 or 10 x 50. The first figure is the magnification and the second the diameter of the lens. For birdwatching, magnifications of 8x, 9x and 10x are the most useful. In woodlands, where birds are often seen close to the watcher, then an 8x magnification is quite adequate but in open places, such as estuaries, where birds are seen at a distance, then a 10x magnification is more helpful.

One drawback with the higher magnification binoculars is that they need a greater lens diameter to gather enough light for clear viewing and, unfortunately, the larger the lens diameter, the heavier the binoculars. When you consider that you might have to walk around all day with a pair of binoculars hanging round your neck then you will understand that weight is a very important factor. Your binoculars can easily become a dead weight by the end of the day. Lightweight models with a higher magnification are available but they tend to be expensive. *Never* be tempted to choose a pair of binoculars with a magnification greater than 10x; they will be heavy and difficult to hold steady without support.

The view through binoculars at 8x and 10x magnification.

## TELESCOPES

Telescopes have much higher magnifications than binoculars but again there are penalties in their high cost and weight. They are heavy and cumbersome and have to be used with a tripod or support. Telescopes are best used at places such as nature reserves where hides or good viewing points are provided and where there is not too much walking to be done.

## CLOTHING

As you are likely to spend many long hours in the field you will need warm, weatherproof clothing and stout walking boots or wellingtons. Avoid bright-coloured clothes which will alarm or disturb the birds you are trying to watch. Choose subdued browns and greens which blend with the countryside and enable you to move about unnoticed.

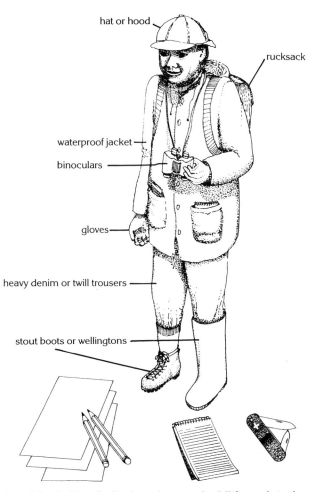

hat or hood

rucksack

waterproof jacket

binoculars

gloves

heavy denim or twill trousers

stout boots or wellingtons

Suitable clothing for birdwatching and wildlife study in the countryside.

# WHERE to WATCH BIRDS

With the present tremendous interest in bird-watching and conservation it will not prove difficult to find good birdwatching sites wherever you are. There are hundreds of nature reserves and bird sanctuaries in Britain, many of them around major cities. Inevitably, though, every birdwatcher wants to see some of the rarer and more unusual birds. The map shows some – most certainly not all! – sites of particular interest, but there really is no substitute for joining your local birdwatching society and finding out about good 'birding' localities through the birdwatchers' grapevine.

## BIRD SITES

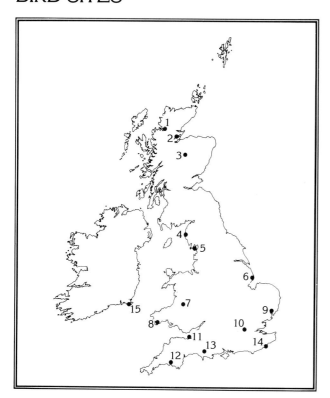

### 1. Beinn Eighe, Ross-shire
A National Nature Reserve. Mountains, moorland and extensive western pine woods. The reserve is typical of the Western Highlands and supports many of the rarer upland birds including golden eagles, hen harriers, ptarmigan, crossbills and possibly dotterel and snow buntings. Black-throated and red-throated divers nest on the numerous lochs in the region.

### 2. Cromarty Firth, Ross-shire
The most important wildfowl site in north-east Scotland. Massive assemblages of geese and large numbers of ducks and waders, particularly at Udale Bay. There is also a wildfowl and wader reserve at Nigg Bay which is under pressure from industrial development.

### 3. The Cairngorms, Inverness-shire
A National Nature Reserve. Mountains, moorland and ancient pine forest. Golden eagles, ptarmigan, snow buntings, crossbills, dotterel, crested tits and possibly snowy owls in winter. The region is the only British nesting locality for the crested tit (at the Forests of Mar and Derry). Excellent communities of upland birds.

### 4. St Bee's Head, Cumbria
A Royal Society for the Protection of Birds reserve. Sheer sandstone cliffs over 90m (300ft high) whose ledges support dense nesting colonies of auks, including black guillemots, puffins and other cliff-nesting birds.

### 5. Morecambe Bay, Cumbria and Lancashire
A major wintering area for waders. Extensive salt-marshes and mud-flats. Nearby is the Royal Society for the Protection of Birds reserve at Leighton Moss which has large areas of reedbeds in which breed bitterns and bearded tits. Walney Island at the mouth of Morecambe Bay is also a reserve and, as well as a large colony of nesting gulls, eider, other sea ducks and waders are abundant.

### 6. Gibraltar Point, Lincolnshire
Local Nature Reserve owned by the Lincolnshire Trust for Nature Conservation. An area of sand-dune and salt-marsh which is an important 'stop-over' for migrating birds, especially wildfowl and waders, and there is a regular flock of wintering snow buntings, with Lapland buntings and shore larks. It is also an observatory site where birds are systematically ringed each year and it is an excellent area for sea-watching.

### 7. Mid-Wales
An area with a rich variety of habitats – woodlands and wetlands, moors and heathland. The only British locality for the red kite.

### 8. Pembrokeshire
The coast around St David's Head and Milford Haven is rich in birdlife. Choughs, ravens and buzzards nest on the cliffs and there are large colonies of sea birds on the off-shore islands of Ramsey, Skomer and

Skokholm. Puffins, razorbills, guillemots, Manx shearwater and storm petrels all nest here.

## 9. Minsmere and Havergate Island, Suffolk

Two Royal Society for the Protection of Birds reserves, relatively close to each other on the Suffolk coast. Reed beds, marshes, islands and scrapes support a great range of waders and wetland birds. Breeding avocets on the scrapes and bearded tits, bitterns and marsh harriers in the reed beds. Stone curlews on fields nearby.

## 10. London

The strings of reservoirs and flooded gravel pits in north and west London support enormous populations of wildfowl and gulls. Several of the lakes are bird reserves. Wintering populations on the River Thames have been increasing steadily in numbers as the river has become cleaner.

## 11. Bridgwater Bay, Somerset

A National Nature Reserve. Extensive areas of salt-marsh and mud-flats rich in waders and wintering wildfowl and geese. The only British site for moulting shelduck; all other shelduck fly out to Germany to moult. Merlins, peregrine falcons and short-eared owls are regularly seen in winter.

## 12. The Tamar Estuary, Devon/Cornwall

A good estuary for wintering wildfowl and geese but it is best known for its wintering flock of avocets. Up to 50 or 60 birds are now recorded every year and a small flock has also become established on the nearby Exe estuary, another important site for wintering wildfowl and waders.

## 13. The Purbeck Heaths, Dorset.

A National Nature Reserve. An extensive area of fragmented heathland that supports a typical community of heathland birds including the rare Dartford warbler.

## 14. Dungeness, Kent

Partly a Royal Society for the Protection of Birds nature reserve. A vast area of shingle with dense clumps of gorse and bramble, which is an important 'stop-over' point for migrating birds. There is an observatory here for watching sea-bird passage and counting the huge flocks of passerines that move through and over the site.

## 15. The Wexford Slobs and Saltee Islands, Wexford

The Wexford Slobs is an important wildfowl and wader reserve on the Irish coast. The Saltee Islands are places of magnificent beauty as well as the site of one of the largest sea-bird colonies on the west coast of Ireland.

# BIRD SOCIETIES AND COLLECTIONS

The British Trust for
   Ornithology,
Beech Grove,
Tring,
Herts.
The bird specialist's society. Numerous newsletters, journals and bulletins issued each year.

The Royal Society for the
   Protection of Birds,
The Lodge,
Sandy,
Beds SG19 2DL
Members receive *Birds*, a quarterly magazine, and are entitled to preferential access to the Society's numerous and often quite outstanding reserves.

The Wildfowl Trust,
Slimbridge,
Glos GL2 7BT
Members receive a quarterly journal. The Trust has a number of reserves and wildfowl collections throughout the country – a few are listed below.

*Caerlaverock*
Eastpark Farm,
Caerlaverock,
Dumfries and Galloway,
Scotland DG1 4RS

*Slimbridge*
Glos.
One of the finest of the Wildfowl Trust's sites. Wildfowl in natural habitats, a very extensive collection of wildfowl and a tropical house.

*Welney*
Pintail House,
Hundred Foot Bank,
Welney,
Wisbech,
Cambs.

# MAMMALS

From cold Arctic wastes to equatorial deserts and jungles, mammals dominate the earth. Worldwide there are nearly four and a half thousand species of mammal. Some, like the Javan rhinoceros are so reduced in numbers that they hover on the brink of extinction. Others, like the wood mouse in Britain are so abundant that they outnumber the human population. Mammals are also extremely varied in form. Man and the higher apes are relatively unspecialised and use their limbs to run, climb or swim, while bats have evolved wings to enable them to fly and whales have become so well adapted to their ocean environment that they are hardly recognisable as mammals at all.

Despite their diversity all mammals have some features in common. In mammals as different as whales and mice, or human beings and giraffes, all have seven bones (vertebrae) in their necks which reveals their common ancestry. Also all mammals are covered in hair. Even the smooth-skinned cetaceans – dolphins, porpoises and whales – are found on close examination to have a very sparse covering of hair on parts of their bodies. But what links all mammals together and separates them from all other animals is their ability to suckle their young with milk produced in mammary glands.

## PRIMITIVE MAMMALS

Mammals are descended from reptiles. They were present on earth during the age of the dinosaurs but were then only the size of rats and mice. They probably fed on insects and worms and lived a life not unlike that of present-day shrews. The most primitive surviving mammals can be found in Australia. The duck-billed platypus and the spiny ant-eater suckle their young like true mammals but lay eggs like their reptilian ancestors. In Australia too can be found the marsupials, mammals like the kangaroo and opossum that give birth to live but very immature young which are suckled in the protection of a special body pouch. Marsupials were once the dominant mammals all over the world, but they were ousted by the more efficient modern mammals. The marsupials survived in Australia and New Zealand because the southern continents drifted away from the Asian landmass long before the evolution of the modern, placental mammals.

Mammals' success is due mainly to their large and complex brains. In comparison with their body size, mammal brains are larger than those of any other group of animals – even the mighty dinosaurs had brains only about the size of a plum. Their increased

kangaroo, a marsupial mammal

Abyssinian cat, a modern mammal

duck-billed platypus, a primitive mammal

brain size has given mammals a greater ability to learn and to solve complicated problems in their everyday lives. Many mammals live in close social groups and are able to act co-operatively — something very rare indeed in the animal kingdom.

# SOCIAL ORGANISATION

Apes and cetaceans (whales, dolphins and porpoises) have the most highly organised social structure among mammals and often show great concern for other members of their group. Cetaceans will actively assist a sick companion to keep up with the group and will co-operate in pushing it to the surface so that it can breathe. Predatory mammals may also display advanced social behaviour. A great deal of skill is required in hunting but, unlike grazing mammals which have to search for food for most of the day, predatory mammals kill only intermittently and spend a great deal of time resting and playing. Play is a very important leisure activity among predatory mammals. It teaches skills, reinforces learning and among social hunters establishes rank at a very early age. Pack hunters like lions, wild dogs and wolves have a very high degree of group co-ordination when hunting and most of them learn their basic skills through play when they are very young.

Increased brain capacity has enabled two groups of mammals, bats and cetaceans, to evolve echo-location techniques for navigation and to search out their prey. They emit a continuous stream of ultrasonic sound which bounces back to them on striking an object. From the returning signal, processed in a fraction of a second, they are able to estimate how far away the object is and if it is suitable prey. Cetaceans also use their wide vocabulary of sound to communicate with other members of their social group. Whales can send massive bursts of high energy sound through the water so strong that it kills or stuns their prey.

A bat bounces sound waves off its prey to locate it.

# WARM-BLOODEDNESS

Their covering of hair and their warm-bloodedness — the ability to maintain a constant body heat — are two other features that have contributed to the success of mammals. Warm-bloodedness enables mammals to remain active, day and night, in all climates, even where the cold is so extreme that it is lethal for most other creatures. In the majority of mammals hair plays an essential role in temperature control and has proved vital for survival in hostile climates. Hair can help to keep a mammal warm or cool. In hot climates a covering of hair shields delicate skin from the burning rays of the sun and aids in the cooling evaporation of sweat, while in cold climates dense layers of hair trap warm air close to the body, preventing too much heat loss. The thick winter coat of the Arctic fox is so efficient that even at −30°C the animal can become overheated after only moderate exercise.

With his advanced social structure and formidable brain power man is the most highly developed of all the modern mammals, yet his increased brain power seems not to have brought compassion for the other creatures that share this planet. Man's greedy quest for meat and fur has brought many species of mammal to the verge of extinction and now the thoughtless and needless wholesale destruction of major habitats is threatening many more. Mammals are adaptable and we must hope that man, the most adaptable of all, will care enough to help them survive.

## MAMMALS FACTS AND FEATS

**THE LARGEST MAMMAL**

| | |
|---|---|
| *Great Britain* | A red deer stag when full grown measures approximately 1.11m (3ft 8in) at the shoulder and will weigh between 104-113kg (230-250lb). |
| *World* | The blue whale. An adult female has been recorded at 33.58m (110ft 2½in). |

**SMALLEST MAMMAL**

| | |
|---|---|
| *Great Britain* | The pygmy shrew, weight 2.4-6.1g (0.084-0.21oz), length of head and body 43-64mm (1.69-2.5in), tail length 31-46mm (1.22-1.81in). |
| *World* | The Kitti's hog-nosed bat, also known as the bumble-bee bat, from Thailand has a wingspan of 160mm (6.29in) and weighs only 1.75-2g (0.062-0.071oz). |

**TALLEST MAMMAL**

| | |
|---|---|
| *World* | A Masai bull giraffe was recorded to be 6.09m (20ft) high. |

**FASTEST MAMMAL**

| | |
|---|---|
| *Great Britain* | The roe deer can cruise at 40-48km/h (25-30mph) over a distance of more than 32km (20 miles). |
| *World* | The cheetah reaches a maximum speed of 96-101km/h (60-63mph) in pursuit of its quarry. |

# MAMMALS of HOUSE and GARDEN

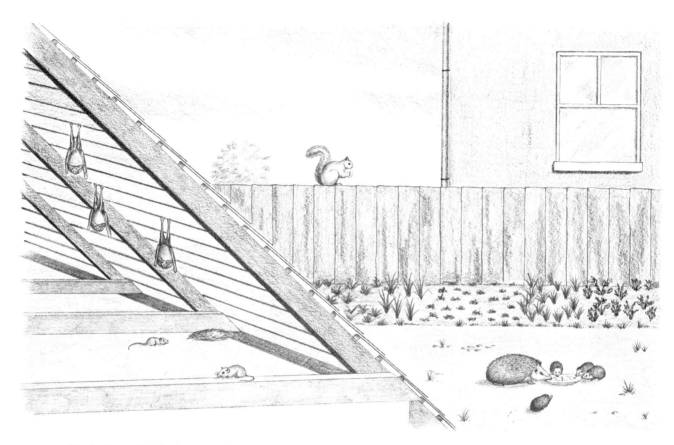

*Squirrels and hedgehogs regularly visit gardens in search of kitchen scraps, and unwelcome mammals such as the house mouse are always searching for ways into a house. Bats in the roof do no harm and ought to be encouraged.*

An average house has a lot of unused space, it is warm and it is secure from predatory animals. Small wonder then that the average house is also home for several mammal 'hangers on'. Provided the roof timbers have not been doused in preservative or insecticide a house loft is not much different from the interior of a hollow tree or a cave entrance and bats are happy to hang from the rafters – even in the heat of summer. They come and go at dawn and dusk, slipping in and out between gaps under the eaves. At times there may be hundreds of bats in a single loft. Not every house attracts bats, however, and they rarely stay in the same house all the time. Mass movements from house to house are common.

Rats and mice have plagued man for centuries. They plunder food stores, damage wood, plaster and electrical wiring and may carry terrible diseases. Once they have gained entry, they travel all over a house, using the space under floorboards or between cavity walls as their runs. For rats and mice,

which come originally from sub-tropical countries, the warmth and shelter of a house may be essential for survival, but they can be remarkably hardy. There is a strain of 'super-mouse' that lives in cold storage warehouses at temperatures below freezing, gnawing their way into frozen meat carcases for food.

A garden cannot offer the same security as a house but there is plenty of food to be found there in a rich and very varied habitat. Many mammals of scrub and woodland find their way into gardens and even large hunters like the fox will forage in gardens or raid dustbins for kitchen scraps. Mammalian pride of place in the garden, however, must go to the hedgehog. Encouraged by is protective armour of spines it is quite tame and can be followed about on its noisy rambles in gardens almost anywhere in the country. Small rodents can also be common, especially where there is an overgrown and neglected corner.

Of all mammals, **hedgehogs** typify the best of wildlife in the suburban garden. With their armour of tough, sharp spines they can hardly be described as cuddly but their comic looks, noisy snufflings and general tameness make them very endearing. They are nocturnal creatures, present in virtually all gardens, sometimes penetrating into those in major cities, where they feed on slugs, worms, beetles and other invertebrates. Hedgehogs, often in family parties, come readily to food left out overnight, especially bread and milk. At the approach of winter their foraging activities increase as they lay down extra layers of fat in their bodies for hibernation. Adult hedgehogs hibernate from October to April in nests of leaves, but young animals may be active as late as December.

At the other end of the spectrum the **house mouse** and **brown rat** typify all that is worst in wildlife inhabiting the home. Both species were accidentally introduced into Britain from Asia by man, the brown rat as recently as the eighteenth century. Both are now universal destructive pests, found in houses, warehouses, sewers and farm buildings. Their diet too is extraordinarily varied – they even eat soap powder and wall plaster, and they are also enormously fertile. A single female house mouse can produce up to eighty young a year while a brown rat female can produce up to forty. The brown rat probably outnumbers humans in many cities.

Bats traditionally have a poor reputation. They regularly roost in roof spaces of houses where they may cause alarm to the householder, but they are actually quite harmless. Their droppings are very dry and do no damage; they are clean creatures and, despite superstitious fears, *never* become entangled in people's hair. The bat most likely to take roost in a house is the **pipistrelle**, Britain's smallest bat. As many as a thousand pipistrelles have been recorded in a favourable roost. They emerge at dusk, flying high, fast and erratically along a regular 'beat' under avenues of trees, at edges of woodlands and in orchards. The **long-eared bat** is another regular user of buildings. It has a weak, fluttering flight, frequently hovering among or landing on branches to pick off insects. At rest, the enormously long ears of this bat are folded under its wings.

The **grey squirrel** was introduced into Britain from North America in 1876 and since then it has spread to almost all parts of England and Wales and to parts of Scotland. It is an animal of deciduous woodland, where it eats buds, bark, nuts and fungi, but it is now well established in parks and gardens where there are plenty of trees. Grey squirrels are active by day and can become quite tame and bold, often visiting bird tables. They make a drey, or nest, of twigs and leaves in a tree fork or in a hole in a tree.

Hedgehog 25.5cm, 10in

House mouse body 7.5cm, 3in; tail 6.5cm, 2.5in

Brown rat body 24cm, 9½in; tail 23cm, 9in

Long-eared bat body 5cm, 2in; wingspan 25.5cm, 10in

Pipistrelle body 5cm, 2in; wingspan 20.5cm, 8in

Grey squirrel body 25.5cm, 10in; tail 20.5cm, 8in

# MAMMALS of WOODLAND and HEDGEROW

*Deer use thick cover in woods to hide themselves and badgers only come out at night. Wood mice climb hazel twigs to get at the nuts and are a favourite prey for weasels.*

Thousands of years ago, when Britain was covered in dense forest, there were mammals to exploit every niche in the woodlands. Since then man has cleared the forest and exterminated many once common species, including bears, beavers and wild boar, and reduced the range of many others such as the pine marten and wild cat. Nevertheless, our woodlands still support a good range of mammals and our hedgerows act as 'highways' for the spread of newly introduced species such as muntjac deer. Woodland deer are browsers, taking advantage of dense cover and using their protective colouring to blend with their surroundings. They emerge, often at dusk, to nibble the tender young shoots of trees and shrubs or to graze in woodland clearings. In natural woodlands deer can prevent the regeneration of trees, so creating temporary scrublands.

On the forest floor, woodmice are the most abundant mammals, running along surface pathways or in underground tunnels. Among the bushes and briar and along hedgerows, woodmice will climb branches to reach nuts and berries at the end of flimsy, swaying twigs and will store them for the winter in old birds' nests. Dormice climb the bushes too, stripping honeysuckle bark from the thick, twining stems to build their nests. In hedgerows, bank voles tunnel into banks where they are pursued by weasels, small and lithe enough to enter their runs. Shrews, too distasteful to be eaten by most predators, scurry along well-used pathways in a constant search for worms and beetles.

Large carnivores such as foxes and badgers roam freely through the countryside but they show their woodland origins by preferring to keep to the cover of hedgerows. They will also, where possible, site their earths and sets in woodland or under a hedge. Cover and seclusion are also important to these mammals when they are rearing young. The cubs are brought to the surface to play but must be able to return instantly to the den at any hint of danger.

Deer were once common woodland mammals but their numbers have been much reduced. However, two small species, the **roe deer** and the **muntjac deer** are still quite common. Curiously, although the roe deer is now widespread and increasing over much of southern England, it had become completely extinct in England (but not Scotland) by the eighteenth century. Its recent spread and recolonisation is due to reintroductions in the nineteenth century. The muntjac is also an introduction. It came originally from south-east Asia but has escaped from collections to become quite widespread in central and southern England and it is still spreading. Both these deer are browsers, eating tree shoots, brambles and low herbage. The muntjac also eats nuts and fruit. They need plenty of cover, favouring areas with thick undergrowth, and they travel along hedgerows, usually during the day. Muntjac and roe deer are rather solitary yet they establish 'family' territories and roe deer often travel in a small party consisting of a doe, a fawn and a yearling.

In contrast to the deer the tiny, nocturnal **common dormouse** is in steady decline, due largely to the loss of its habitat. Once quite widespread, it is now rare and confined to southern England. It prefers woods, scrub and hedges with thick cover and plenty of nut-bearing trees and bushes. Dormice climb well and build round nests made from honeysuckle bark above the ground in dense scrub. Hibernation nests are usually built at or below ground level and the animal curls up inside with its long, furry tail wrapped over its head.

Most abundant of all mammals in Britain is the **woodmouse**. It has large, distinctive eyes and ears and occurs in a wide range of habitats where there is tree cover. Woodmice are active climbers but they also dig tunnels for their nests. They eat mainly seeds, nuts and berries, some of which they store for winter use. Being so abundant, they are a major prey for a variety of predators, especially tawny owls.

**Common shrews** are also extremely abundant, reaching very high numbers in woodland. They are, however, not eaten by most predators because of their strong, musty scent; only owls take them with any regularity. Shrews are active day and night, searching for worms and beetles in runways under surface litter or soil. Contact with other shrews during their regular foraging expeditions usually results in noisy fights. Shrews are short-lived and few survive beyond a second autumn.

Voles, though similar to mice, differ from them in having blunt noses, short tails and small eyes and ears. **Bank voles** prefer habitats with dense cover and are most common in thick, scrubby woodlands, hedgerows and forestry plantations. They are active in the daytime, climbing to reach their food of seeds, bark and berries. In winter they supplement their diet with dead leaves. Their numbers vary throughout the year and in years of abundance they may cause damage to tree seedlings by stripping bark.

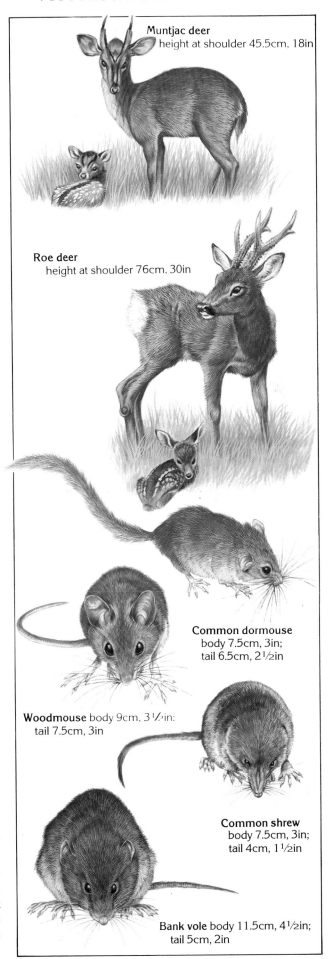

Muntjac deer
height at shoulder 45.5cm, 18in

Roe deer
height at shoulder 76cm, 30in

Common dormouse
body 7.5cm, 3in;
tail 6.5cm, 2½in

Woodmouse body 9cm, 3½in;
tail 7.5cm, 3in

Common shrew
body 7.5cm, 3in;
tail 4cm, 1½in

Bank vole body 11.5cm, 4½in;
tail 5cm, 2in

Squirrels are the best adapted of all British mammals for life in trees. Their bodies are built for climbing and leaping, and they display great agility and surefootedness on even the slenderest of twigs. The **red squirrel** is native to Britain but its numbers have been reduced by disease and competition from the introduced grey squirrel. The red is shyer and smaller than the grey. It is a richer red colour in summer and has prominent ear tufts in winter. It is most abundant in large areas of coniferous woodland where there is an ample supply of pine cones. Pine seeds stripped from the cones are its staple diet but it also eats fungi, tree foliage and on occasion birds' eggs and fledglings.

The weasel and the stoat, those sinuous and merciless hunters, are found on the woodland floor. The **stoat** is larger than the weasel and it has a permanent black tip to its tail. Northern populations

hedgerows and lanes, pursuing them down their burrows. Weasels are very inquisitive creatures and are active by day. If one is seen it will quickly hide but it soon reappears, standing on its hind legs to watch you. Like the stoat, it will raid birds' nests and nest boxes, taking both eggs and young.

Surprisingly, the large, powerfully-built **badger** is also a member of the weasel family. Its black and white head gives clear warning of its power to other creatures and it has no enemies except man. Yet despite its formidable strength the badger exists mainly on a diet of earthworms. An enormous range of other animal and vegetable food is also eaten and it uses its strong claws to dig out wasps' nests and young rabbits from nest holes. The badger set, an extensive system of tunnels and chambers, is usually sited among cover in woods and hedgerows.

When cubbing, **foxes** often make use of part of a

Red squirrel body 20.5cm, 8in; tail 18cm, 7in

Stoat body 25.5cm, 10in; tail 11.5cm, 4½in

Weasel body 20.5cm, 8in; tail 7.5cm, 3in

Fox body 61cm, 24in; tail 40.5cm, 16in

Badger 61–76cm, 24–30in

moult into a white coat in winter and are then known as **ermine**. Largely nocturnal, the stoat prefers to hunt from dense cover, tracking prey by scent. Small mammals (especially rabbits) and birds are the main items of its diet. Birds are attracted within reach by a strange, twirling, somersaulting dance which apparently fascinates them and overrides their sense of caution. In the autumn family groups hunt together, giving rise to stories that stoats hunt in packs. The **weasel** is an inhabitant of more open countryside where it hunts for voles and mice along

badger's rambling set as their den or earth as it is called. The fox's occupancy can usually be detected by the untidy litter of food remains and droppings strewn around the entrance hole. Except during the mating season, foxes are solitary and tend to lie up on the surface. They live and thrive in a variety of habitats, including many of our major cities, but are most abundant in habitats with good cover and plenty of prey. Rodents, moles, toads, insects and fruit are all part of their diet and in recent years they have taken to raiding rubbish bins.

# MAMMALS of GRASSLAND, HEATH and MOOR

*Field voles make runways through the grass and harvest mice make a nest of grass and leaves among tall stems. Below ground, moles patrol their tunnels, while hares live entirely above ground.*

Because Britain was once a forested country, most of our grassland mammals are also found in clearings and woodlands. One of the few true British grassland species is the mountain hare, restricted to cold, bleak mountain tops where the climate is too severe to allow trees to grow. It was probably much more widespread at the end of the last Ice Age when cold, windswept tundra grasslands covered most of the country. The wild cat, another species restricted to upland heath and moor, hunts for prey in the sparse grass cover and thick heather.

Thick grass covers the feeding runs of many small mammals, particularly the very abundant field vole, a major source of food for many grassland predators. Like a number of other grassland mammals, field vole populations may increase dramatically, resulting in mass movements and in places causing economic damage to trees and crops. Tall grasslands in the lowlands and, less commonly in recent years, tall crops provide cover for harvest mice that clamber among the stems. Lowland pastures are frequented by the brown hare which

likes open space to enable it to run at speed from its pursuers. Close-mown airport grasslands are one of its favourite habitats. Where there is cover for burrows the rabbit will be found in all types of grassland and the same is true for the mole. Being an underground dweller it is not so dependent on grass as are other species but it is rare or absent on the thin, sandy soils of true heaths.

Grass is difficult to digest so the herbivorous mammals of grassland all have special digestion chambers in their stomachs to break down the large quantities of fibre and cellulose. They also have teeth that grow throughout their lives, to cope with chewing rough grass stems. Grass is also rather poor in nourishment so most grass-eating species have to eat large amounts to meet their bodies' needs.

Tunnelling either below ground or in the dense mat of vegetation is another common feature of herbivorous grassland mammals. Hidden from view, they gain protection from predators in an otherwise open landscape. Even hares hide beside a tussock of grass in a low depression known as a form.

57

On mountain moorland and in upland forests the **wildcat** makes its den among rocks and fallen trees. Once widespread all over Britain, persecution has now reduced its range to only the Scottish Highlands. A shy, secretive animal, the wildcat is often mistaken for a feral tabby cat, but it is larger than a tabby and has well-defined rings on its blunt-ended, bushy tail. Domestic tabby cats always have pointed tails. The wildcat is a largely nocturnal and solitary creature that stalks or ambushes its prey, principally rabbits, hares and small rodents.

**Rabbits**, while being animals of open, grassy areas, prefer some tree or shrub cover in their habitat for the siting of their underground warrens. **Hares**, in contrast, live permanently above ground. The rabbit excavates a blind burrow or nest stop for its naked, helpless young, but the young of hares – called leverets – are born above the ground, active and fully furred. Hares can be distinguished from rabbits by their longer, black-tipped ears and longer hind legs. The mountain hare of high upland moors is smaller than the brown hare and in northern areas turns white in winter. In the spring, hares indulge in furious courtship chases and comic boxing matches, giving rise to the saying 'mad as a March hare'. Rabbits, originally from Spain and Portugal, were introduced into Britain by the Normans who kept them for food. They eventually became established in the wild in Britain and multiplied enormously, becoming a serious agricultural pest until myxomatosis, a viral disease of rabbits, first appeared in this country in 1953 and decimated the population.

**Field voles** are extremely abundant but not often seen. They make runways through grass, above the ground, keeping under cover and making nests under logs and in thick grass tussocks. Their populations undergo dramatic cycles of abundance and scarcity and not surprisingly they are eaten by a variety of bird and mammal predators. Field voles are active all day and they feed mainly on grass, leaves, stems and bark. Voles differ from mice in having a short tail, small ears and a blunt nose.

The smallest British mouse is the tiny, chestnut-coloured **harvest mouse**. It was once common in cornfields but mechanical harvesting and changing agricultural practices have brought about its decline. Now it is a rare and local species confined to reed beds and dense, grassy areas, especially near hedgerows. Harvest mice are agile climbers with prehensile tails and they clamber among grass stalks and low vegetation in search of insects and seeds.

Below ground, the **mole** moves along its tunnels in search of beetles and worms. With a cylindrical body, small eyes and ears and large digging claws it is perfectly adapted for life underground. Moles are present in most grassy habitats and are surprisingly common in deciduous woodland. Molehills, heaps of freshly dug soil, are the best indication of the mole's presence. Food is stored in chambers during the autumn and winter.

Wildcat body 76cm, 30in; tail 15cm, 6in

Rabbit 40.5cm, 16in

Brown hare 61cm, 24in

Harvest mouse body 5.5cm, 2¼in; tail 5cm, 2in

Field vole body 10cm, 4in; tail 2.5cm, 1in

Mole 15cm, 6in

# MAMMALS of the WATER'S EDGE

*The introduced mink preys heavily on water voles. The mink is an agile and active swimmer.*

Aquatic habitats, although a good source of food, are demanding for mammals which are largely land-based animals. Most aquatic mammals have water-repellent fur that prevents waterlogging and avoids the dangers of chilling, and layers of fat under the skin to protect them from the cold. Swimming species such as otters also have webbed feet and paddle-shaped tails that help propel them through the water. The food taken by water-dwelling mammals is also very varied, ranging from bankside grasses and water weeds to invertebrates and fish. None of them, however, depend completely on the water. All species on occasion forage for food far away from water and some, such as water shrews, can often be found in hedgerows long distances from the swift-flowing streams they usually inhabit.

Not surprisingly, most aquatic mammals seek shelter in natural holes or in burrows they excavate for themselves in river banks. Mink and otters occupy and raise their young in temporary dens, known as holts, beneath tree roots in the river bank. Water voles dig tunnels with one entrance in the river bank, one entrance below water and another entrance coming out on the surface of the land near the river. Their clever nests have an airtight chamber which traps a life-saving pocket of air during times of flood. The introduced coypu is also an avid and destructive tunnelling species. In East Anglia, where it is common, its activities can undermine ditch banks and the dikes which are defences against flooding, and for this reason it is heavily persecuted.

Other species of mammal are regularly attracted to water because of the availability of food. Foxes search waterside reeds for ducklings and rodents, and some bats constantly fly over ponds and lakes to catch the gnats and small flies that swarm there. They have also been seen skimming over the surface of lakes to scoop up water to drink.

Daubenton's bat and the water shrew are two insectivores with greatly contrasting lifestyles and habits yet both are attracted to water. Although found in many habitats the **Daubenton's bat** is often seen over water, flying low and fast in pursuit of insects, occasionally touching the water's surface. The **water shrew** is mostly aquatic, living in clear, unpolluted streams where it feeds on frogs, fish and water invertebrates. Prey is detected by sensitive, mobile whiskers on the snout as the shrew swims along the surface of the water. It dives only with difficulty, despite the presence of stiff bristles under the tail and along the hind legs which assist it in swimming. Unique among British shrews, the water shrew produces venom in its saliva which probably helps in subduing prey.

The very large, introduced coypu and the native, rat-sized water vole have many similarities in their behaviour and choice of habitat. Both live in weedy waterways, both eat a variety of grasses and both are active during the day. **Coypus**, originally from South America, were bred on farms in Britain for their dense, water-repellent underfur. There were many escapes and several colonies were established, but these are now confined to reed swamps and marshes in East Anglia. Strenuous efforts are made to control the animals' numbers because of their habits of invading farmers' fields to nibble crops, especially sugar beet, and tunnelling into the banks of dikes. **Water voles** cause no economic damage and are regularly seen along most waterways in Britain, though they are rare or absent in much of western Scotland. They dive and swim well and nest in tunnels excavated in banks.

The North American **mink** is another species which has escaped from fur farms to become widely established in Britain. Breeding in the wild was first recorded on the River Teign in Devon in 1956 and since then colonies have become established in most parts of England and much of Scotland and Wales. Nocturnal, solitary and excellent swimmers, they are ferocious hunters of fish, small mammals and birds. In places they have seriously reduced the numbers of moorhens and water voles.

It was once thought that mink were responsible for the recent dramatic decline in the **otter** population. The sad truth, however, is that pesticides, pollution and disturbance, not the mink, have brought about the loss of the otter from most parts of Britain. In fact, otters have even been known to kill and eat mink! With their streamlined bodies, thick, tapering tails and webbed feet, otters are superbly adapted for aquatic life. Under water they propel themselves by powerful undulations of their bodies. Fish is their main food but they also eat aquatic insects, birds and small mammals.

**Daubenton's bat** body 5cm, 2in; wingspan 24cm, 9½in

**Water shrew** body 9cm, 3½in; tail 6.5cm, 2½in

**Coypu** body 61cm, 24in; tail 45.5cm 18in

**Water vole** body 20.5cm, 8in; tail 10cm, 4in

**Mink** body 45.5cm, 18in; tail 15cm, 6in

**Otter** body 66–84cm, 26–33in; tail 30.5cm, 12in

# MAMMALS of the SEA

More than three-quarters of the earth's surface is covered with water, in places up to three miles deep. Exotic and wonderful creatures are found in these uncharted depths, while teeming populations of plankton, invertebrates and fishes roam the fertile, sunlit waters near the surface. The oceans are the home of the cetaceans, including the whales, among the most awsome of all living creatures. The blue whale at up to 30m (100ft) long is the largest animal in the world. Despite it size, this mammal, like most other whales – a group that includes dolphins and

contrast, the **common dolphin** is sleek and fast-moving, with a snout drawn into a pronounced 'beak'. They are active, inquisitive and playful, often leaping out of the water or following ships at sea. Dolphins move into British waters from the south-west, following migrating shoals of herring and mackerel, their major prey.

Seals also feed extensively on fish, but apart from far-ranging juvenile wanderings, the two British species are relatively sedentary and show no migratory behaviour. The **common seal** is an animal

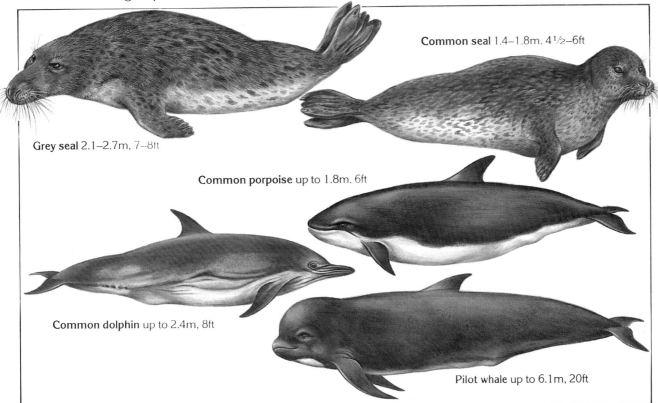

Common seal 1.4–1.8m. 4½–6ft

Grey seal 2.1–2.7m, 7–8ft

Common porpoise up to 1.8m. 6ft

Common dolphin up to 2.4m, 8ft

Pilot whale up to 6.1m, 20ft

porpoises – feeds on the vast populations of small creatures known as krill that drift in the open sea.

Each year the **pilot whale** migrates from sub-polar regions to the warmer waters of the temperate south following shoals of fish and squid. They are seen regularly in the coastal waters around Scotland and north-east England. They usually swim slowly in 'schools' of twenty or so individuals but on occasion 200 or more may be stranded together on beaches.

Porpoises and dolphins are often mistaken for each other but they can be easily distinguished. The **common porpoise** is the smallest British cetacean and is found around all parts of the British coast, especially in the late summer and autumn. It has a blunt snout and swims slowly in large schools, feeding on a variety of fish and crustaceans. By

of sheltered waters, sandbanks and estuaries. The largest British colonies are to be found in East Anglia and there are smaller colonies in the Scottish firths. Common seal pups are born on temporarily-exposed sandbanks in mid-summer and are able to swim and dive as soon as they are born. The pups will clamber on to their mothers' backs when they get tired. Fish are their main prey, and this brings them into conflict with man when they take salmon from nets. The larger **grey seal** is a more serious pest of salmon fisheries, and both species have been culled regularly in the past but a close season now operates during their breeding time. In Britain the grey seal is common on all rocky coasts. Fish are hunted by means of sensitive vibrissae (bristly hairs) on their long muzzles.

# MILK BOTTLES, PELLETS AND PATIENCE

The study of mammals needs patience and a good working knowledge of practical fieldcraft. All mammals rely, to a greater or lesser extent, on their senses of sight, smell and hearing to tell them what is happening around them. Mammal watchers must know how to avoid giving away their presence to the animals they are tracking. So if you want more than just a chance, fleeting glimpse of wild mammals follow these few simple but vital rules:

- Always dress in subdued colours, preferably brown or dull green.
- Always move slowly and quietly, pausing frequently to look around you.
- Never allow yourself to become exposed on the skyline and never make sudden or excited movements.
- Never make any unnecessary noise and *don't talk*.
- Always try to remain downwind of your quarry.

Most mammals have very keen eyesight. Dull-coloured clothing helps break up your outline, making you less noticeable and enabling you to blend into the background. Bright colours, sudden movement and noise will attract attention. The modern, so-called 'camouflage' clothing is in reality far too bright to wear when mammal watching. Wearing gloves and a hat or hood will help to conceal the surprisingly bright patches of skin on the hands and head. Your scent, though, is one of the greatest giveaways of your presence. Eyesight and hearing may be poor in some species but all mammals have an acute sense of smell. When watching or stalking it is essential to approach into the wind so that your scent is not carried to your quarry.

## CLOTHING

Inevitably, much of your mammal watching will take place in cold weather. You will certainly find yourself in rough terrain and probably end up crawling along a wet ditch. Tough, warm and waterproof clothing is, therefore, a must. Get a windproof, waterproof jacket, preferably with a hood and roomy pockets. Heavy denim or twill trousers will protect you from the vicious barbs of bramble, thorn and gorse. Wellington boots are best for most conditions but if you prefer to wear stout walking boots they must be waterproofed regularly.

Never underestimate the weather. When you stop moving or sit watching for long periods it's surprising how cold you can become, even in summer. Thermal underwear and socks are invaluable, as is an extra jumper carried in your rucksack. A pair of nylon over-trousers which fold to fit your pocket or rucksack will protect you from the uncomfortable effects of sudden showers.

## EQUIPMENT

Generally, the less you have to carry around with you the better. A small rucksack is useful for carrying your sandwiches and flask, plastic bags, a penknife and any specimens you collect. Many mammal watchers also carry a small inflatable cushion to ease the burden of sitting on cold, hard or wet ground. A notebook and pencil will be needed for taking notes – remember, a pencil will write even when it is wet, a ballpoint pen won't.

Finally, every serious mammal watcher should have a pair of binoculars. For general work a small,

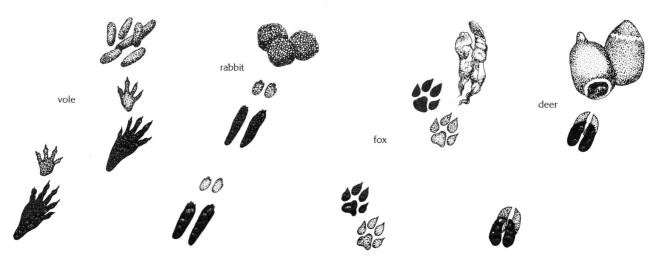

vole

rabbit

fox

deer

mammal tracks and droppings

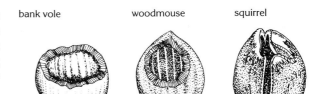

bank vole · woodmouse · squirrel

hazelnuts opened by small mammals

lightweight pair with a magnification of 7x or 8x is ideal (see the section on birdwatching for more information). Binoculars not only allow you to watch mammals without the need to move in too close, but they also enable you to locate your quarry at a greater range and with less likelihood of disturbance.

# LOOKING FOR MAMMALS

Finding mammals isn't just a matter of walking about the countryside in the hope of bumping into them. This can happen, but it usually requires care, quiet and a lot of time and patience. It is far better to look for the signs that mammals leave and then go out to look for them, confident not only of knowing which species are likely to be seen in a particular area but also knowing just where you have a chance of seeing them. The easiest signs to look for are burrows, footprints, droppings and signs of feeding.

Holes in the ground with lots of earth outside could indicate rabbit, badger or fox. Rabbit holes tend to be higher than they are wide, while badger holes tend to be wider than they are high, though this isn't always so. Foxes often leave a smelly collection of carcases outside their holes and they sometimes make their earths in badger sets. One way to tell if a hole is in use and what species is using it is to lightly rake over the soil outside the burrow and return the next day to look for footprints. The homes of smaller mammals are harder to find. When searching for the riverside burrows of water voles look for small areas of neat, green, close-cropped grass just above the water level – a water vole 'lawn' – and you'll soon locate the hole. Field voles and shrews make runways in thick grass. Tease apart the grass to follow the runways and look for fresh droppings which might indicate that the runs are still in use.

Droppings may be scattered at random, as with deer and hedgehogs, but very often they are deposited to mark territorial boundaries. Rabbits make distinctive dung piles, usually on a raised spot like an ant mound, and badgers create regular lines of dropping pits. Territorial dropping places are used regularly and may lead to good sightings for the observant mammal watcher, but randomly scattered droppings can also give you a clue as to which species are in the vicinity.

Feeding signs are a little more difficult to interpret. Each species of rodent has a characteristic way of opening nuts and most of them strip bark from trees. Places regularly browsed by deer are revealed by the neatly clipped appearance of bushes and trees.

Lastly, always look for animal pathways. Most larger mammals prefer to follow a regular route when crossing roads or open fields and, with practice, it becomes easy to spot a well-used path. Look for hair caught in barbed wire or on thorn bushes to confirm you suspicions. Mammals also use human footpaths. Look for their tell-tale footprints in soft earth and mud.

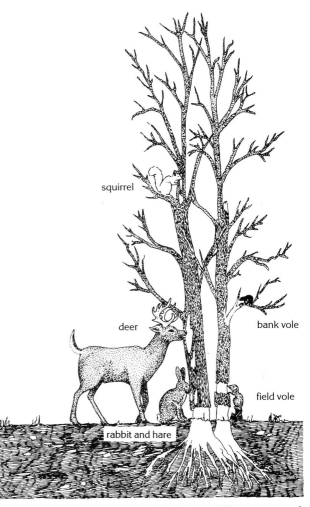

squirrel

deer

bank vole

field vole

rabbit and hare

Various mammal species strip bark from different parts of trees and shrubs.

Collecting all this information is in itself great fun but now, and most importantly, with this knowledge you will have a much greater chance of seeing and watching wild mammals. Dawn or dusk are the best times to watch but some mammals such as deer and water voles can be seen during the day. Choose a place, perhaps overlooking a burrow or an animal pathway, select a comfortable vantage point in good cover and patiently sit and wait. Sometimes you won't see the animals you want, though baiting can be helpful (see Projects). But there are many other creatures in the countryside besides mammals and watching them can be just as rewarding as you sit in wait for a sight of your 'real' quarry.

## OWL PELLETS and MILK BOTTLES

Because of their small size and secretive habits mice, voles and shrews are not often seen. Their feeding signs can be scarce and their droppings hard to find and identify. However, there are two fascinating, if somewhat messy, ways of finding out about the small mammals in your area. The first involves the examination of owl pellets for the presence of skulls and jaws and the second requires you to search hedgerows and roadsides for discarded bottles into which small mammals have crawled, been trapped and died.

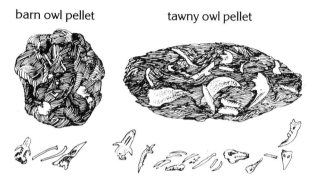

barn owl pellet          tawny owl pellet

mammal bones and skull removed from a pellet

Owl pellets are the disgorged remains of prey – the fur, feathers and bones – that the bird cannot digest. Owls, and other birds of prey, cast their pellets at their regular daytime roosts, usually an old barn or tree, where they rest in quiet security. Owl pellets readily break up in warm water and armed with a hand lens and a suitable key to jaws and teeth it is easy to identify which mammals the owl has been eating (see Projects: Making a Skull Collection). Once you have located a roost you can collect pellets at different times of the year. Eventually you will build up a picture not only of what species are being eaten but also how many and at what time of year.

Carelessly discarded empty milk bottles are lethal for small mammals. Thinking the bottle mouth is a tunnel they crawl in, only to find the slippery glass and narrow neck form a death trap from which they cannot escape. When searching for bottles containing mammal remains it would be a kindness to take home any empty bottles you find. A bottle partly filled with a smelly, semi-liquid ooze is most likely to contain mammal remains. Repeatedly rinse the ooze through a sieve – it is dangerous to break the bottle – until you find skulls or jaws.

# WHERE TO WATCH MAMMALS

Watching mammals in the wild can be done in the comfort of your own back garden or in the wealth of habitats in the countryside. Most mammals are quite widely spread and present in any suitable habitat but some are more local and choosy and you will need patience, fieldcraft and sound information if you are to track them down. The map shows some of the areas where the more unusual and exciting mammals can be found in Britain.

Safari parks are good places to study the behaviour of some species of exotic animals such as primates or the big cats. In open, free-ranging conditions many species retain their natural behaviour patterns and are interesting to watch. Zoos also provide an opportunity to study mammals at close quarters where much can be learned about their lifestyles and adaptations. Most zoos now have very good educational departments that can make your visit much more rewarding and enjoyable.

## MAMMAL SITES

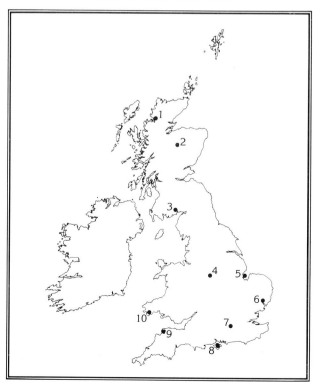

1. Beinn Eighe, Ross-shire

A National Nature Reserve. Mountain, moorland and western pine woods containing red deer, pine marten, red squirrel, wild cat, wild goat and mountain hare. There are several nature trails in the area and a visitors' centre at the village of Torridon.

2. The Cairngorms, Inverness-shire

A National Nature Reserve. Mountain, moorland and ancient pine woods. Red squirrel, mountain hare, wild cat and a herd of semi-domesticated reindeer – the only herd in Britain – thrive in the National Nature Reserve.

3. Leighton Moss, Lancashire

A Royal Society for the Protection of Birds reserve close to Carnforth. Otters are seen regularly from the hides that overlook the meres on the reserve.

4. The Peak District

A National Park. Mountain hares can still be found here and the introduced red-necked wallaby can be found in heather moorland and thick scrub in areas north-west of Leek in Staffordshire and near Hoo Moor in Derbyshire.

5. The Wash

Houses the largest British colony of common seals. Common seals can also be found at Dornoch Firth and the Firth of Tay on the east coast of Scotland and along much of the west coast of scotland.

6. East Anglia

This area is the stronghold of the introduced coypu. They are found in fens and wetlands over the whole area and are occasionally seen from the hides in the Royal Society for the Protection of Birds reserves such as Minsmere, a coastal reserve south of Dunwich.

7. Richmond Park, Surrey

An extensive tract of parkland close to London which has a herd of red deer and resident badgers as well as many of the common mammals.

8. Isle of Wight, Hampshire

The island is one of the last strongholds for red squirrels in southern England. They can also be found in the Breckland of East Anglia, in parts of northern England and extensively in Scotland and Wales.

9. Exmoor, Devon and Somerset

A National Park. The Exmoor heaths and wooded valleys are home to red deer, and the rivers are havens for otters. There is also a famous herd of feral goats in the Valley of the Rocks, Lynton.

10. Pembrokeshire

The Pembrokeshire coast and islands have a large colony of grey seals, especially on the islands of Skomer, Skokholm and Ramsey. They are best seen here in October, during the breeding season. There are also extensive grey seal colonies in the western Scottish isles and around much of the coast of Ireland.

# MAMMAL MUSEUMS AND COLLECTIONS

Birmingham Nature Centre,
Cannon Hill Park,
Birmingham.
Run by Birmingham Museum.
An interesting collection of small mammals, insects and birds in natural conditions.

British Museum (Natural History),
Zoological Museum,
Akeman Street,
Tring,
Herts.
An extensive collection of stuffed mammals and birds.

Edinburgh Zoo,
Zoological Park,
Murrayfield,
Edinburgh,
Scotland EH12 6TS

# REPTILES and AMPHIBIANS

Nowadays reptiles and amphibians are lumped together under the rather ugly name of herptiles. They are usually considered together because of their close similarities in structure and evolution but they are in fact very different both in lifestyle and form. Amphibians have soft, moist skins and must return to water to breed, but reptiles have dry, scaly skins and are completely independent of water for breeding, instead laying eggs which are protected from drying out by tough shells.

Amphibians were the first vertebrates (animals with backbones) to leave the water for the land. In time they gave rise to reptiles and eventually to birds and mammals, yet they themselves never completely gave up their watery habitat. For a very brief period during the Carboniferous era 300 million years ago they ruled the world: giant amphibians lived in the swamps and steamy jungles among the plants that time has turned into coal. The amphibians were soon overtaken by the more efficient reptiles, a line of evolution that eventually led to the mighty dinosaurs and the greatest blossoming of reptile life.

In the modern world herptiles are sadly reduced in numbers. Of the amphibians only frogs, toads, newts and salamanders remain. Of the reptiles, the turtles, crocodiles, lizards and snakes have survived. The turtles, including tortoises and terrapins, are an order older even than the dinosaurs, while crocodiles and alligators are hardly changed from their ancestors who inhabited muddy rivers and creeks in the world of the dinosaurs.

## NEED FOR WATER

The amphibians' need for water does restrict their distribution but they have evolved some remarkable ways of surviving drought and rearing their young. One tropical tree frog releases its tadpoles into the tiny puddles of rainwater trapped in the leaves of plants, while the Surinam toad rears its young on its back! As the eggs are laid the male Surinam toad presses them into special brood pouches on the female's back where they remain until fully developed.

British frogs and toads spawn in shallow pools and ponds and the eggs are fertilised in the water by a male clasped on to the female's back. The mating process can be noisy and spectacular. Toads also make mass migrations to the same piece or water every spring and hundreds can be seen moving towards their ponds on favourable nights. Strangely, frogs and toads are almost the only herptiles with a voice – the most that other species can muster is a low hiss or a thin squeak. Male frogs and toads use air-filled sacs of skin on the face and throat to amplify their croaking voices. The expanded sacs turn them into grotesque and comic sights but the real purpose of croaking is to attract a mate and they will 'sing'

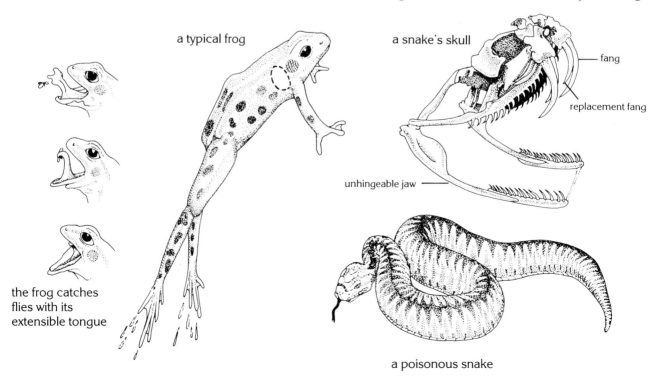

a typical frog

the frog catches flies with its extensible tongue

a snake's skull

fang

replacement fang

unhingeable jaw

a poisonous snake

continuously to lure a female to them. It has been found that females are generally attracted to the larger males with the deepest croaks. The remaining herptiles use bright colours or attractive scents in their courtship.

## FEEDING

Most herptiles are carnivorous. Frogs and toads have long, sticky tongues which can be shot out some distance to catch prey, and snakes have evolved powerful poisons to subdue fast-moving prey. Snake venoms attack the nervous system or dissolve vital tissues, causing paralysis and death. Venoms are delivered through needle-sharp hollow fangs that are folded back into the mouth until the snake is ready to strike. The prey is silently stalked and then struck at with lightning speed, the fangs buried deep into the flesh to deliver the poison rapidly into the body. The venom does not act immediately and the stricken animal may have time to run away. The snake, however, just follows its scent trail at a leisurely pace, confident in the knowledge that the poison will soon take effect and immobilise its victim. Snakes are able to swallow very large prey by unhinging their jaws and allowing their mouths to stretch wide. Waves of muscular contractions push the prey into the snake's stomach where it lies as a noticeable lump until it is digested.

One apparent disadvantage for reptiles and amphibians is their cold-bloodedness. Low temperatures send reptiles into an inactive torpor but many amphibians are quite resistant to cold. To remain active reptiles must bask in the sun to raise their body temperatures. The one advantage of cold-bloodedness which has enabled herptiles to survive alongside the more active and efficient mammals is that torpor and a low body temperature reduce the amount of energy used. This means that less food has to be eaten to remain alive, and so herptiles can fill niches that mammmals cannot because of the mammals' need for a large and constantly available supply of food.

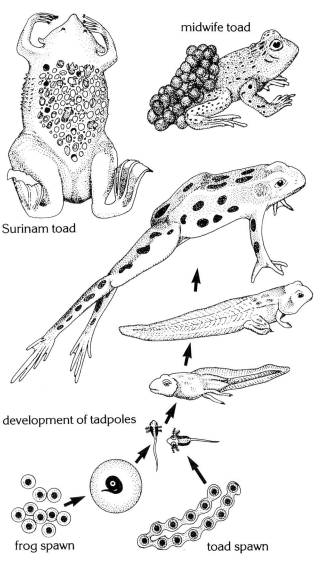

midwife toad

Surinam toad

development of tadpoles

frog spawn

toad spawn

Garter snakes give birth to live young; grass snakes hatch from eggs.

## HERPTILE FACTS AND FEATS

MOST POISONOUS

| | |
|---|---|
| World | The most venomous reptile is the sea snake of north-western Australia. The most poisonous amphibian is the golden arrow-poison frog of South America. An average adult specimen contains enough poison to kill 2,200 people and it is even dangerous to handle. |
| LARGEST | |
| World | The largest reptile is the salt-water crocodile of Australia and south-west Asia. An adult male measures 4.2-4.8m (14-16ft) in length and weighs about 408-520kg (900-1150lb). The largest amphibian is the Chinese giant salamander which lives in marshes and mountain streams. One specimen measured 180cm (5ft 11in) in length and weighed 65kg (143lb). |

# FROGS, TOADS and NEWTS

Two toads, one frog and three newts are native to the British Isles, though a number of other frogs and toads have been introduced with varying success. In the past few decades all the British amphibians have declined in numbers, largely because of land drainage, changes in agriculture and pond infilling. Two species, the natterjack toad and the great crested newt are now so uncommon that they are protected by the Wildlife and Countryside Act.

The **common frog** varies in colour from yellowish to olive, has spotted flanks and a distinct eardrum. Frogs leap rather than walk or hop as do toads, and their webbed feet make them strong swimmers. They feed on slugs, beetles and other insects which they catch with a long, sticky tongue.

Of the toads, the **common toad** is the most widespread and is found even in fairly dry habitats. Its body is heavily warted and the colour varies from greyish to brown, and sometimes brick red. The eyes are a striking gold or copper colour. The common toad is largely nocturnal and feeds on insects, especially ants and worms, which it crams into its mouth with its forelegs.

Both the common toad and the **natterjack toad** have an amazing defence against predators, particularly grass snakes. They adopt a head-down, rump-up posture and puff up their bodies with air to make them appear much larger than they really are. Grass snakes often decide they are too big to swallow and move on! The natterjack toad is easily distinguished from the common toad by the prominent yellow stripe down its back. It is also much rarer, being found only in areas of dune and heath where it spawns in shallow, sandy pools.

The three British newts are very different from frogs and toads and rather resemble lizards, especially during their land-living phase when they can be found away from water under logs and stones. During the breeding season males sport large, showy crests and develop bright courtship colours.

The **great crested newt** is a very dark species that prefers to breed in deep ponds. Breeding males develop bold patterns of yellow or orange on their underbellies and a spiky crest along their backs. The bright colours may also warn predators that this newt secretes a mild poison from its skin as a means of defence.

The **smooth newt** is the commonest newt in Britain. It is also the most terrestrial and outside the breeding season it can be found in a variety of habitats including cultivated ground, woods and gardens.

The **palmate newt** is less common, preferring acid pools and even brackish ponds by the sea.

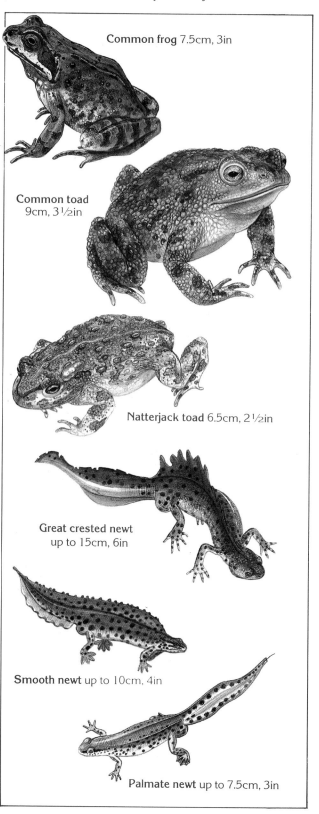

Common frog 7.5cm, 3in

Common toad 9cm, 3½in

Natterjack toad 6.5cm, 2½in

Great crested newt up to 15cm, 6in

Smooth newt up to 10cm, 4in

Palmate newt up to 7.5cm, 3in

# SNAKES and LIZARDS

There are three snakes and three lizards native to the British Isles, though none of the snakes and only one lizard, the viviparous lizard, are found in Ireland. The slow-worm has a superficial resemblance to a snake but it is really a legless lizard. All these reptiles have a forked tongue, which they flick constantly in and out to 'taste' the air, drawing it back over scent-sensitive organs in the mouth. Two heathland reptiles, the smooth snake and the sand lizard, are becoming increasingly rare due to the break-up and destruction of their habitat and they are now protected by the Wildlife and Countryside Act.

Britain's only poisonous snake is the **adder** or **viper**. Its bite, though painful, is rarely fatal. The venom is stored in a gland in the upper jaw and is pumped through the hollow fangs after they have been embedded in the victim. After use the fangs can be folded back into the mouth out of the way. Adders are active during the day and live in a wide variety of habitats. They lie in wait to ambush their prey – small mammals, birds, lizards and other animals.

The slow-moving **smooth snake** also ambushes its prey, mainly other reptiles – especially lizards and slow-worms – which it holds and tightly squeezes in its coils. It is a snake of dry, sandy heathland though it seldom strays far from water.

The **grass snake** prefers damp habitats and is a good swimmer. It is the largest British snake and is easily recognised by the yellow, black-bordered collar behind the head. If handled it will often feign death, drooping its head and body and usually giving off a foul-smelling secretion from its anal gland.

**Slow-worms** can be distinguished from snakes by their movable eyelids and their ability to shed their tails when attacked, which is typical of lizards. They prefer damp habitats with plenty of ground cover and an abundance of their main food – slugs and snails. They bask under warm, flat stones rather than in the open and are surprisingly long-lived.

The rare **sand lizard** inhabits dry, sandy heaths and sand-dunes, particularly where there is a dense cover of low vegetation. It is quite inconspicuous as it clambers among the plants in search of spiders and insects and can be easily overlooked.

In contrast, the **viviparous lizard** inhabits more humid habitats in open woodland and scrub as well as fields and hedgerows. It forages close to the ground for a wide variety of invertebrate prey and is the lizard most often seen basking in the sun. The female gives birth to live young and basks to maintain her temperature as her young are developing. In unfavourable summers she will carry the foetuses over winter during her hibernation.

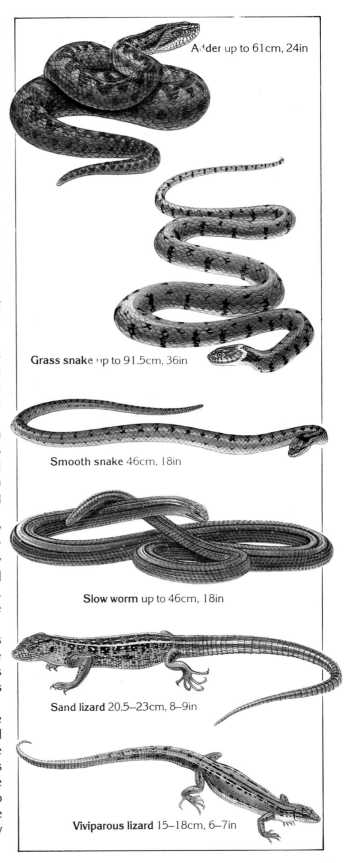

Adder up to 61cm, 24in

Grass snake up to 91.5cm, 36in

Smooth snake 46cm, 18in

Slow worm up to 46cm, 18in

Sand lizard 20.5–23cm, 8–9in

Viviparous lizard 15–18cm, 6–7in

# FISHES

More than seventy per cent of the earth's surface is covered by water and here the fishes are undoubtedly the dominant vertebrates. There are at least 25,000 species and they number in tens of thousands of millions. They are most abundant in the shallow seas along the margins of continents where life-giving nutrients are poured into the sea by muddy rivers. In the icy cold depths of the oceans where light cannot penetrate food is sparse and there are few fishes. The fish that do live here have enormous stomachs capable of accommodating prey much larger than themselves for no chance of a meal can be missed. Many of these deep-sea fishes have bizarre shapes and usually carry arrays of light-emitting organs to lure prey, or perhaps to distract predators. Away from the sea, fishes are quite at home in every kind of watery habitat from rushing streams to deep, slow-flowing rivers. They can even be found, blind and colourless, in dark pools deep in underground caves. Fishes can be very hardy, surviving not only the great pressures in the depths of the sea but also the intense cold of the frozen wastes of the north and south polar regions. The black fish of Siberia and Alaska is reported to survive unharmed, frozen into winter ice, until released by the spring thaw. A kind of 'anti-freeze' in the blood of Antarctic fishes keeps them active even when the sea reaches freezing point. Yet fishes are also very sensitive. They may be killed by quite small changes in the chemical composition of the water in which they live and are susceptible to disease in polluted or semi-polluted water.

Fishes were among the first vertebrates to evolve, appearing some 400 million years ago, and they swarmed into the oceans to become the dominant form of life there – the position they still hold all these millions of years later. During their long history they have evolved into a number of strange and incredible forms, the best-known fossils of which are the

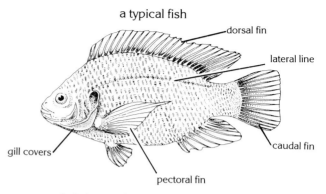

a typical fish
dorsal fin
lateral line
caudal fin
pectoral fin
gill covers

armoured fishes which were covered all over in protective bony plates. These must have been heavy, slow-moving creatures which fed on sluggish or sedentary animals on the sea bottom. The forerunners of our modern fishes did not appear until the end of the Cretaceous period some 80 million years ago.

## GILLS and SPECIAL SENSES

What special features of fishes have enabled them to survive unchallenged through the ages in their watery habitat? Perhaps the most important is that most fish have very highly efficient gills for extracting oxygen from the water. Fishes' gills are a marvel of animal engineering. There are several banks of them on each side of the head, each bank supported by an arch of cartilage. From each arch there extends a mass of delicate, finely-folded filaments made up of extremely thin blood vessels. The blood in these filaments, which contains the red pigment haemoglobin just like human blood, flows in the opposite direction to the flow of water. This 'contraflow' system is extremely efficient. Fishes' gills can extract eighty per cent of the available oxygen from water whereas man can extract barely twenty-five per cent of the oxygen from the air he breathes. Fish without gills breathe through their

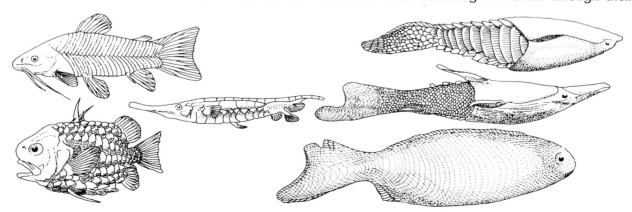

Some modern armoured fishes (left) compared with fossil armoured fishes (right).

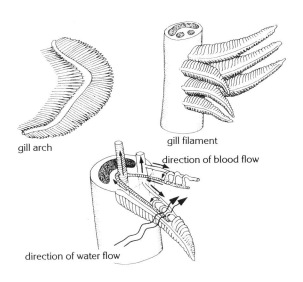

how fish gills work

gill arch

gill filament

direction of blood flow

direction of water flow

highly permeable skins, the second of their unique features. Their skin is thin, transparent and covered in slime. Embedded in it are scales – thin, bony plates with a variety of shapes and uses. Scales and slime are of vital importance to a fish. The slime maintains the chemical balance of the skin, sometimes of the whole body, and if large areas of scales are rubbed off then the fish becomes prone to bacterial and fungal attack on its exposed skin. In some fishes scales have been modified into a covering of horny armour, similar to the armour of fossil fishes, while in others scales have been adapted as weapons of defence. An example of this are the scales on the whip-like tail of the sting-rays. The 'whip' is long and flexible and has projecting scales with saw-like edges which can inflict a vicious, jagged wound. Another special feature is the organ known as the 'lateral line' that runs the length of each side of the body of a fish. It is a slime-filled canal with a series of openings at the surface, well supplied with sensitive nerves. The lateral line can detect even small changes in pressure in the water for some distance around the fish. It serves to warn of obstructions and the movements of other fish and predators in the water and is often regarded as a fish's 'sixth sense'. Finally, there are fins, webbed outgrowths of cartilage that fish use to steer and propel themselves through the water. Over millions of years of evolution these fins have been modified for other uses – into legs for walking, as cruel 'stings' that can inject painful venom or, as is the case in flying fish, into wings for short, gliding flights over the ocean's surface.

# FEEDING and BREEDING

As would be expected from such an ancient and diverse order of animals, fishes feed in a variety of ways on a wide range of foods. Other fish and animals, crustaceans, insects, weed and plankton are among the commonest foods. Flesh-eaters have arrays of sharp teeth which are continuously replaced as they are lost or worn away. Sharks, legendary for their feeding exploits on man, have a continually growing conveyor-belt system for their dagger-like teeth. Sharks may be fearsome but for sheer ferocity and voraciousness there is little to beat the Atlantic blue-fish. These fish hunt in vast, ravening packs which are estimated to eat ten thousand million fish every day during a summer season! Fishes feeding on hard corals or molluscs have grinding teeth and hard, biting jaws while in plankton feeders the teeth are reduced to stumps and instead 'gill-rakers' are used to sieve plankton from the water.

Despite the great variety of fishes, their reproduction is remarkably similar. Virtually all of them lay eggs which are fertilised in the open water. In oceanic species it is quite common for the eggs to drift on the sea currents, at the mercy of predators and the elements. Freshwater species often build nests or lay eggs in sticky clumps and strings among water weeds, and brood care by one of the parent fish is common. Tropical cichlid fishes brood their eggs in their mouths and also shelter their young in their mouths when danger threatens.

Inevitably, through their very abundance, fishes have attracted the attention of man. Many fishes are good to eat and in the past some primitive communities lived almost entirely on fish caught from the sea or from huge inland lakes. In modern times new technology has presented man with the possibility of unlimited harvesting of the ocean's fishes. Unhappily, one by one, fish populations have been depleted and this destruction of fish stocks has also caused the decline of the birds, sea mammals and predatory fishes that feed on them. The sea is a fragile world largely closed to us. We cannot see the damage we inflict, we can only see the results.

## FISH FACTS AND FEATS

**LARGEST FISH**

| | |
|---|---|
| *Great Britain* | In 1937 a common sturgeon 2.74m (9ft) long was taken from the River Severn. It weighed 230kg (507.5lb) |
| *World* | The whale shark, widespread in warm parts of the world's oceans. The largest recorded was 18.5m (60ft 9in) long and its weight was estimated to be 43 tonnes (42.4 tons). |

**SMALLEST FISH**

| | |
|---|---|
| *World* | The dwarf pygmy goby is a colourless and nearly transparent fish of streams and lakes in the Philippines. An adult male meaures only 7.5-9.9mm (0.28-0.38in) in length and weighs 4-5mg (0.00014-0.00017oz). |

**FASTEST FISH**

| | |
|---|---|
| *World* | The sailfish. One off Florida, USA, was recorded at a speed of 109.7km/h (68.1mph). |

# STREAM FISHES

The tumbling upper reaches of rivers and the swiftly-flowing waters of tributary streams course over beds of rock, sand and gravel with little vegetation cover. These well-oxygenated waters are home for a number of small fishes that hide under stones by day and hunt for aquatic invertebrates at night.

The **brown trout** is the largest of the stream fishes and with the bullhead will live in streams at an altitude of over 2000m (6000ft). It is active during the day, though rather sedentary, preferring to take up and defend a feeding station behind a bubbling riffle or in a deep pool below an overhanging bank. Brown trout are not migratory; they remain in the streams all their lives and spawn in the loose gravels and sand.

Bullheads and stone loach are strictly nocturnal and remain hidden during the day. The **bullhead** has earned the alternative name of 'miller's thumb' from the likeness of its broad, flattened head to the flat thumb developed by millers as they rubbed wheat grains between thumb and forefinger. Bullheads feed on the larvae of mayflies, blackflies and caddis flies but will also eat the eggs and fry of other fish. Their own eggs are laid in a hollow excavated under a stone and are guarded by the male. **Stone loach** eat similar prey but they also take worms and snails. Stone loach are very sensitive to pollution so their presence is regarded as a sign that a river or stream is in good health.

Commonest of all British river and stream fishes is the **minnow**. It is present, living in small, tight-packed shoals, in most waters with a sand or gravel bottom but it is much rarer in lakes. Minnows feed on small crustaceans and aquatic insects and are themselves an important source of food. They are eaten not only by other fishes, kingfishers and herons but also, in parts of eastern Europe, by man.

In the lower reaches of streams lives the **gudgeon**, a bottom-dwelling fish that also occurs in lakes provided they have sandy or gravelly beds. It is easy to keep in captivity and it too was a source of food for man. Gudgeon feed on insects, snails and worms which they detect by means of barbels around the mouth which are used as 'feelers'.

Probably the most familiar of stream fishes, equally at home in the lower reaches of streams, in rocky pools on the sea-shore or in a jam jar, is the **three-spined stickleback**. During the breeding season the males develop bright red underbellies to attract the females. They are territorial and aggressively defend their territories against other males. Passing females are enticed into laying eggs in nests of plant debris built by the males and glued together with a secretion from their kidneys. More than one female may lay in a nest which can contain up to a thousand eggs. The male fans fresh water over these and guards them until they hatch.

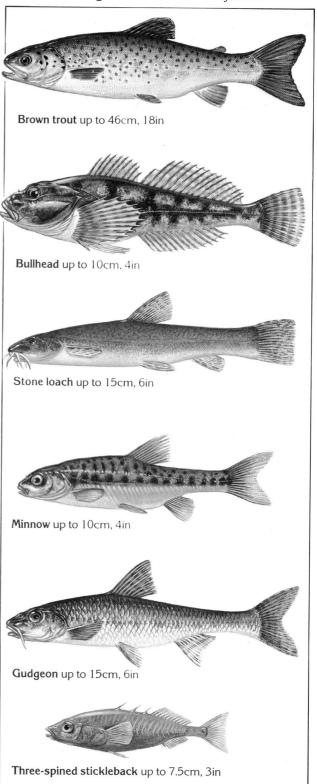

Brown trout up to 46cm, 18in

Bullhead up to 10cm, 4in

Stone loach up to 15cm, 6in

Minnow up to 10cm, 4in

Gudgeon up to 15cm, 6in

Three-spined stickleback up to 7.5cm, 3in

# RIVER and LAKE FISHES

As they tumble off the hillsides, leaping streams and tributaries merge to form the slow-flowing rivers of the plains. Smooth, muddy and weedy, they meander through backwaters and deep weir pools. Large lakes and canals with little flow resemble the quiet backwaters of a river. These are the habitats of large fishes that hide among weeds or gather in shoals in the turbid water.

Largest of all the British fishes is the **pike**, which grows up to 1.2m (4ft) long and has a huge mouth

spawn in the Sargasso Sea in the middle of the Atlantic and the small larvae drift for two to three years on the Gulf Stream before reaching the European coast. Eels can live out of water for a time and often travel over wet ground in the autumn.

Two species that are very common in rivers and lakes but have very different feeding habits are roach and perch. **Roach** are largely plant feeders, though they also take small invertebrates and snails, and they form large shoals. They tolerate some degree of

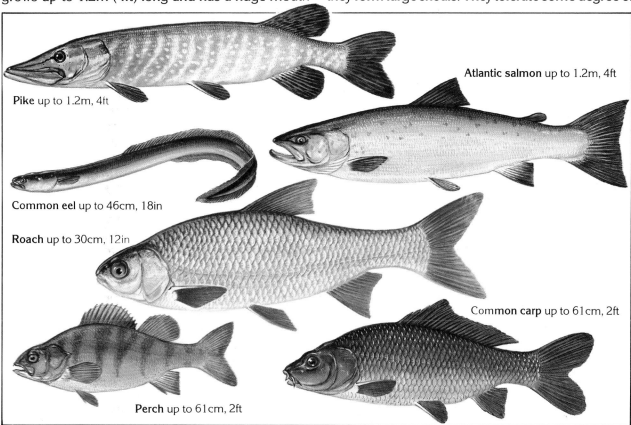

Pike up to 1.2m, 4ft

Atlantic salmon up to 1.2m, 4ft

Common eel up to 46cm, 18in

Roach up to 30cm, 12in

Common carp up to 61cm, 2ft

Perch up to 61cm, 2ft

able to gulp down prey almost as big as itself. Hidden by its barred, mottled colouring it waits motionless among weeds ready to dart out and ambush passing prey. Other fish, frogs, ducklings and even moorhens are swallowed whole.

Almost as large, and certainly of immense importance to fishermen and gourmets, is the **Atlantic salmon**. The salmon's feat of migration is legendary. It spends from one to four years at sea and then returns to the river where it was spawned, guided by an incredibly sensitive sense of smell. It spends very little time in the lower reaches of the estuary, not even pausing to feed as it fights its way upstream to its spawning grounds.

Another migratory species is the **common eel**, a long slender fish of both fresh and salt water. Eels

pollution and are therefore an important angling fish near major cities. **Perch** also form 'schools' but only in the early stages of growth when they feed on small crustaceans and water insects. As they get larger they become more solitary, feeding on small fish and quite regularly on the young of their own species. Perch spawn in April and May and one female may lay strings of hundreds of thousands of eggs around vegetation and tree roots.

The **common carp** is a large, bottom-dwelling fish, probably introduced into Europe by the Romans who valued it as a food fish. It is sluggish, tolerant of stagnant conditions and prefers warm, densely-weeded waters where it often comes to the surface to bask in sunshine. The barbels around its mouth help it detect worms and insects in the bottom-mud.

# INVERTEBRATES

Invertebrates are the most abundant animals on earth. Insects alone account for more than half of the world's known animals and tiny, soil-dwelling nematode worms, which most people never see, number in countless billions. Invertebrates can affect the lives of other animals, including man, in devastating ways. Locust swarms, hundreds of miles in extent, and containing so many insects that they blot out the sun, can completely devastate crops over vast areas leaving behind them entire nations condemned to starvation. Malaria, a disease caused by a microscopic invertebrate blood parasite, is transmitted by another invertebrate, a mosquito, and has been responsible for the deaths of more people than any other disease known to man.

What then are the main characteristics of invertebrates? They are quite simply animals without backbones, creatures lacking an internal skeleton like those of, for instance, mammals. The term invertebrate covers an enormous variety of animals from jellyfish, which are just bags of fluid floating in water, to the arthropods, such as spiders and insects, which have tough external skeletons.

## TYPES OF INVERTEBRATES

Invertebrates have a long and ancient history. The first invertebrates dominated the earth 1,200 million years ago and their descendants left the seas to live on land 380 million years ago, long before the vertebrates (animals with backbones) began their clumsy explorations. Because of their long evolution and incredible diversity of form there are really no other common characteristics. They can, however, be divided into two groups, the lower invertebrates and the higher invertebrates.

Lower invertebrates are those without a full external skeleton, such as jellyfish, squids, worms or snails, which are never completely independent of the need for moisture in their environment. Most of the lower invertebrates live in water or soil where there is plenty of moisture. A few, like snails, have evolved partial skeletons, in this case a shell, into which they can withdraw for protection from desiccation or cold. Higher invertebrates are those that are completely enclosed in a tough external skeleton (the exoskeleton) which prevents water loss and allows them to live in almost any climate, from Arctic wastes to burning deserts. These are the arthropods: animals such as crabs, spiders, centipedes and the spectacularly successful insects.

Although the arthropod exoskeleton has been of enormous evolutionary importance it does have two major disadvantages. The first is that it restricts the ultimate size that an individual arthropod can attain. The exoskeleton does not let in water or air and the animal has to obtain its oxygen by diffusion through

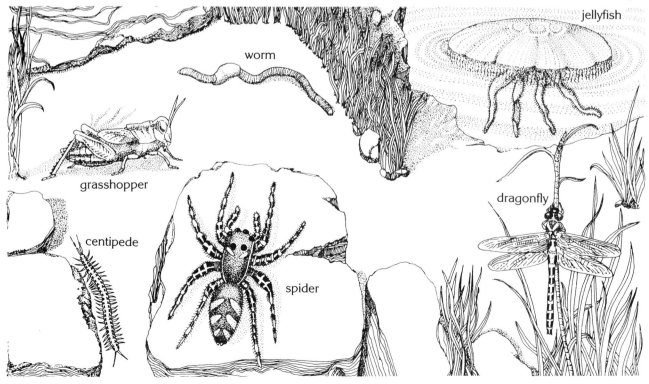

worm

jellyfish

grasshopper

centipede

spider

dragonfly

a number of openings on its body called spiracles. The greater the body size the more difficult it becomes for air to diffuse into the body. Present-day insects can never become the giants of the film-makers' imaginations and the largest insect ever known to have lived – an extinct dragonfly – only had a 60cm (2ft) wingspan. The second disadvantage is that the exoskeleton cannot increase in size throughout life as the animal grows. Instead it has to be shed periodically, a dangerous procedure since it leaves the arthropod soft, weak and defenceless. The new exoskeleton grows beneath the old. Shortly before the old one is about to be shed a chemical is released which causes it to soften. At the same time the arthropod's body swells with fluid or air and bursts the old skin open. The body remains swollen until the new exoskeleton hardens and then shrinks back to normal size leaving plenty of room for growth inside the new skin.

## METAMORPHOSIS

The so-called 'higher' insects such as beetles, flies, butterflies and moths have adapted the process of skin-changing to astonishing advantage. In these insects the intermediate stage, the larva, is completely different from the adult. The larva may be worm-like, or a grub or caterpillar, or a fast-moving, active creature. The larva usually eats different food from the adult and lives in different habitats. It will have its own camouflage and defence mechanisms and will shed its exoskeleton periodically like other insects, but with one important difference: at the approach of maturity the larva develops into another form, the pupa. At this stage the whole body of the insect is literally dissolved and re-formed into the adult, which eventually breaks free of the pupal case. This incredible process is known as metamorphosis, from the Greek word meaning 'changed form'. Together with the insect power of flight, this is possibly the greatest evolutionary achievement of the invertebrates.

Flight probably developed first as an aid in escaping from predators but it eventually enabled insects to colonise new habitats and increase their powers of dispersal. Metamorphosis enabled a single species not only to colonise completely different habitats but also to live completely different lifestyles, all within a single generation.

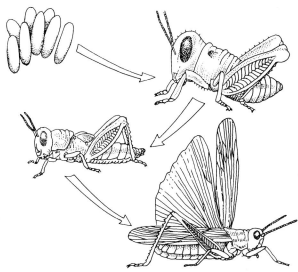

moulting stages of a grasshopper

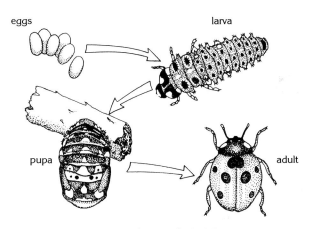

metamorphosis of a ladybird

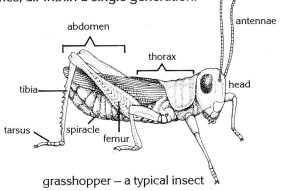

grasshopper – a typical insect

## INVERTEBRATE FACTS AND FEATS

BIGGEST APPETITE

*World*    The larva of the polypnemus moth of North America eats an incredible 86,000 times its own weight in food in the first 48 hours of its life.

COMMONEST INSECT

*World*    Springtails are found all over the world, even in the Antarctic. It has been calculated that the top 22cm (9in) of soil in one acre of grassland contains 23 million springtails.

LARGEST SPIDER WEB

*World*    The tropical orb web spiders *Nephila* spin webs 573cm (18ft 9¾in) in circumference.

SMALLEST INSECT

*World*    Common 'hairy-winged' beetles measure only 0.2mm (0.008in) in length, smaller than some single-celled protozoan animals.

LONGEST-LIVED INSECTS

*World*    The larvae of the tropical splendour beetles survive for up to 30 years before becoming adults.

# INVERTEBRATES of HOUSE and GARDEN

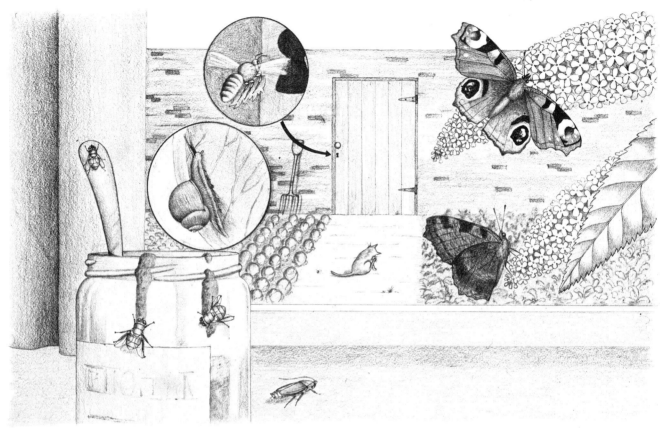

*Inside the house, flies are attracted to exposed food and cockroaches thrive in the warmth of the kitchen. In the garden, snails attack our crops, butterflies feed on the nectar from flowers, and solitary bees sometimes use keyholes for their nests.*

We usually think of wildlife as something to be found outside the home, but an enormous number of creatures live and thrive, often unnoticed, inside our houses. All nest-building animals share their homes with a host of uninvited guests, and what is a house if not a large nest? Nests are made of wood and wool, mud and moss and in them, for a brief period, live a group of helpless young. The invertebrates that attack animal nests and their occupants also attack our homes and us. There are moths that eat the wool in our carpets and clothes, beetles that bore holes in our furniture and house timbers and fleas and lice that suck our blood. The general warmth and dryness of a house, however, makes our homes a difficult habitat for our native invertebrates and so it is no surprise to find that many of the house-dwelling invertebrates that thrive here have been accidently introduced from the warmer lands of the Mediterranean and the Middle East. In recent times, the expansion of world trade and the ease with which

we can travel from one continent to another has increased the numbers of pests that have been introduced into our warehouses and homes.

Gardens, surprisingly, are now considered to be Britain's biggest nature reserve. Lumped together, they cover an enormous area of land on a great variety of soils in areas with very different climates. Despite the abundance of imported and introduced plants and shrubs, more than half the known British insects have been recorded in gardens and more are being constantly discovered. The ready supply of nectar from a succession of flowering plants is probably the main reason why insects are drawn to gardens — as we might visit petrol stations on our travels to fill up our fuel tanks, so many invertebrates visit flowers to 'top up' with nectar. Invertebrates also live and breed in neglected, weedy corners, or in compost heaps and among rotting vegetation in undisturbed areas. The more varied the garden, the greater the number of predators that can live there.

Of all the creatures found in the house few cause more revulsion – and a lot of involuntary scratching at the mere mention of them – than **fleas**. The human flea is thought to be extinct in Britain but cat and dog fleas are becoming more common in the home and have become a real public health problem. The cat flea readily bites man, leaving irritating red spots. Adult fleas are wingless and have a flattened form that enables them to slip easily and rapidly among hair and fur. Female fleas need a blood meal to complete the development of their eggs. The eggs are then scattered at random about the host's living quarters and the resultant larvae feed on house dust and flea faeces. Fortunately for us the vacuum cleaner is the greatest enemy of the flea.

Another common pest in buildings that also arouses disgust is the **cockroach**, an insect generally associated with dirty, ill-kept kitchens. The cockroach was accidentally introduced from the tropics and its need for warmth confines it to buildings in this country. It brings itself to the attention of man by its characteristic and offensive odour which taints the food it crawls over as it scavenges in the kitchen. Large numbers can build up unnoticed behind skirting boards and loose panelling. They are nocturnal, fast-running and have a rapid rate of reproduction. The female produces eggs contained inside a protective case, the *ootheca*, which she carries beneath her abdomen until the young are ready to hatch.

Another insect that feeds on kitchen scraps in the home but which has been given a friendly welcome is the **house cricket**, the original 'cricket on the hearth'. It came from Africa or the Middle East and thrives in the warmth of our homes, bakeries and factories, even colonising rubbish tips. The high-pitched 'song' of the cricket is produced only by the male. He raises his wings above his body and rubs a toothed ridge on the right wing across the hind edge of the left wing. Some recent experiments have shown that the cricket 'sings' faster as the temperature rises.

**Silverfish** and **booklice** too have been companions of man for a very long time. They feed on kitchen scraps and spilled food, the mould that grows on paper and the glues that bind books together – a habit which has earned the booklouse its name. Booklice are not true lice. They are small and move rapidly for their size. Occasionally enormous populations build up in the damp conditions of new houses. Silverfish are nocturnal, fast-moving and very agile. They are small, primitive, wingless insects with three-pronged tails and are covered in silvery scales which rub off easily if they are handled.

The **tortoiseshell butterfly** by contrast is not a permanent resident in the home. It enters houses in the autumn to find a cool, dry place to spend the winter, and in this respect a house to this butterfly is no different than a hollow tree.

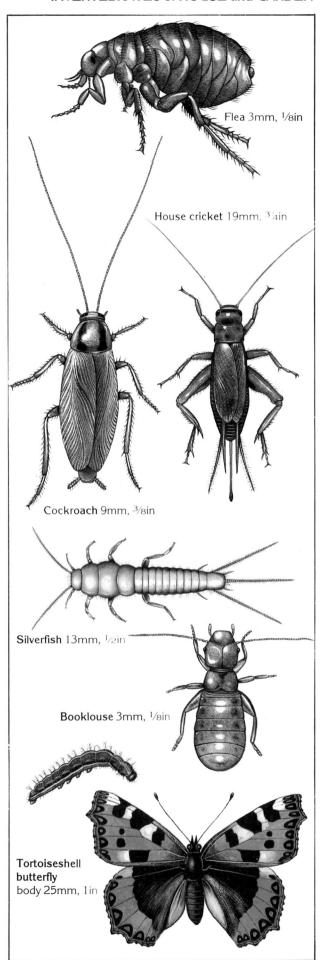

Flea 3mm, 1/8in

House cricket 19mm, 3/4in

Cockroach 9mm, 3/8in

Silverfish 13mm, 1/2in

Booklouse 3mm, 1/8in

Tortoiseshell
butterfly
body 25mm, 1in

The **house spider** too finds conditions in the home not much different from the stony banks and hollow trees where it can be found outdoors. The spider spins a hammock web with a silken tube retreat – often in the corners of rooms – and is seldom noticed until it begins to wander about the house in search of a mate or becomes trapped in a bath or wash basin. They never reach the bathroom by climbing up the drainpipe as is popularly supposed. Houses are very dry habitats and the spiders simply become trapped when searching for water to drink.

The **furniture beetle** finds the man-made house a good alternative to the trees in its natural habitat of woods and hedgerows. House timbers, floor joists and furniture are little different from the dead wood of the countryside to this beetle. The female lays her eggs in crevices, on rough surfaces or in the beetle exit holes that already pock-mark the wood. The larvae live for about three years inside the wood, gradually eating it away and rendering it useless.

Houseflies and blowflies are opportunists also, coming into the house in search of sweet food to eat, or meat on which to lay their eggs. The **housefly**, once a tropical insect, now occurs worldwide and is a serious threat to public heath. It carries a number of disease-causing bacteria which are picked up when it feeds on dung or carrion. These are then spread to uncovered food by the fly's legs or in the fluid it regurgitates as it feeds. Houseflies reproduce rapidly, completing development from egg to adult fly in as little as 10–14 days in hot weather, so numbers can build up quite rapidly in unhygenic surroundings. Winter cold kills off most houseflies but some always manage to survive the winter by hibernating indoors. The **blowfly** or **bluebottle** has similar habits to the housefly but it is usually only the female which enters the house, buzzing loudly as she searches for meat or scraps on which to lay her eggs. Male blowflies feed on nectar from flowers.

Rotting fruit and vegetables attract the **fruitflies**. These small flies can be seen circling idly or crawling around dustbins and rubbish bags.

**Mosquitoes** breed in pools of stagnant water and their wriggling larvae and pupae can often be found in water butts or neglected watering cans in the garden. Two species regularly enter houses but only one habitually bites man; the other prefers to feed on birds. They come into the house to overwinter in cool, damp cellars and lobbies. Only the female bites, piercing the skin with a long, tough proboscis. Like the flea, she needs the blood to complete the development of her eggs.

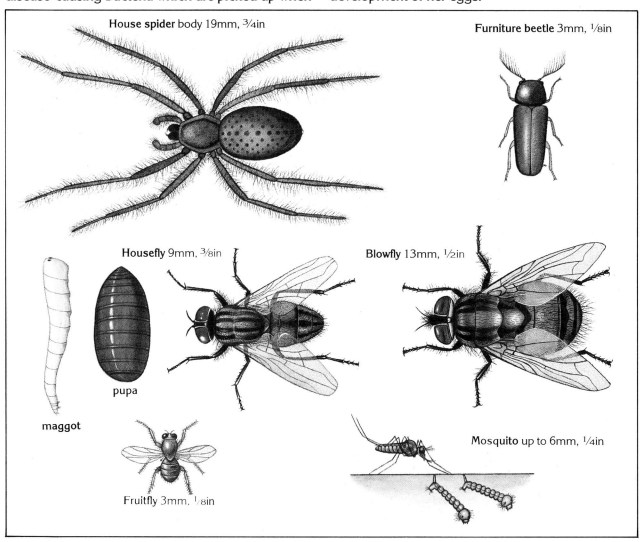

House spider body 19mm, ¾in

Furniture beetle 3mm, ⅛in

Housefly 9mm, ⅜in

pupa

maggot

Blowfly 13mm, ½in

Mosquito up to 6mm, ¼in

Fruitfly 3mm, ⅛in

Most invertebrate species in a garden are harmless and come only to feed on the nectar from flowers, the decaying debris in the soil or to prey on the rich variety of other invertebrate life. Some species, however, can be very destructive indeed. The **large white butterfly** causes considerable damage to kitchen garden plants. It lays clusters of small yellow eggs on the underside of the leaves of cabbages and other brassicas – from which it gets its other name, the cabbage white. When hatched, the caterpillars feed communally, soon reducing infested plants to ribbons. Caterpillars of the large white are often parasitised by a small wasp whose young develop inside the still-living caterpillar. Their yellow, woolly cocoons can be found clustered round the body of the dead caterpillar.

**Aphids** or, as they are more popularly known, greenfly and blackfly, can be just as damaging but in a less obvious way. They occur in such large numbers that they weaken the plant by drawing off its life-giving sap, causing distortion of the leaves and growing shoots and transmitting a number of harmful virus diseases. Aphids overwinter as eggs which hatch into wingless females in the spring. These give birth to large numbers of live young, some unwinged which remain on the host plant and some winged which fly off to find other plants. Some species of aphid are tended and protected by ants who 'milk' them of honeydew, a sugary secretion they exude while feeding on plant sap.

**Frog-hoppers** also cause damage to plants, not as adults but as immature, wingless nymphs. The nymph surrounds itself in a protective, sticky, bubbly froth, commonly known as cuckoo-spit, which hides it from the eyes of predators. They feed on the sap of the plant, often causing distortion at the feeding site. The adult insect derives its name from its resemblance to a frog and its leaping habit.

The **earwig**, often regarded as a pest because it eats flower petals, actually does more good than harm by scavenging on decaying debris and eating other insects. Its fearsome-looking pincers are quite harmless to people and are used mainly for folding the insect's delicate wings back under its wing cases.

Despite their conspicuous colouring the caterpillars and adults of the **magpie moth** are easily overlooked. The caterpillar feeds on a variety of garden bushes and shrubs but they draw attention to themselves by their unwelcome attacks on gooseberry and currant bushes. The bright colours of the moth and caterpillar advertise their distastefulness to foraging birds.

The **peacock butterfly**, a regular visitor to the garden, also uses warning coloration to deter birds. Prominent eye-spots on the hind wings are flashed to frighten predators away. The dark, spiky caterpillars feed on nettles left in neglected corners of the garden.

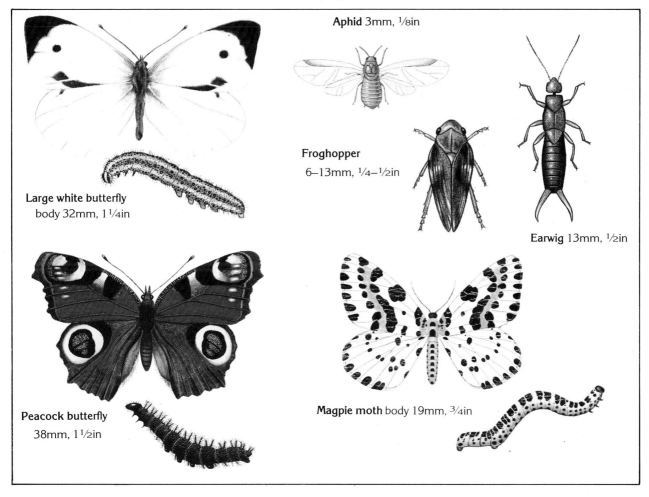

Aphid 3mm, 1/8in

Froghopper 6–13mm, 1/4–1/2in

Earwig 13mm, 1/2in

**Large white butterfly** body 32mm, 1 1/4in

**Peacock butterfly** 38mm, 1 1/2in

**Magpie moth** body 19mm, 3/4in

One of the most useful of all garden invertebrates is the **honey bee**. Its long tongue reaches deep into flowers to sip up the nectar, which is turned into honey, and its hairy body pollinates the flowers as it feeds. The hairs on a bee's body are feathery and ideal for trapping pollen. Some pollen is transferred to other flowers but much of it is combed off the bee's body into a cage of hair on each hind leg called a pollen sac. So nutritious is honey and so successful is the bee at pollinating man's crops that it was domesticated centuries ago, probably first in south-east Asia. A hive founded by a single queen may contain as many as 60,000 worker bees. The drones(males) are tolerated only until the queens are mated, after which they are thrown out of the hive.

In contrast, the **leaf-cutter bee** lives a solitary life. It digs tunnels up to 30cm (1ft) long in rotting wood, though it sometimes also nests in keyholes! The burrows are lined with rolled-up segments of rose

useful as they prey on caterpillars and other common insect pests. It is only towards the autumn as the colony begins to break up that they turn their attention to fruit. Each winter the wasp colony dies off leaving only the mated queens which seek out sheltered places to hibernate. They emerge in the spring and each queen constructs a small nest made of wood pulp and saliva in a tree, building or old mouse hole. They tend the first workers who will eventually expand the nest until it contains 2,000 or more worker wasps.

The familiar **ladybird** is another beneficial predator, feeding on aphids both as adults and larvae. Their bright colouring is a warning to birds that they are distasteful.

**Rove beetles** are secretive but quite common inhabitants of the garden, feeding on other insects or decaying vegetation and fungi. One large species, the 'devil's coach horse', raises its abdomen and

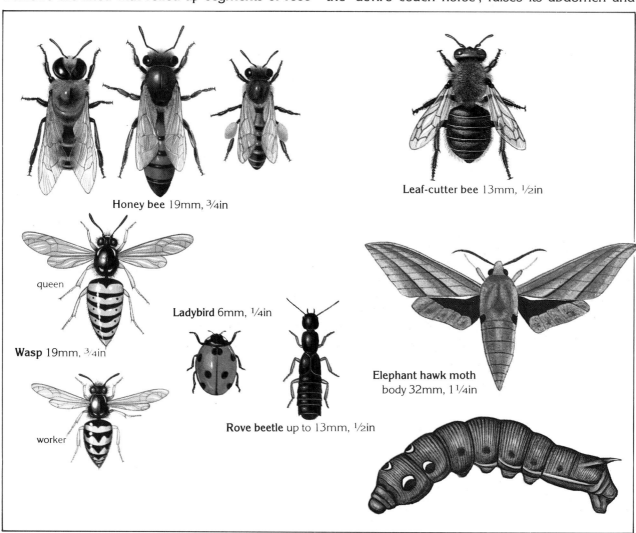

Honey bee 19mm, ¾in

Leaf-cutter bee 13mm, ½in

queen

Wasp 19mm, ¾in

worker

Ladybird 6mm, ¼in

Rove beetle up to 13mm, ½in

Elephant hawk moth
body 32mm, 1¼in

leaves which the bee slices off in semi-circles with its strong cutting jaws. The bee then divides off its burrow into a series of chambers filled with pollen and honey, depositing an egg in each one.

**Wasps** are colonial, but unlike the honey bees they are not welcomed in the garden. Yet, despite their aggressive readiness to sting, they are generally

releases an unpleasant vapour into the air if attacked.

The **elephant hawk moth** is not uncommon in gardens where its large caterpillar feeds on willowherb and fuschia. The caterpillar has an extensible 'elephant's trunk' and conspicuous eyespots which it uses to frighten off predators. The adult moth is often attracted indoors by house lights.

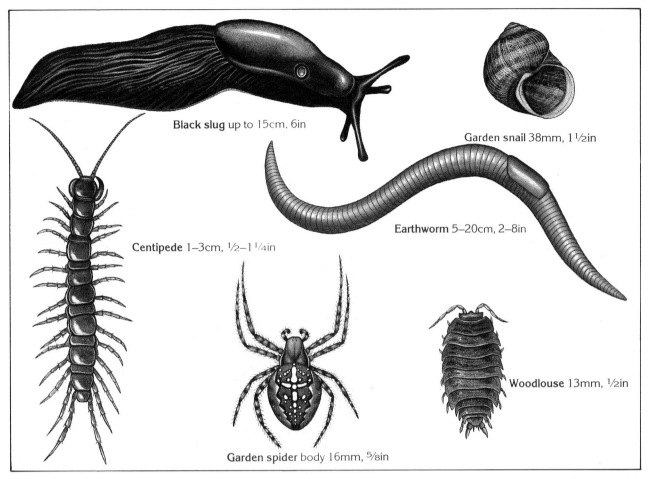

Black slug up to 15cm, 6in

Garden snail 38mm, 1½in

Earthworm 5–20cm, 2–8in

Centipede 1–3cm, ½–1¼in

Woodlouse 13mm, ½in

Garden spider body 16mm, ⅝in

Slugs and snails in the garden are likely to meet a range of death-dealing baits and traps. The **black slug** (a misleading name since there is a red variety) is one of our largest slugs. It has no visible shell and has a breathing aperture on the mantle behind its head. Like snails, slugs have eyes on the ends of retractable stalks. The **garden snail**, again one of our larger species, has a handsome, mottled-chestnut shell which affords it some protection from predators and the elements. The garden snail is able to withdraw into its shell and seal the entrance with a papery film to avoid the hardship of dry weather or winter cold. Without an external shell for protection, slugs must retreat deep into the soil to avoid drying out. Slugs and snails feed on decaying matter and tender young seedlings. Movement on their strong, muscular foot is aided by a secretion of slime.

**Earthworms** use mucus to help them slide up and down their galleries in the soil. They eat soil and leaf litter, digesting the organic content and aerating the soil as they tunnel. At night, especially in damp weather, they emerge at the surface in search of leaf litter which they drag into their tunnels. Worms are killed by exposure to sunlight. Specimens found apparently drowned in puddles have unsuccessfully sought the shelter of the water to protect themselves against the damaging rays of the sun.

The fast-moving, predatory **centipedes** feed extensively on worms as well as on spiders and insects. They have powerful, sickle-shaped jaws which deliver a paralysing venom that quickly subdues their prey. Their name refers to the number of the creature's legs, popularly supposed to be one hundred, but the number varies from thirty in the short brown species illustrated to 177 in pale, soil-dwelling species.

Spiders too have sickle-shaped jaws which deliver a potent venom. The **garden spider** or **diadem spider** (because of the cross-like pattern on the abdomen) is most noticeable at the end of summer when the females have grown to a large size. They sit in the middle of a complex orb web, the construction of which is directed entirely by instinct, and wait for prey to blunder into the sticky threads. Prey entering the web is immediately bitten and wrapped in silk. Silk was probably used originally as a protective wrapping around egg cocoons. Garden spider egg cocoons can be found attached to bark or hidden in crevices in walls or rocks. When the tiny yellow and black young hatch they remain clustered together on a small web for a few days before dispersing.

Spiders' eggs are eaten by a wide variety of creatures including **woodlice**, which normally feed on decaying vegetation. These familiar crustaceans have at least sixty-five common names, possibly more than any other animal in the British Isles. Woodlice are nocturnal and seek shelter under stones and logs during the day. They carry their young in a brood pouch until they develop sufficiently to lead an independent life.

# INVERTEBRATES of FIELD and MEADOW

*Dung beetles roll up balls of dung and bury them in chambers to feed their larvae. Some moth caterpillars feed on poisonous leaves so that they too will be poisonous to creatures that eat them, displaying their dangerous nature to predators by bright warning colours.*

On still, warm, sunny days butterflies flit from flower to flower over gently-waving grasslands and multi-coloured flies cluster on the showy flowerheads of tall-growing plants. Sadly though, as farming becomes more mechanised, such scenes are becoming rarer. Old flower-filled meadows are being ploughed and reseeded, or sprayed with weedkiller. Grasslands still remain in unworkable, neglected corners but increasingly roadsides and commons are becoming the last refuge for the once-common invertebrates and other animals of fields and meadows. Roadside verges wind through the countryside, their flowers changing as the soil changes and every possible niche is colonised by the teeming invertebrates. Butterflies and flies visit flowers, caterpillars and grubs eat leaves and roots, seeds are attacked by weevils, and spiders weave webs between stems to catch unwary passing prey. In general, the taller and more varied the grassland, the greater the number of invertebrates that can live in it.

Close-mown grass supports only ground-living invertebrates that can hide under stones or in cracks in the soil by day, but in tall grassland there are hiding places among the tall stems, dead leaves or grass tussocks. Young, juicy leaves are eaten by bugs, beetles and grasshoppers, and beetles tunnel into dry seeds. Predatory invertebrates clamber among the tangle of stems searching for prey. Beetles or bugs feeding among the stems can drop down into the vegetation to hide when danger threatens. Other invertebrates will 'freeze' where they sit, relying on colour and camouflage to conceal them. Flowers towering above or peeping out of the dense tangle of plants are visited by flying insects.

In grazed grasslands dung adds something special to the habitat. It supports its own mini-community of beetles, flies and worms, and battles of life and death are fought constantly within the dung heaps until the dung finally decays and returns its nourishment to the soil. The last remains of the tough grass stems, that are very resistant to decay, are quickly consumed by vast populations of detritus feeders, the woodlice and millipedes and the incredible numbers of microscopic mites that inhabit the soil.

A large number of species of butterfly are abundant in grassland habitats and three of the most common species are illustrated here. The **orange tip** is a member of the white family of butterflies and is often seen flying along roadsides and in country lanes in the spring. Only the male sports the bright orange tips to the wings. Both sexes have dappled, greenish underwings which provide them with a protective camouflage when they rest among low-growing plants. Like the other whites, the caterpillars feed on plants related to domestic brassicas such as cuckoo-flower and jack-by-the-hedge, but unlike them the caterpillars of the orange tip feed on the seed pods. The caterpillars are also carnivorous, the larger ones eating the smaller if they happen to be on the same plant. The full-grown caterpillar pupates for up to eleven months, one of the longest periods of pupation among British butterflies.

The slug-like caterpillars of the **common blue** feed on low-growing herbs such as bird's-foot trefoil and clover. This species is double-brooded, with adults emerging in May and June and again in August and September. The male is a handsome pale blue but the female is a dull indigo-brown with orange spots along the borders of its wings.

The **meadow brown**, commonest of all the brown butterflies, is typical of all kinds of overgrown grassland. It has a lazy, floppy flight and is often reluctant to fly when flushed from resting places in the grass. It has a very long flight period, from June to September, and is one of the few butterflies that can be seen on the wing in dull weather as well as fine.

Of the many hundreds of moths that live and feed in grassland, three are especially conspicuous. They all have bright warning colours and two species, the **cinnabar** and the **six-spot burnet**, are common day-flying moths. Adults of both species have black and red warning colours and their caterpillars black and yellow. The caterpillars accumulate distasteful poisons in their bodies from the plants on which they feed and the poisons are retained in the adult moth. The cinnabar moth extracts its poison from ragwort and the six-spot burnet moth extracts hydrogen cyanide from bird's-foot trefoil. If attacked, the six-spot burnet releases the cyanide as a repellent fluid.

The handsome **garden tiger**, although nocturnal, can often be found resting on vegetation by day. Its caterpillar, the familiar 'woolly bear', feeds on dock, nettles and dandelions. The long hairs are a means of defence, causing severe irritation in birds' gullets if they are swallowed – only the cuckoo is immune. The moths do not feed, they live off the body reserves of food stored during their phase as a caterpillar.

**Orange tip butterfly** body 25mm, 1in

**Common blue butterfly** body 19mm, ¾in

**Meadow brown butterfly** body 32mm, 1¼in

**Cinnabar moth** body 19mm, ¾in

**Garden tiger moth** body 38mm, 1½in

**Six-spot burnet moth** body 19mm, ¾in

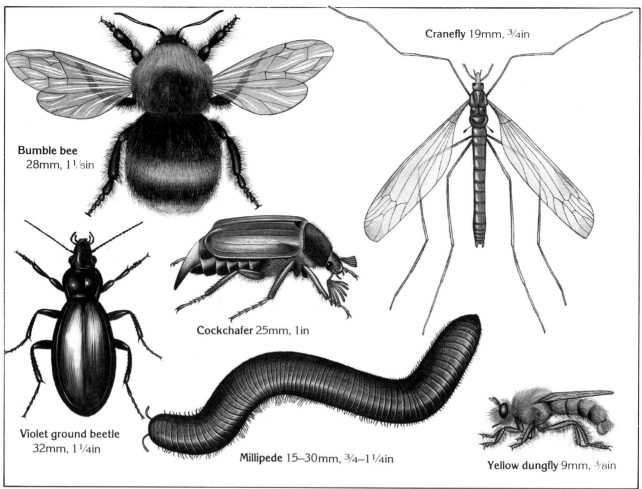

Cranefly 19mm, ¾in

Bumble bee
28mm, 1⅛in

Cockchafer 25mm, 1in

Violet ground beetle
32mm, 1¼in

Millipede 15–30mm, ¾–1¼in

Yellow dungfly 9mm, ⅜in

The **bumble-bee**, with its hairy body and brightly coloured stripes, is one of the most familiar creatures of the countryside. There are a number of different species, most of them living in fields and meadows or open woodland. Only the queens survive the winter, emerging from hibernation in spring to build a nest of moss and grass inside an old mouse hole. The queen constructs about a dozen chambers filled with pollen and nectar into which she lays her eggs; she even sits on the eggs to keep them warm! From this nucleus of developing bees the nest will eventually expand to contain up to 150 workers.

The **violet ground beetle**, which lives not only in fields and meadows but also in woodlands and gardens, hides by day under stones and logs. It is a large, voracious, carnivorous beetle with a metallic violet sheen. It hunts by night, eating worms, snails and a wide variety of insect prey.

The larvae of **craneflies** and **cockchafers** are probably better known than the adult insects, though the cranefly is familiar to all as the 'daddy-long-legs'. Cranefly larvae are the notorious leatherjackets that can sometimes build up in such numbers as to destroy whole areas of grass or young crops. Cockchafer larvae can be equally destructive at times. The fat, white grubs have sickle-shaped jaws that can slice through strong roots. They live in the soil for up to three years and are a favourite food of birds, especially rooks, which has earned them the

name of rookworm. The adult cockchafer has a slow, bumbling flight and is also known as the 'maybug'. It is a favourite food of bats.

**Millipedes**, which normally live on decaying vegetation, can also be destructive on occasion, attacking young plants or tubers. This behaviour is usually triggered off by drought, forcing the millipedes to obtain much-needed moisture from plants. Drought also seems to stimulate millipedes into extraordinary mass migrations involving hundreds of thousands of individuals. Like centipedes, their name refers to their numerous legs. They have two legs to every segment compared to one in centipedes, but even so the largest British species has only 150 legs. Millipedes move their legs in a series of waves, easily seen in a captured specimen, and the more common cylindrical species curl up when disturbed. They also produce an acrid, oily secretion as a means of defence.

No meadow is complete without its complement of cowpats and horse dung and neither is it complete without the variety of creatures that help break the dung down and return its nutrients to the soil. The commonest of these are **yellow dungflies**. The males swarm around fresh dung waiting to mate with visiting females. Eggs laid in the dung hatch into maggots, whose feeding helps to break down the pats. The adult insects feed on nectar, insects and other dungflies.

Rather than expose their larvae to the risks of living unprotected in cowpats, **dor beetles** dig a series of chambers underneath the pat, each filled with a rolled-up pellet of dung for the young to feed on. The beetle has a loud, buzzing flight and is also known as the 'lousy watchman' because it usually carries a number of small, pinkish-red parasitic mites on its underside.

The **green tiger beetle** is an insect of dunes, heaths and moors. It is a fast-running, carnivorous beetle that snatches up insects and other invertebrate prey. Its larvae excavate burrows in the soil, up to 30cm (1ft) deep, where they sit in wait for passing insects with only their cruel jaws protruding out of the burrow.

**Weevils**, another branch of the beetle family, have their heads extended into a snout or 'beak' with the mouthparts placed at the very tip. They are plant eaters and many species cause serious damage to crops. Species with very long 'beaks' are able to bore, or more precisely chew, their way into seed-pods or individual seed grains where an egg is laid. The larvae eat out the inside of the grain, leaving only an empty shell.

The **common field grasshopper** is also a plant eater but it prefers to feed on the leaves of grass. Grasshoppers are best known for their prodigious leaps and high-pitched 'song'. Each species makes its own characteristic song by rubbing a series of pegs on the large hind legs against a thick vein on the forewings. The song is used primarily to attract a mate and both males and females can 'sing'. When egg-laying, the female is able to extend her abdomen into soft soil where the eggs are laid in batches protected by a case of hardened froth.

**Spiders** and **harvestmen** are quite closely related; both are arachnids and they are often lumped together as 'spiders'. They are, however, very different creatures. The spider has a divided body and spins silk for egg cocoons and for trapping its prey, but the harvestman has a rather round, unsegmented body and has no ability to spin silk. Spiders are wholly carnivorous but harvestmen, as well as killing other invertebrates, also eat vegetable matter and scavenge on other dead creatures. The tiny money spiders are the most common spiders, many of them spinning minute webs among the grass; larger species of money spider spin conspicuous hammock webs among bushes and low herbage.

**Ants** are among the most abundant insects in the world, equally at home in tropical rain forests or parched deserts. They are omnivorous, feeding on an astonishing variety of plant and animal matter and all are sociable, living in communal nests. In Britain the best-known ants are red ants, with their vicious bites, and wood ants which live in colonies many thousands strong. The wood ants build large nest mounds of twigs and pine needles along the edges of paths and rides and in woodland clearings.

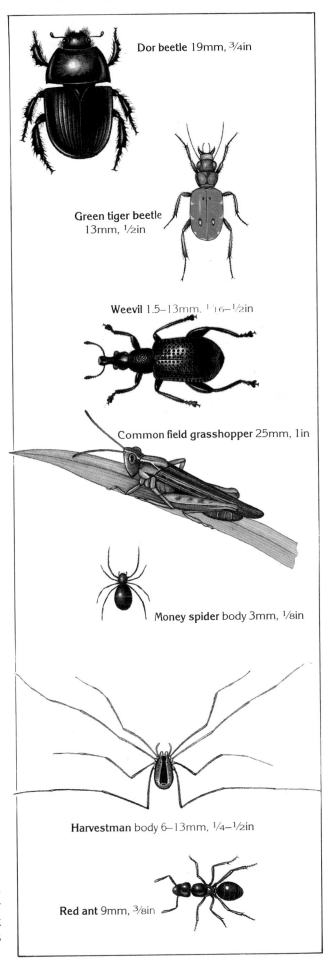

Dor beetle 19mm, ¾in

Green tiger beetle 13mm, ½in

Weevil 1.5–13mm, ¹⁄16–½in

Common field grasshopper 25mm, 1in

Money spider body 3mm, ⅛in

Harvestman body 6–13mm, ¼–½in

Red ant 9mm, ⅜in

# INVERTEBRATES of WOODLAND and HEDGEROW

*Caterpillars strip the leaves from trees, bugs suck the sap of plants, and beetles and butterflies visit hedgerow flowers to feed. The formidable ichneumon fly drills through wood to lay its eggs in a wood-boring larva.*

The oak, one of the commonest woodland trees, directly supports nearly 300 species of insect, more than any other British tree except willow. Birch and the hedgerow hawthorn also support many insects. Including the predators that feed on these insects and the creatures that eat dead leaves, bark and fallen wood, the number of species of invertebrates that are supported by woodland and hedgerow runs into many thousands.

Every part of a tree or shrub is under constant attack. It is impossible to turn over a leaf or pull off a piece of loose bark without finding invertebrates or signs of their activities. Trees may be stripped bare of leaves by hungry caterpillars, but they respond by putting out a fresh crop of leaves when the caterpillars have pupated. Beetles tunnel beneath bark leaving distinct galleries etched in the soft, growing, outer layer of wood. Snails and slugs climb the tree trunks to graze the algae and nibble the tender shoots sprouting low down on the bole. Dead wood, either on the trees or as fallen, decaying logs,

is especially important to woodland creatures as more than a fifth of the total invertebrate population rely on it for food and shelter. Moth and beetle larvae bore into the soft, pulpy wood and other creatures, such as woodlice, hide under the loose bark by day to emerge at night to feed on the wood or the dead leaves and fungi of the woodland floor.

Beneath the shade of tall, spreading woodland trees there is little undergrowth, so most of the large, visible invertebrates live among the leaves of the tree canopy, while on the woodland floor an army of often unseen creatures munches its way through fallen leaves and woodland debris. A break in the canopy lets in light which allows shrubs, herbs, grasses and climbers to grow thickly and flower profusely, enabling sun-loving insects to thrive.

A hedgerow is, in fact, a very long strip of woodland scrub, not only a rich community in itself, but also a pathway between larger areas of woodland across cultivated land that would normally be impassable to most woodland invertebrates.

The **brimstone** is the original 'butter-coloured fly' which gave butterflies their name. These large yellow butterflies emerge from hibernation in February and are usually the first species seen each year. They hawk along hedgerows and woodland rides searching for buckthorn or alder buckthorn, the only food plants of their bluish-green caterpillars.

Butterfly caterpillars rarely occur in numbers great enough to cause serious damage to the plants on which they feed but many moth caterpillars will completely strip trees of their leaves. Both the **green tortrix moth** and the **buff-tip moth** feed communally and in some years they reach plague levels. Green tortrix moths, which feed on oak leaves that they roll around themselves for protection, are regular defoliators of oak, sometimes stripping several acres of trees quite bare. Buff-tip caterpillars are usually only a problem on young trees and saplings. They feed on a variety of deciduous trees and shrubs, the clusters of caterpillars stripping one branch bare before moving on to the next.

Caterpillars can cause damage in other ways. Those of the **pine shoot moth** bore into the buds of pine trees causing them to be deformed and distorted. Inside the bud the caterpillar spins a silk-lined cell to protect it from the tree's sticky, oozing resin and it later pupates in the stem.

**Goat moth** caterpillars tunnel deep into the trunk and branches of the tree, feeding on the wood much in the manner of the larvae of wood-boring beetles. They are tough and leathery and give off a distinct smell of goats. They may live in the wood for up to three years. The adults do not feed. The female is attracted by sap seeping from wounds in the tree, usually poplar and willow, where she lays her eggs.

The caterpillars of two other tree-feeding moths have some potent defences against predators. The **puss moth** caterpillar is a strange shape. It has a swollen fore end bearing two false 'eyes' and a tapering rear from which protrude two extensible 'whips' which can be waved at predators (these are, in fact, modified legs). As if that weren't enough, this formidable creature will also eject formic acid from behind its head if attacked! The puss moth caterpillar feeds on poplar and willow and pupates inside a hard cocoon made of chewed-up wood cemented to the bark of the tree. The emerging moth secretes potash, a caustic chemical that softens the cocoon as it breaks free.

Both the caterpillar and adult moth of the **vapourer** rely on a covering of irritating hairs to deter birds. The caterpillars hatched from over-wintered eggs feed on various deciduous trees and shrubs. The female moth is wingless and when ready to mate she releases a *pheromone*, a powerful scent which will attract males from over a mile away.

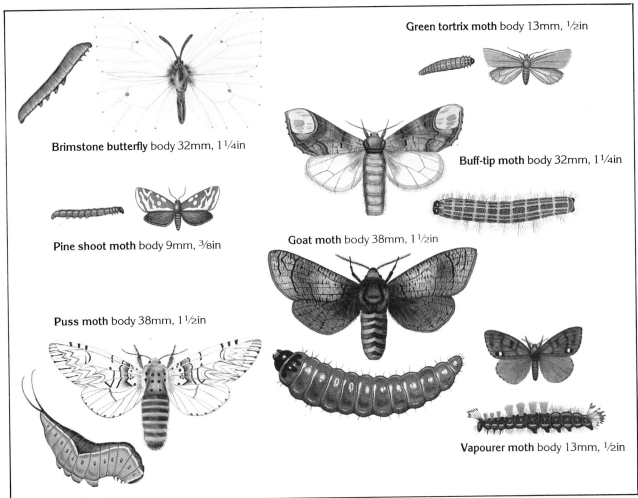

Green tortrix moth body 13mm, ½in

Brimstone butterfly body 32mm, 1 ¼in

Buff-tip moth body 32mm, 1 ¼in

Pine shoot moth body 9mm, ⅜in

Goat moth body 38mm, 1 ½in

Puss moth body 38mm, 1 ½in

Vapourer moth body 13mm, ½in

Along the edges of woodlands or in wide, green woodland rides, out of the dense shade of the trees, there is a more prolific growth of grasses and flowering plants. This is the habitat of the glow-worm and the red-brown skipjack beetle. The **glow-worm** is one of Britain's most fascinating insects, having the ability to emit light through all the stages of its life cycle – even the egg glows! The male and the larvae emit a weak light but the flightless female has a light-emitting organ under her tail which can glow quite

catapults them into the air with an audible click.

**Bark beetles** are very common, living in trees in woodlands or hedgerows. They tunnel under the bark of trees and feed on the sap. Each species makes a characteristic pattern of tunnels, the male boring the original tunnel from which the females and larvae tunnel off at angles. Some species, known as ambrosia beetles, introduce a fungus into their tunnels as an additional source of food. It is the fungus introduced by bark beetles that is responsible

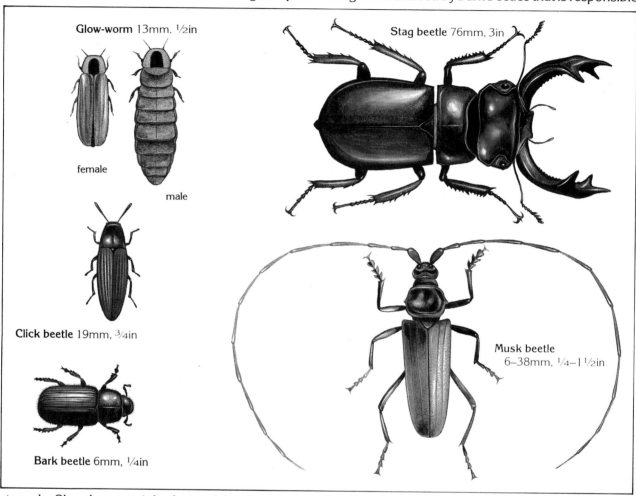

Glow-worm 13mm, ½in

female

male

Click beetle 19mm, ¾in

Bark beetle 6mm, ¼in

Stag beetle 76mm, 3in

Musk beetle 6–38mm, ¼–1 ½in

strongly. She glows at night during July when she is ready to mate, climbing on to low vegetation and twisting her body to display the light. The light is generated by the oxidation of luciferin and the reaction can be stopped quite simply by cutting off the supply of oxygen to the light-emitting organ. Adult glow-worms do not feed and live for only eight or nine days. The larvae, however, survive for three years, feeding on slugs and snails which they kill by injecting them with a paralysing digestive fluid and sucking out the body contents.

The **red-brown skipjack beetle** or **click beetle** is one of a group of about sixty species of beetle whose members include those with destructive root-eating larvae, known as wireworms. Their names come from their ability, when overturned, to right themselves by springing into the air. This they do by arching their backs to engage, on their undersides, a small peg into a pit. When this is released under tension it

for Dutch elm disease. The fungus grows so vigorously that it blocks off the sap flow in the tree and eventually kills it.

Rotten timber, and sometimes the strong heartwood of living trees, is attacked by a number of beetles. The male **stag beetle**, a south-eastern species, is the largest and most fearsome-looking of all British beetles but his fine display is a sham. The formidable, antler-like pincers are too weak to inflict a painful bite and in any event the adult beetles rarely feed. The male's pincers are probably used in mating. The female, which has considerably smaller jaws, lays her eggs in rotten wood where the larvae, large white grubs, live for up to three years.

The **musk beetle**, a species of longhorn beetle, lays its eggs in the bark of living or dead willow trees, where the larvae tunnel for two years or more before emerging as green or copper-coloured adults. The adult beetle exudes a strong smell of musk.

**Ichneumon flies** are not flies, but parasitic wasps. They cause alarm because they appear to have a long 'sting' but they are, in fact, quite harmless, their terrible 'sting' being merely a very long egg-laying device – an ovipositor. The ichneumon is able to detect the presence of the tunnelling larvae of wood wasps and other insects and it bores through the wood, perhaps for several inches, to lay eggs inside its helpless victims.

Another member of the wasp family which has a fearsome reputation that is undeserved is the **hornet**; it is a docile insect that very rarely stings. It is a rare species found mostly in southern England, coloured brown and orange instead of the typical black and yellow of the wasp. It builds a nest of wood pulp in hollow trees, or sometimes in buildings, where it feeds its larvae on grubs and flies. The adult feeds on nectar and the juice from rotting fruit.

Bush crickets are very large grasshoppers that live among trees and bushes in hedgerows and scrub. The **great green bush cricket** has a long, sword-like ovipositor which gives it a menacing appearance though the ovipositor is used only to lay eggs in soil or bark. Far more unexpected is its sharp bite! The jaws are tough, enabling it to eat a mixed diet of other insects and vegetable matter. The **oak bush cricket** is wholly carnivorous and, as the name implies, is never found very far from trees. Bush crickets are often active at dusk and the oak bush cricket regularly enters houses, attracted by light. They also 'sing' loudly in the evening by raising their forewings and rubbing them together.

Shield bugs are so named because their flattened bodies have the form of a medieval shield. They are also known as stink bugs because they give out a characteristic but not unpleasant odour. The **common shield bug** feeds on various plants but especially on birch and alder, piercing the stems with its beak-like mouthparts to reach the sap.

**Banded snails** are common along hedgerows throughout Britain. There are several species and each occurs in a variety of band types and colour forms. Their diet consists mainly of live and rotting vegetation which they browse with a rasping tongue called a radula. At the onset of winter banded snails hibernate, burying themselves in the ground and sealing off the entrance to their shell with mucus hardened with calcium carbonate.

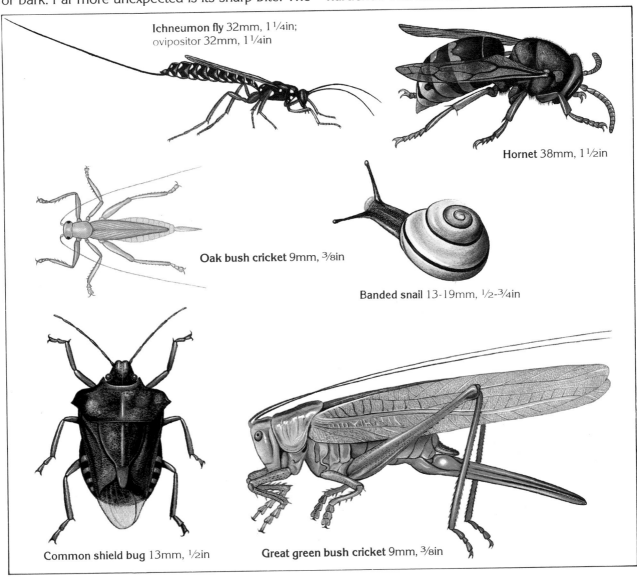

Ichneumon fly 32mm, 1 1/4in; ovipositor 32mm, 1 1/4in

Hornet 38mm, 1 1/2in

Oak bush cricket 9mm, 3/8in

Banded snail 13-19mm, 1/2-3/4in

Common shield bug 13mm, 1/2in

Great green bush cricket 9mm, 3/8in

# INVERTEBRATES of PONDS, LAKES and RIVERS

*Beneath the water's surface lurk ferocious predators that prey on water creatures hiding among the weeds. Great diving beetles and water boatmen will even take small fish. Above the water dragonflies hawk for flying insects and mayflies rest on waterside vegetation before taking part in aerial mating dances.*

Invertebrate animals are able to live in almost all freshwater habitats, from the largest lakes to just the cupful of water contained in a tree hollow! In swiftly-flowing streams invertebrates often have a flattened form and press close to stones to avoid being washed away by the strong currents. To find them, you will need to look under stones and rocks. Slow-flowing rivers and canals and the still waters of ponds swarm with invertebrate life that can easily be observed from the bank. Look for pond-skaters and whirligig beetles skimming the surface of the water. Below the surface, water-beetles and water-boatmen swim jerkily amongst the water plants seeking their prey.

Freshwater habitats with a lot of plant growth support the most life. So long as the weed is not too thick it will provide food and shelter for many aquatic creatures. Some eat the living weeds or the minute algae that grow on them. Others feed on the dead leaves and stems that fall to the mud below. Hungry predators hide among the plants and ambush any prey that comes too close.

Emergent plants are important for several species. These have their roots and stems below the water and their leaves above, and are useful pathways to the surface for the larvae of damselflies and dragonflies. Where the water is too deep, or where bankside trees cast a dense shade, plant growth is poor. But even here interesting species such as the crayfish hide under the banks. The deep, cold waters of upland lakes are not favourable to life. Apart from microscopic plankton near the surface, most invertebrates can only be found in the thin band of vegetation around the lake edge.

Mussels live in the mud at the bottom of rivers and lakes, and occasionally in small ponds. These molluscs are filter feeders. They sieve plankton and debris from the water, which they pass in a constant stream over their gills. Although easily overlooked, mussels can be abundant and the swan mussel can reach a length of 20cm (8in).

Please remember that exploring freshwater habitats can be dangerous. Beware of boggy and crumbling edges, swift currents and deep water.

**Dragonflies** and **damselflies** are the largest and most striking of freshwater insects. Dragonflies in particular are powerful and acrobatic fliers. They can hover and fly backwards, and in fast forward flight can reach speeds of up to 60mph. Damselflies have a fluttering flight, darting back and forth from waterside vegetation. At rest, damselflies fold their wings over their backs whereas the dragonfly rests with wings outstretched. Both groups have exceptional eyesight and capture a variety of prey on the wing. Some species of dragonfly are strongly territorial, clashing noisily with any competitors that fly into their 'beat'. Their aquatic larvae are big eaters, feeding on crustaceans and worms when young and water lice, shrimps, tadpoles and even small fish as they grow larger. Dragonfly larvae can propel themselves forward by squirting a jet of water from behind.

The **great diving beetle** is well adapted for its life in ponds and lakes. It has a streamlined body, paddle-like legs and an oily, water-repellent covering over its body. It rises to the surface to take air under its wing cases (elytra), breaking the surface tension of the water with a claw. Both the adult and the larvae are fierce predators, with pincer-like jaws to suck the juices of their prey.

**Caddis flies** are most familiar as the moving sticks at the bottom of ponds! The caddis larva spins a silken tube which it camouflages with pieces of sand and gravel or plant debris and tiny sticks. Each species makes its own characteristic case into which it withdraws when danger threatens, gripping the end of the case with hooks on its tail. Nearly all species are vegetarian, feeding on algae and plant fragments. The adult fly is very moth-like, flying at dusk and living for only a week.

**Water-boatmen** are quite large carnivorous bugs that swim upside-down with a jerky movement. This and their habit of rising upside-down to the surface of the water to collect air has earned them the name of 'back-swimmer'. They attack prey with long, piercing mouthparts called a 'beak' or 'rostrum', which can also deliver a painful and venomous bite to humans. The adults can fly.

**Great pond snails** inhabit ponds and slow-flowing rivers. They are grazers and scavengers, feeding on plants and carrion. Much of their time is spent at the surface where they take in air via a breathing aperture. This gives them buoyancy as well as an oxygen supply. If disturbed they will expel the air from the aperture and sink like a stone.

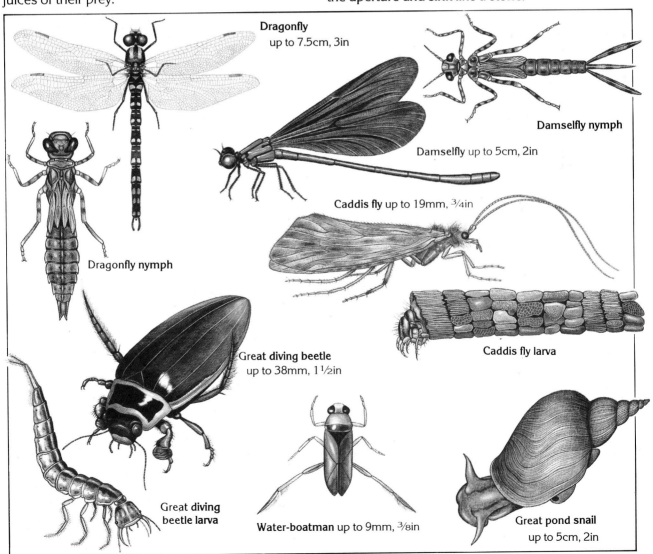

Dragonfly up to 7.5cm, 3in

Damselfly nymph

Damselfly up to 5cm, 2in

Caddis fly up to 19mm, ¾in

Dragonfly nymph

Great diving beetle up to 38mm, 1½in

Caddis fly larva

Great diving beetle larva

Water-boatman up to 9mm, ⅜in

Great pond snail up to 5cm, 2in

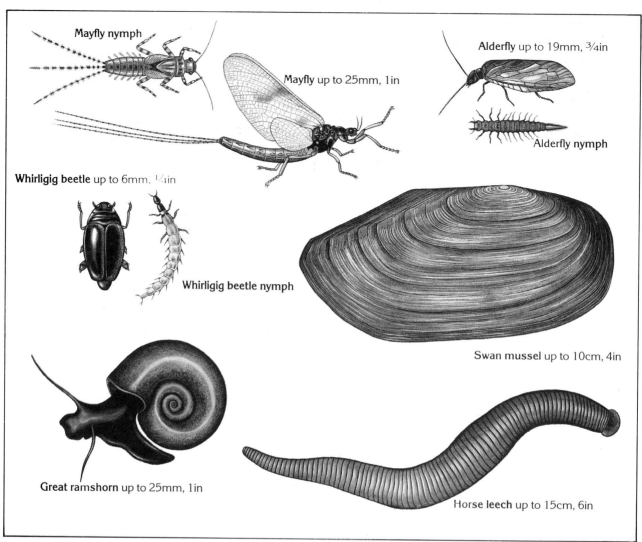

Mayfly nymph

Mayfly up to 25mm, 1in

Alderfly up to 19mm, ¾in

Alderfly nymph

Whirligig beetle up to 6mm. ¼in

Whirligig beetle nymph

Swan mussel up to 10cm, 4in

Great ramshorn up to 25mm, 1in

Horse leech up to 15cm, 6in

**Mayflies** are among the commonest of flying insects around rivers and streams in the early summer. They do not feed and are very short-lived, resting on waterside vegetation or flying in large mating swarms over the water. The aquatic nymphs of mayflies have flattened bodies enabling them to hide under or press close to stones to avoid being washed away. Dislodged nymphs are eagerly snapped up by fish as are nymphs rising to the surface to emerge.

Similarly, **alderflies** have an aquatic nymphal stage but their nymphs are carnivorous. The dark adults emerge in May and June. They are reluctant fliers, resting on waterside vegetation with their wings folded tent-wise over their backs.

Whirling rapidly in circles on the surface of ponds and of quiet streams, the **whirligig beetle** is unmistakable. Its fringed legs make perfect paddles and it is one of the fastest-moving pond insects. The eyes of the whirligig are divided, one half adapted for seeing in air, the other for seeing in water, so that the beetle misses no chance of sweeping up prey that fall in the water or rise to the surface.

**Swan mussels** are the largest British freshwater molluscs. They live at the bottom of ponds and lakes, filtering plankton through siphons that protrude from the shell. If threatened, swan mussels withdraw the siphons and pull the two halves of their shells tightly closed, making them very difficult to prise open. They have a strange reproductive cycle – their eggs are developed inside a special brood pouch and ejected as larvae which attach themselves to fish, where they remain for a time as parasites.

The **great ramshorn**, more familiar as an aquarium snail, is also a bottom-dweller. It inhabits stagnant waters and lives mainly on detritus. A characteristic of ramshorn snails is the presence of the red oxygen-binding pigment, haemoglobin, in their blood – a useful adaptation to the airless conditions of the ponds they live in.

Leeches tend to draw a shudder of horror from most people, mainly because they are believed to enjoy human blood. In fact, in Britain, only the medicinal leech will suck human blood and that species is extremely rare, confined to just a few ponds in northern England. The other leeches, such as the **horse leech**, common in lakes and rivers, feed on fish, small aquatic animals and snails. The horse leech swims with strong and graceful undulations but will also move 'looper' fashion, using its front and rear suckers as holdfasts. Leeches store food in internal body pouches so one meal may last for many months.

# BUTTERFLY NETS and BAITED TRAPS

Despite their abundance, invertebrates can be very hard to find. Species with defences such as poison or a sting deliberately advertise their presence to avoid being mistaken for a good meal, but most invertebrates hide under the cover of darkness or in a protective disguise. They can be found by careful searching, a rewarding if slow process, but other methods are needed for the collection of agile or secretive species. Hand searching provides a lot more information about the habits and habitats of invertebrates than does trapping.

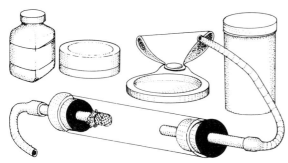

basic equipment for the invertebrate collector

## BASIC NECESSITIES

Every invertebrate collector ought to carry some small glass specimen bottles or pill boxes with transparent tops in which to hold and examine a 'catch'. They are particularly useful for containing a find happened on by chance. A 'pooter' is also very useful, allowing insects to be sucked up from difficult places or out of a net without harming them or struggling to entice them into a specimen bottle. A small, folding biological lens is essential for the close examination of a catch. Eight times (8x) or ten times (10x) magnifications are the most commonly used. Armed with these few basic pieces of equipment any walk in the country — or around the home! — can become a voyage of discovery. However, those with a more serious interest will need more complicated equipment.

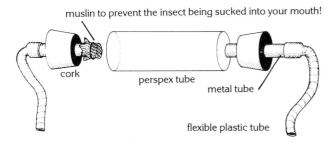

muslin to prevent the insect being sucked into your mouth!

cork

perspex tube

metal tube

flexible plastic tube

a pooter

## CATCHING METHODS

There are four basic ways of catching invertebrates: with traps, with nets, with lights and with sieves. Each method samples particular groups.

### TRAPS

These are used mainly to catch ground-living invertebrates or flying insects. The most commonly-used trap is the pitfall trap, a jam jar sunk up to its neck in the ground and charged with bait. Baited with meat, pitfall traps are ideal for catching the predatory and carrion-feeding ground beetles which are active at night. Once they fall inside the jar they cannot climb up the smooth sides to escape. Care must be taken to check the traps at regular intervals — perhaps every hour or so — to prevent the beetles killing each other. Make sure that no sticks fall inside the jar as the beetles will climb up these and make good their escape. A flat stone propped up above the jar prevents shrews from getting in and eating your catch. When not in use, traps should always be removed.

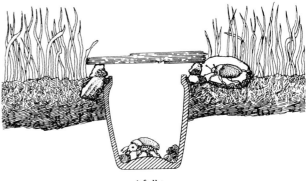

a pitfall trap

Sugar traps attract nectar-feeding insects, especially moths. A thick solution of treacle and sugar is painted on to a tree trunk, wall or fence post and visiting moths can be examined by torchlight, though there are often daytime visitors too. A sugar trap resembles the natural weeping sap wounds on trees which are sometimes visited by clouds of butterflies.

### NETS

Butterfly nets may be a standing joke to many people but they are one of the most useful tools for catching flying insects that you can possess. With practice, butterflies, moths and flies are easily caught and transferred to a pill box for examination at close quarters. Butterfly nets with a toughened rim, usually

93

known as sweep nets, can be swept through long grass and herbage to catch a mass of unseen creatures which would otherwise remain hidden from even the most careful searcher.

A variation on the butterfly net is the pond net or dip net. Pond nets are strong nets with a gauze mesh that offers little resistance to water but which strains out aquatic invertebrates that are then trapped in the bottom of the net. They can be swept back and forth in open water or pushed through beds of water weeds.

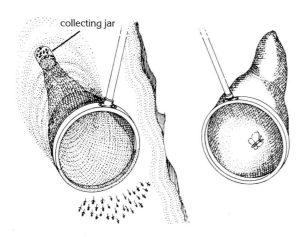

pond net                    butterfly or sweep net

A beating tray is a square of light-coloured cloth, or even a light-coloured umbrella turned upside down. It is positioned under a branch to catch falling insects dislodged by giving the branch a few sharp taps with a stick.

## LIGHT TRAPS

Light traps attract night-flying insects, especially moths and flies, although beetles and bugs are also attracted. A fairly powerful beam is needed – a household torch is not bright enough – which is shone on to a white sheet to diffuse the glow. Insects flying on to the sheet are easily picked off or examined. Oil-fired Tilley lamps or camping-gas powered lamps are quite bright and easily carried but a small headlamp run from a car battery is most effective. For best results site a light trap where there is little interference from street lamps or house lights. More sophisticated light traps using powerfully attractive mercury vapour lamps can be bought from suppliers but they can be awkward and heavy to transport.

## SIEVES

Sieves are used mainly for sifting through leaf litter for snails or soil-dwelling invertebrates such as centipedes and millipedes. The leaf litter is passed through a series of sieves with a gradually decreasing mesh size and the animals picked out from the sieve which they are too big to pass through. Professional sieve kits are expensive but soil sieve kits from garden centres are cheaper. However, their use is limited as the mesh would not be fine enough to catch the very smallest creatures.

# WHERE TO FIND INVERTEBRATES

Invertebrates are all around us so there can be no hard and fast rules about where to look, and in any case even the most unpromising places can turn up major surprises. Woodland, hedgerow, grassland, and ditches are obvious places to look but do not ignore the more unusual places such as under stones, in dung, on carrion or in bird and animal nests. 'Special' habitats like bog or heathland can produce exciting finds but familiar areas are often least explored. Roadside verges, local parks and your own garden are all worth investigating. The map shows some of the more famous and interesting sites around Britain where rare and unusual invertebrates can be found. Many of these sites are ancient habitats rich in species. Most of them are National Nature Reserves or are in the care of nature conservation bodies so permission may be needed for entry and for collecting. It is no accident that most of the localities lie in the south. Many of the more interesting species are unable to survive the cold of

## INVERTEBRATE SITES

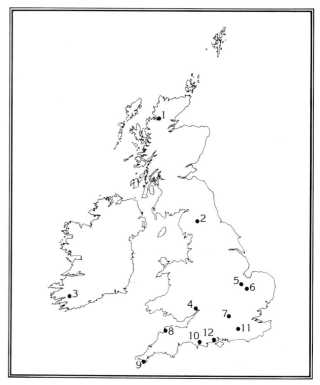

the north. The sites marked, however, are only the best-known ones. Similar habitats elsewhere may be just as interesting and may repay investigation.

### 1. Beinn Eighe, Ross-shire

A National Nature Reserve. Mountains, wooded valleys and moorland. Numerous mountain species and a very interesting community of insects in the Caledonian Forest woodlands and on mountain moors.

### 2. Upper Teesdale, Cumbria and Durham

Part National Nature Reserve. Botanically rich lowland hay meadows and ancient upland grasslands on limestone. Has probably never been forested since the last Ice Age and has a fascinating invertebrate community.

### 3. South-west Ireland

A part of Britain little explored by naturalists, yet rich in rare species. The climate is mild and supports Mediterranean types of plants and invertebrates found nowhere else in the British Isles.

### 4. Forest of Dean, Gloucestershire

An extensive area of woodland on acid and limestone soils. Pedunculate oak woods and ash woods with many rare species. Good woodland communities of invertebrates.

### 5 and 6. Woodwalton Fen and Wicken Fen, Cambridgeshire

Woodwalton Fen is a National Nature Reserve and Wicken Fen is a National Trust Reserve. Both reserves are relict sites of the fenland that once surrounded them but which has now been drained and converted to arable farmland. Dikes, drains, fens, wet woodland and small meres very rich in plant and invertebrate life. Many very rare species. Woodwalton Fen requires a permit for access.

### 7. Aston Rowant, Oxfordshire

A National Nature Reserve. Beechwoods – the best example of Chiltern hillside woodland, chalk scrub and chalk grasslands containing many rare and characteristic species of chalkland plants and invertebrates.

### 8. Braunton Burrows, North Devon

A National Nature Reserve near Braunton. A very extensive system of sand-dunes backed by marshland and scrub. A botanically rich site with a great number of rare and unusual invertebrates. Part of Braunton Burrows is a military training area, so do not enter when the red flags are flying.

### 9. The Lizard, Cornwall

Partly a National Nature Reserve. Formed of serpentine rock, an uncommon rock type in Britain. An exceptionally good grassland and heathland site with many rare and unique plants and a rich invertebrate community with many rare species.

### 10. The Purbeck Heaths, Dorset

An extensive but fragmented area of heathland and wetland containing rare plants, insects and reptiles. There are three National Nature Reserves and a Royal Society for the Protection of Birds reserve in this area.

### 11. Chobham Common, Surrey.

An extensive dry heath with many rare plants and invertebrates. It has been continuously studied by London naturalists for decades.

### 12. The New Forest, Hampshire

A huge area of common land containing a great range of habitats including woodland, heathland, bog and mire. There are many rare species of plants, reptiles and invertebrates. There is unrestricted public access over most of the New Forest.

# INVERTEBRATE MUSEUMS & COLLECTIONS

The British Museum (Natural History),
Cromwell Road,
South Kensington,
London SW7 5BD
Insect exhibitions recently renovated and modernised.

Cotswold Wildlife Park,
Bradwell Grove,
Burford,
Oxon.
Contains a well laid out and very interesting insect collection.

London Zoo,
Regent's Park,
London NW1 4RY
The London Zoo's insect and invertebrate collection is the finest in Britain with living specimens from all over the world.

Natural History Museum,
Wollaton Hall,
Nottingham.
This museum has a new insect and invertebrate gallery.

Worldwide Butterflies Ltd
(see Suppliers)

# PLANTS

Plants are the basis of all life on earth. There are about half a million known species and their ranks include algae, fungi, mosses, ferns, flowering plants and trees. Without plants animal life could not exist. At the base of every animal 'food chain' there is a plant: an owl may feed on a mouse but the mouse feeds on the seeds of a plant; a ladybird may feed on a greenfly but the greenfly has sucked the juices of a plant. Plants themselves make food by harnessing the energy from the sun. In a process known as photosynthesis plants intercept sunlight with a coloured pigment called chlorophyll and use it to convert water and carbon dioxide into glucose, the building block from which plants make stems, leaves, roots, wood, flowers and seeds.

The first true plants were the algae and today there are thousands of species. Some are minute, single-celled organisms that drift in unimaginable numbers in seas and lakes, while others, such as the seaweeds, are multi-celled and can grow to great sizes. Giant kelp, the largest seaweed, forms vast underwater forests with fronds up to 30m (100ft) long.

## FUNGI, MOSSES and FERNS

Not all plants are photosynthesisers. Fungi, often not regarded as true plants at all, contain no chlorophyll and instead obtain all their nourishment from decaying vegetation. Fungi normally live unseen in the ground or within the tissues of the decaying matter on which they feed but in some groups, mushrooms for example, the reproductive spores from which new fungi will grow are shed from strange and exotic fruit bodies which grow above ground, for this purpose alone. The root-like hyphae of the fungi penetrate and digest decaying wood, leaves and plant debris with remarkable speed. Some species feed on living animal tissue — the fungus that causes athlete's foot is one such species.

Mosses, small, low-growing, creeping plants, were, like the amphibians in the animal world, the first to take up a truly terrestrial life. They live completely out of the water but have no roots to supply them with their food and water so, like the amphibians, they are largely restricted to moist, humid and shady habitats. Clubmosses were among the first plants to achieve true independence from water, evolving root-like structures and stems able to conduct water to all parts of the plant. Today's clubmosses are small but in the swampy, steam forests of the Carboniferous era some 300 million years ago clubmosses grew to heights of 30m (100ft) or more.

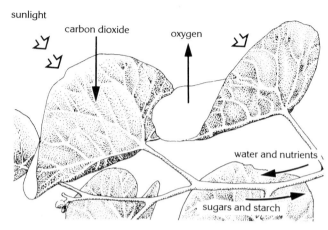

photosynthesis

Next in the evolution of land plants came the ferns. Ferns have a much more complicated leaf structure than the mosses and true roots and stems, but like the clubmosses they are still dependent on surface water for the fertilisation of their spores and they grow best in moist, humid habitats. The spores are carried on the undersides of the leaves in small capsules called sporangia. They can easily be mistaken for insect eggs or the signs of disease. An astonishing 52 million ripe spores may be released from the sporangia on *each leaf*. By the Permian era, about 28 million years ago, the climate had changed dramatically — humid conditions and swamps were followed by widespread drought, and glaciers advanced over the land as the climate cooled. In these conditions plants needing free water for fertilisation were at a disadvantage and those that had developed seeds now came to the fore.

## FLOWERING PLANTS

Seed-bearing ferns were probably the direct ancestors of all our modern plants, the gymnosperms and the angiosperms. The gymnosperms are the oldest group, most familiar to us as the conifers or cone-bearing trees. Conifers have separate male and female cones. Male cones release huge quantities of pollen which is carried by the wind to the female cones. These bear the female spores, or eggs, now highly modified, in a tough protective ovule. The ovule secretes a sticky liquid that traps any pollen grains blown on to it by the wind. Nourished by the sticky liquid, the pollen grains grow into the ovule to fertilise the egg. After fertilisation, the wall of the ovule hardens to become the seed. Most conifers have winged seeds that are widely distributed on the wind when they are released from the cone.

The angiosperms are relatively recent arrivals in

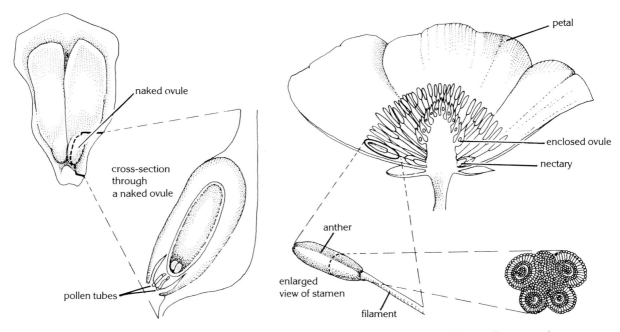

a gymnosperm seed (pine nut)

an angiosperm flower (buttercup)

the plant world, appearing in large numbers only some 75 million years ago as the dinosaurs were vanishing from the earth and the mammals made their first appearance. Angiosperms are familiar to us as the wonderful variety of flowering plants that dominate our planet. Broadleaved trees, grasses, fruits, vegetables, nuts and spices are all angiosperms. Flowers and fruit distinguish angiosperms from all other plants. The flowers may be fertilised (pollinated) by wind, insects, birds or even bats and small rodents. The ring of brightly-coloured, often scented and sometimes strangely-shaped petals clustered around the ovary serve to attract insects to pools of sugary nectar at the base of the flower. To get to the nectar, the insects have to push their way past an inner ring of male stamens which shower the insect with pollen. When the insect

visits the next flower some of this pollen is brushed off on to the stigma which leads to the ovary where there is a cluster of eggs, the ovules. After fertilisation the ovules develop into seeds while the ovary swells into a fleshy fruit that surrounds the seeds — for example, in an apple the ovary forms the flesh while the ovules form the pips. Fruits may be sweet and fleshy, tempting animals to eat them, while the seeds pass unharmed through their digestive tracts to be expelled some distance away many hours later. Burred fruits cling to animal fur, and in some plants such as the vetches, the ovary develops into a seed case that shoots the seeds clear of the parent plant as it splits open.

SEEDS

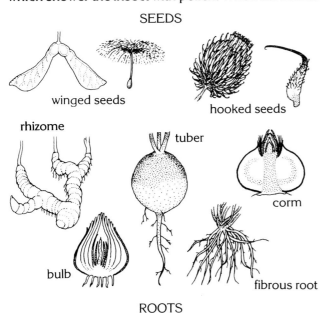

winged seeds

hooked seeds

rhizome

tuber

corm

bulb

fibrous root

ROOTS

## PLANT FACTS AND FEATS

**OLDEST PLANT**

*World*      A clone of the creosote plant of south-west California, USA, is estimated to be 11,700 years old.

**BIGGEST BLOOM**

*World*      The parasitic stinking corpse lily (named after its smell!) has a flower that measures 94cm (3ft 9in) across and weighs 7kg (15lb).

**BIGGEST LEAVES**

*World*      The leaves of the raffia palm that grows on the Mascarene Islands and the Amazonian bamboo palm of South America grow up to 81m (65ft) in length.

**SMALLEST SEEDS**

*World*      The seeds of some epiphytic orchids are so tiny that 35 million of them weigh only an ounce.

**TALLEST CACTUS**

*World*      In 1978 a saguaro cactus in Arizona, USA, measured 24m (78ft) in height.

# PLANTS of WASTE GROUND

*There is no shortage of waste ground anywhere in Britain and a surprising variety of plants grow there. Thistles and nettles rapidly colonise the disturbed ground and buddleia grows abundantly on old walls and railway tracks.*

The term 'waste ground' covers a great range of habitats but they all have in common the fact that they are constantly disturbed by man, or were once used for industry or building, were later abandoned and have reverted to wildness. Old industrial yards and buildings, land cleared of slum housing and left undeveloped, abandoned railway sidings, disused quarries and mineral workings can all be regarded as 'waste' ground. These sites have impoverished soil which is poor in nutrients and contains large amounts of stone, concrete and rubble. What soil remains is usually so broken up and compacted as to be almost useless. Some sites may also be poisoned by industrial chemicals that are lethal for most plants.

There are thousands of acres of waste ground in Britain and the acreage continues to grow. The closure of heavy industry is creating more and more sites that have been abandoned or levelled. Industries such as coal and mineral mining produce vast amounts of left-over rock – spoil – which is often poisoned or lifeless and is just dumped in heaps in convenient places. Today, great efforts are made to sow these wastes with plants bred to be tolerant of the lethal chemicals in the spoil but old or small heaps are still left for nature to cover.

Waste-ground plants, uncharitably referred to as 'weeds', have to be hardy to survive. They are pioneer plants, able to flourish in these blighted lands, yet usually unable to survive competition with other plants in rich meadows or shady woodlands. Some waste-ground plants were introduced to Britain as arable weeds by the Romans and other invaders. Many others were already present, remnants of the great populations that colonised the shattered earth after the last Ice Age. As the land became more fertile they survived in small numbers on crumbling sea-cliffs, shifting sand-dunes and cold, high hillsides. Man's activities gave them a new lease of life and they spread rapidly into their new habitats, invading land ploughed for agriculture as well as colonising abandoned villages, buildings and rubbish tips.

**Shepherd's purse** is one of the most successful of the waste-ground weeds. It grows vigorously in cultivated and waste ground, in gardens and fields and on roadsides, and has been taken to other continents with emigrating settlers. It flowers throughout the year and its flowers are self-pollinated, probably one of the keys to its success. As a self-pollinator it can set seed efficiently and spread rapidly in disturbed habitats. Its common name, shepherd's purse, or money bags, was given because of the likeness of the seed cases to medieval purses. If you pluck a ripe 'purse' it breaks in two and the seeds pour out like money out of a bag.

**Chickweed** is another green winter plant, flowering in even the coldest months of the year. The petals on the small white flowers are very deeply divided, giving the appearance of many more petals than there are in reality. The leaves of chickweed are fleshy and succulent and can be eaten as a salad or boiled as a vegetable. Birds relish the seeds, hence the country name of chicken's meat or chicken weed. The leaves and seeds are often fed to cage birds as a 'tonic' supplement to their diet. Chickweed grows commonly in gardens and on waste ground and has a low, spreading growth. The stems are covered in water-absorbing hairs.

Two other early-flowering plants are the **red** and **white dead nettles**. Their flowers appear in February or March and are very attractive to bees. Both species have a nettle-like appearance, especially the white dead nettle, though neither of them possesses stinging hairs. Their resemblance to the stinging nettle is possibly an evolutionary trick, the plants gaining protection from browsing animals by their clever masquerade. Both the nettles are plentiful in waste ground, on roadsides and on disturbed ground.

On overgrown waste ground the long, twining and climbing stems of the **greater bindweed** reach up to 3m (10ft) high over bushy vegetation, smothering it in a mass of large, dark-green, arrowhead-shaped leaves. It has a long flowering season, the large, trumpet-shaped flowers blooming throughout the summer. It is also called old man's nightcap, because of its bell-shaped flowers, and morning glory. The name morning glory was probably given to the similar trumpet-shaped flowers of the cultivated morning glory by early settlers in America.

The **daisy** is too familiar a plant to need much description. It is found everywhere, on lawns, roadsides, waste ground and on mountains up to 1000m (3000ft) above sea level. The name daisy is a corruption of 'day's eye', an apt name coined from its habit of closing up at night and during dull weather. It was also called bruisewort because of its reputation for curing wounds. A common country proverb says that when you can put your foot on seven daisies at once then summer has come. One curious belief was that if daisy juice is fed to a child it will stunt the child's growth.

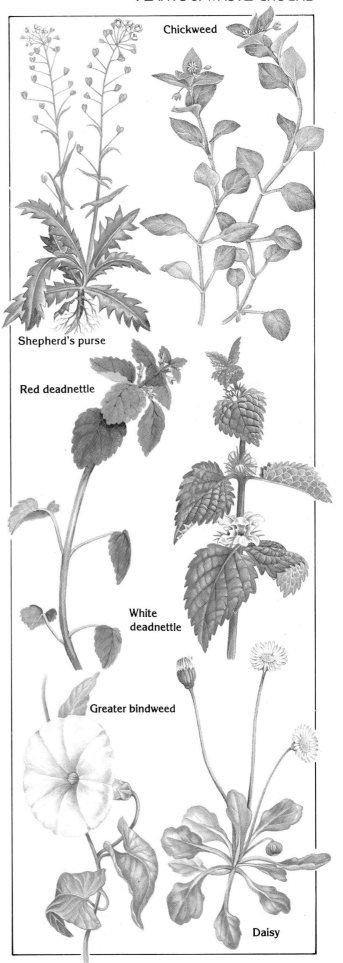

Chickweed

Shepherd's purse

Red deadnettle

White deadnettle

Greater bindweed

Daisy

Many of the most persistent and troublesome of garden weeds are those with deep tap-roots or those which seed freely over long periods of the year. These species take advantage of the opportunities offered by disturbed or cultivated ground.

**Pineapple mayweed** is the perfect example of such an opportunist plant. It was accidentally introduced into Britain from South America in 1871 and has since established itself over most of England and Wales. Some smart botanical detective work showed that its tiny seeds were carried from farm to farm in mud caught in the tread of vehicle tyres. It is common around farm gateways, on footpaths and waste ground. The pineapple-shaped flowers have no petals and the whole plant gives off a strong, pleasant scent of pineapple.

**Groundsel** flowers also lack petals. In Old English groundsel means 'ground swallower' and certainly any piece of neglected, recently-tilled ground will soon become swamped in its seedlings which develop into plants up to 23cm (9in) high. It produces fluffy seeds in large numbers all the year round when temperatures are right for germination, and these are dispersed widely by the wind. In the past it found some value as food for rabbits and cage birds.

Coltsfoot and dandelion produce large quantities of seed but these plants also have deep roots that are difficult to remove. Pieces left behind after the plants are pulled or dug out will often grow again into a complete new plant. **Coltsfoot** flowers early in February, long before the large leaves appear. These are popularly supposed to be in the shape of a colt's foot. It is common on waste ground, especially clay. A country name for coltsfoot was 'baccy plant' because its leaves were used as a herbal tobacco to relieve coughs. In medieval times and later the seed-down of coltsfoot mixed with saltpetre was used as tinder to light fires.

The parachute-like seedheads of the **dandelion** were the country children's clock – the number of puffs it took to blow all the seeds off the head told the time of day. Another common story was that if you picked the dandelion flowers you would wet the bed. This, however, had some basis in truth because in folk medicine the dandelion is a herb that makes the patient pass water. The leaves make a good, if somewhat bitter, salad and the dried roots are used to make a kind of coffee. Dandelion wine, made from the flowers, has passed into modern folklore as the traditional 'tipple' of country ladies.

The long, creeping runners of the **creeping buttercup** root wherever they touch, rapidly turning one plant into a veritable colony. It is a common plant in gardens and on waste ground but it is also found in large numbers in pastures and woods.

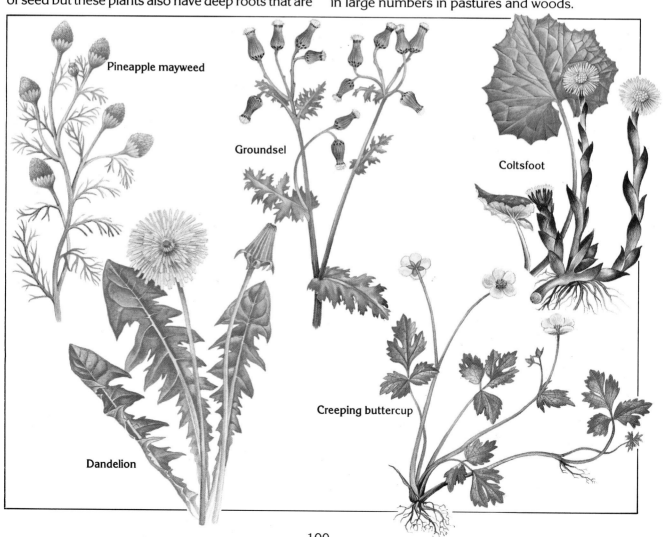

Pineapple mayweed

Groundsel

Coltsfoot

Dandelion

Creeping buttercup

At least two waste-ground weeds owe their success to their habit of readily invading burnt ground. **Rosebay willow herb** was a rare plant in Britain until about 1860 when it appeared to undergo a genetic change that made it much more hardy and invasive and it began to spread rapidly on disturbed ground. It appeared in woodland clearings and along railway lines where the ground had been burnt, and in London during the Second World War it became so common on bombed sites that it was known as 'bomb weed'. In America it is known as 'fireweed', a name probably imported from Britain's West Country.

Oxford ragwort also owes its spread to fire. It is a Mediterranean plant and grows there on parched, poor, volcanic soils. Introduced into the Botanic Gardens in Oxford in the seventeenth century, it soon escaped on to walls in the town. The coming of the railways, however, exported it to most parts of Britain. At first it grew in cinders on the tracks but it soon began to colonise the newly-burnt banks on the sides of the tracks and then its seeds were wafted along the lines by the draught from passing trains.

This plant too was a spectacular invader of the bombed sites of London during the Second World War. It is still common in waste ground in cities and along railway lines.

**Spear thistle** is so invasive that it has become a notifiable weed – one that every effort must be made to destroy if it appears on your land. For all that, it is a handsome plant reaching over 1.3m (4ft) in height and sporting clusters of red-purple flowers. The stiff, sharp spines of the thistle are a very effective defence against grazing animals. The flowers are very attractive to butterflies and later in the year flocks of goldfinches tear out the thistledown to get at the seeds in the flower head.

Though it has no spines the **burdock** is closely related to the thistles. There are two common species, the great burdock of woods and hedgerows and the smaller lesser burdock of waste ground and waysides. Its clinging, hairy seed heads are well known to children who throw them at each other because they stick on their clothes. It is also an ingredient of the soft drink, dandelion and burdock, which is popular in the North Country.

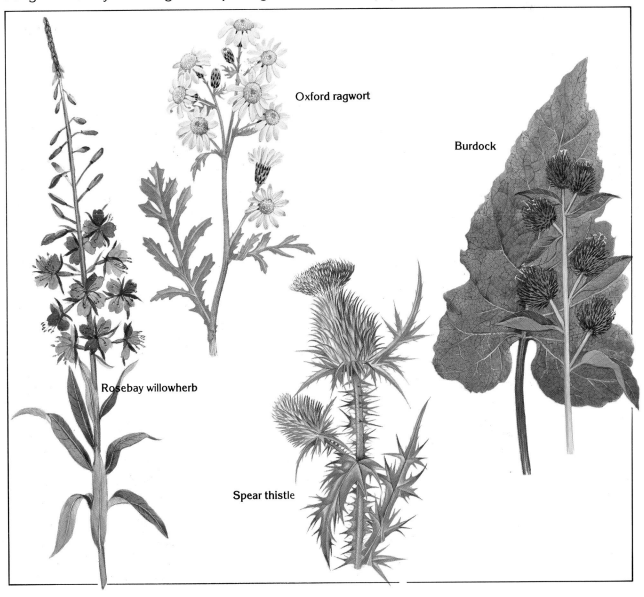

Oxford ragwort

Burdock

Rosebay willowherb

Spear thistle

At some time or another almost all gardeners must have wished that the fast-growing, rampant weeds in their gardens had some practical uses. Surprisingly, most of them have, but in the modern world they are considered old-fashioned and out of date.

In ancient times **fat hen** was one of many edible plants. Both the fat seeds and the tender leaves were eaten as a vegetable and the leaves yielded an orange dye. It is an untidy plant common throughout Britain, growing on arable land and in waste places. A similar plant, Good King Henry, has larger, more succulent leaves.

The **nettle**, one of the commonest and best-known of all weeds, grows in all kinds of disturbed and enriched ground, woodlands and grassy places. It is persistent and its stinging hairs cause a painful, burning irritation. Most grazing animals avoid it but cattle are immune to its sting. Nettle is one of the most useful of all wild plants. It contains vitamin C and more essential minerals than any other wild herb. The young tops were gathered to be boiled as a dish of spring vegetables, the dried leaves were used for tea and the young stems were boiled and eaten like asparagus. The fibre of the stem is tough and strong, like hemp or flax, and was used to make cloth. The name nettle is a corruption of the Anglo-Saxon word *noedl*, a needle, possibly from its sting but more likely because it was the most widely-used thread and cloth in northern Europe. The beleaguered German nation grew thousands of acres of nettles for the production of cloth for its soldiers during the blockades of the First World War. Nettle leaves give a permanent green dye and the roots, boiled with alum, produce a yellow dye.

The **common poppy** of waste ground and cultivated fields has a simple beauty unmatched by most other wild flowers. Before weedkillers wiped out wild flowers from the cornfields whole areas of the countryside were scarlet with its mass of blossoms in the summer. The poppy's thousands of tiny black seeds are held in an enclosed seed case with a series of holes around the rim and they are scattered by the wind like pepper from a pepperpot. The seeds yield an excellent edible oil and also an oil used in mixing artists' paints.

The seeds on the long rat's-tail stalk of the **common plantain** contain a kind of starch and were gathered as food for cage birds. Young plantain leaves are edible, though rather coarse, and the plant was the Anglo-Saxon 'waybread', a magical plant of healing and divination.

The small, bright-red flowers of the **scarlet pimpernel** are common in all types of waste ground. This straggling plant is the 'poor man's weather glass', its flowers opening and closing according to the weather, an open flower predicting a fine day. A variety with deep blue flowers, common on the Continent, is sometimes found in Britain.

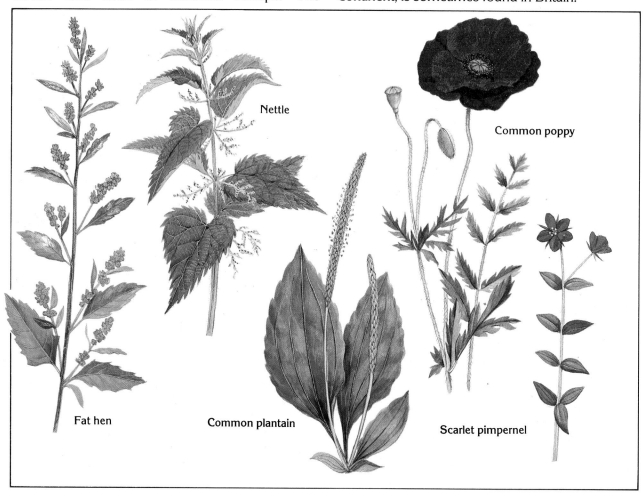

Nettle

Common poppy

Fat hen

Common plantain

Scarlet pimpernel

One of the most attractive and fast-growing plants of waste ground is the **buddleia**. It can grow to a height of over 4m (15ft) in only a few years and readily colonises old walls, railway embankments and ruined buildings. It was introduced into Britain from China in the nineteenth century and can now be found naturalised in most of our major cities and towns. Also known as 'the butterfly bush', its long spikes of scented flowers are particularly attractive to peacock, tortoiseshell and red admiral butterflies. A

can be eaten as a salad or boiled as a vegetable — they were also used in the past as a hot poultice on wounds. 'Cheeses' or 'bread and cheese' are two other common names given to the plant because its large, flat seeds look like cakes or round cheeses. The seeds are edible and have a flavour not unlike peanuts. Dwarf mallow, a smaller, trailing plant with small, pale pink flowers is also a common plant of waste ground.

**Fumitory** is found all over Britain where the

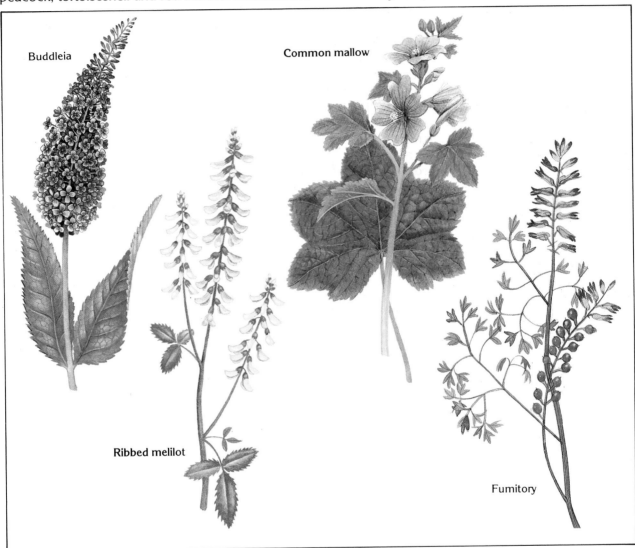

Buddleia

Common mallow

Ribbed melilot

Fumitory

number of garden varieties are cultivated but those with purple flowers are the most attractive to insects.

The melilots are also an introduced group of plants. They were brought from Europe by sixteenth-century herbalists who cultivated them for their value as ingredients of healing plasters and poultices. **Ribbed melilot** is a tall, mainly southern plant of waste places, roadsides and grasslands, especially over chalk where it grows so thickly it may smother more delicate, low-growing plants. When cut and dried, melilot has a strong scent of new-mown hay.

The **common mallow** is another tall plant of waste places, especially near the sea. It often grows quite bushily and has large, handsome, five-petalled purple flowers. The broad, lobed leaves of mallow

ground is cultivated. It is a variable plant, low and bushy or erect and climbing. The leaves have a bluish, hazy appearance suggesting smoke, hence the old Latin name for the plant — *fumus terrae*, smoke of the earth. Even its roots have a strong smell of smoke when pulled from the earth and the juice of the plant dropped into the eyes is supposed to cause tears and smarting, as woodsmoke does. In the Middle Ages it was believed that by burning the leaves evil spirits could be driven away. The small, round seeds of the fumitory are a favourite food of the collared dove and this bird's distribution over the countryside is mainly dependent on the amount of arable land in the area containing fumitory and other particular weed plants.

# PLANTS of FIELD and MEADOW

*Chalk grasslands support some of the most beautiful and rarest of our wild flowers. In spring, cowslips crowd the meadows and bee orchids grow among the grass.*

An enormous area of Britain is under grass. There are meadows grazed by cows and sheep, meadows where the grass is left to grow long, to be cut for hay, and pastures in low-lying river valleys that are kept wet to encourage a lush growth of grass for grazing stock. In addition, alongside our roads, railways and canals, there is a vast and varied acreage of grassland that stretches the length and breadth of Britain. Grasslands vary considerably according to soil and climate. Many plants are common to all types of grassland but there are also those that grow only on particular types of soil. These are so-called 'indicator' plants because they tell you at a glance what type of soil is in a particular area.

With the increasing pressure of agriculture the traditional meadow rich in wild flowers is becoming a thing of the past. Fertilisers and herbicides, ploughing and reseeding have turned our flower-decked meadows into monotonous swards of dark-green grass. The remnants that persist are protected in nature reserves or held in trust by nationwide conservation bodies. In some heavily farmed districts roadside verges are increasingly becoming a final refuge for many species.

The richest and most fascinating of all grasslands are those that lie over chalk. Chalky soils are thin, are easily drained, and warm quickly in the summer sun. It is no accident that ancient man first cleared the forests from the chalk to practise his primitive agriculture. Chalk grasslands have been grazed for centuries and where there has been no grassland 'improvement', or where it has never been ploughed, a wonderfully intricate community of plants has formed. Many of our rarest flowers grow on chalk grassland, some of them protected by law. Ancient hay meadows in damp, fertile river valleys are another rich grassland habitat. Hay is not cut before early summer so a great variety of plants have a chance to flower and set seed among the grass.

The grass verges of roadsides are always worth examining. They slice through every soil type in the country, very often exposing soils that may not otherwise occur in the area. These are the places to look for rare and unusual plants.

Of all the wild flowers, the **cowslip** is the one most associated with old, established cow pastures. The name cowslip is a corruption of 'cowslop', a reference to the plant's habit of growing in places where cowpats have fallen. Even its scent is said to smell like cows' breath. Another of its common names is 'bunch of keys', presumably because its bright yellow clusters of flowers hang like a bunch of keys. The widespread use of fertilisers and herbicides has unfortunately caused the loss of the cowslip from much of our countryside. It does still grow on roadsides, however, and where it is abundant on limy pastures it is worth searching for the pink flowers of the green-winged orchid, a companion flower which has also been severely reduced in numbers by modern farming methods.

Another species of old, established pastures is the **broomrape**, a brown or reddish plant which is parasitic on clover. It has no need of the green substance chlorophyll, instead it gets all its nourishment from its host plant. There are several species of broomrape, most of them quite rare. The greater or common broomrape, though, is widespread in the south and east and was once a serious pest on clover crops, sometimes growing by the thousand in fields. It produces enormous amounts of dust-like seeds which are carried for miles on the wind, so where it does grow it is often very persistent.

**Meadow cranesbill**, one of the largest of the cranesbills, is a tall-growing plant that makes a splendid display on limy roadsides, especially in the north of England. It is rarely found in Scotland and Ireland. The striking pale-blue flower gives way to a large, pointed seed pod which is said to resemble a crane's bill and is the feature which gives the name to all cranesbills. In the autumn the leaves turn a tawny orange and red, producing a second display of glorious colour.

The flowers of the **germander speedwell** are a deeper blue and just as attractive as the saucer-like flowers of the meadow cranesbill. Despite their tiny size their brightness draws attention and their abundance on every roadside and field edge makes them an obvious candidate as the travellers' flower, 'speeding them well' on their journeys. In Ireland a stem from this low, trailing plant was sewn into the clothing to keep the wearer from accident. Another name for germander speedwell is bird's eye and in the south-west there was a belief that if you plucked the flowers of bird's eye, enraged birds would come to pluck out *your* eyes!

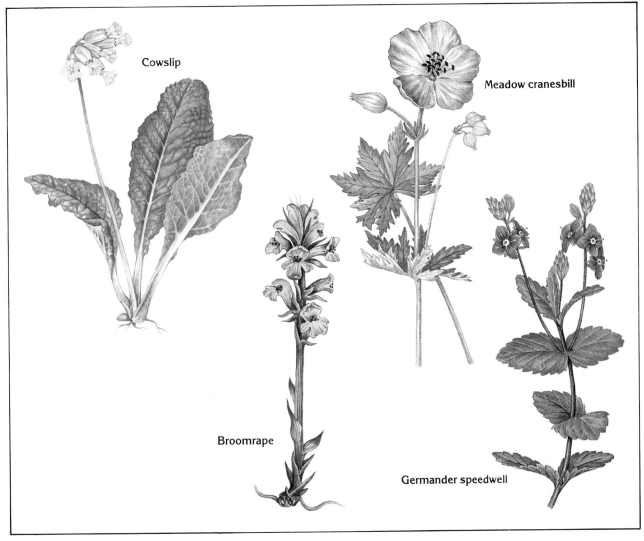

Cowslip

Meadow cranesbill

Broomrape

Germander speedwell

# PLANTS of FIELD and MEADOW

The dry pastures of chalk and limestone support a wealth of flowers, and the most fascinating of these are the orchids. Their strange life cycles have long puzzled botanists and even now many wild species still have not been grown successfully by horticulturalists. Orchids may take years to germinate and when they do it may be several years more before they flower. It has been discovered recently that germination depends on a close association with particular types of fungi.

**Bee orchids** are common on limy soils, appearing in thousands one year and hardly at all the next. The flower resembles a large female bumble-bee, so much so that male bumble-bees will attempt to mate with the flower. The orchid is not dependent on insects for pollination, however, as it has become self-pollinating and its evolutionary link with the bumble-bee is no longer necessary.

**Fragrant orchids** and **pyramidal orchids** grow in the same chalky pastures and dune turf. The fragrant orchid, with its graceful spike of flowers, blooms earlier in the season than the pyramidal orchid and also has several forms, one of which grows in wetland habitats of marsh and fen. Both orchids are strongly scented and are pollinated by butterflies and moths. Fragrant orchids have a smell of clove carnation while pyramidal orchids have a markedly strong, sweet, 'foxy' smell. All orchids produce masses of dust-like seeds which are dispersed over hundreds of miles and the pyramidal orchid is a ready coloniser of new, chalky pastures.

The **common spotted orchid** is one of the most widespread of the orchids, growing in most types of grassland and also in the clearings, glades and grassy rides of woodlands. It is rare in Scotland, however, and does not grow in acid grasslands. The common spotted orchid is very variable in colour, ranging from a very pale pink to almost purple.

Also common on the lime-rich soils of downs and dunes is the **yellow wort**, or blackstonia. It is unique among the gentian family in having eight petals instead of the usual four or five. The leaves too are curious, joined together at the base and pierced through the centre by the long stem. It grows in dry, sunny places, the flowers opening with the sun and closing in the afternoon. Yellow wort is widely distributed in England and Wales but is absent from Scotland.

**Wild thyme** is a low, creeping plant of dry grasslands, heaths and dunes. In flower it becomes a glorious carpet of strongly-scented purple flowers which are very attractive to bees. In the Middle Ages thyme was believed to have antiseptic properties and, together with other strongly-scented flowers, was carried in posies by magistrates and other public dignitaries to blot out the supposedly disease-carrying smells from the streets and the common people. Very strangely, considering its attractiveness to bees, wild thyme was also formerly used as an insect repellent.

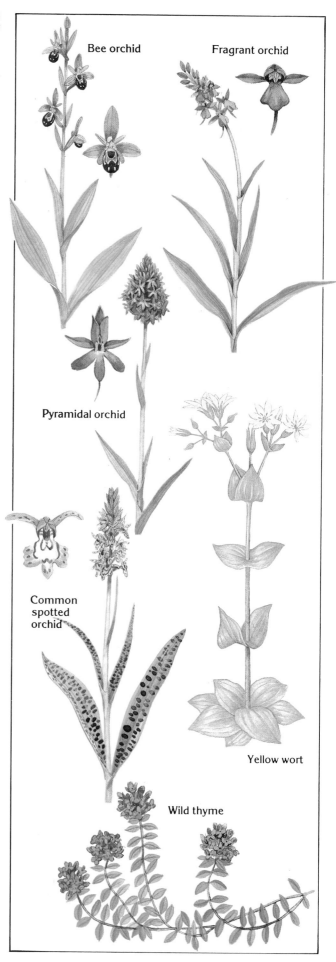

Bee orchid

Fragrant orchid

Pyramidal orchid

Common spotted orchid

Yellow wort

Wild thyme

The **carline thistle** is another plant of dry grasslands. It is a widespread flower but prefers soils containing chalk or lime. This unusual thistle has a strange, dried-up appearance and the tight, whitish-pink flowerheads have no true petals. Instead there is a rosette of modified bracts which close up in dull weather just like the petals of many other flowers. The dead, dried-out flower stems of this plant persist throughout the winter and it is popular with flower arrangers.

Where the land is heavier and damper **yellow rattle** is abundant in old, established grasslands although it occasionally grows on roadsides as well. It is a semi-parasitic plant, tapping into the roots of the grasses it grows with for some of its nourishment. The yellow flowers grow out from large bladders which also hold the seeds after germination. When the stem is

been specially cultivated for its edible leaves. In the Lake District and other parts of the north of England, bistort leaves are the most important ingredient in the traditional Easter Ledger Pudding, which is made almost entirely of wild plants. The aquatic form, usually called amphibious bistort, has floating leaves, and its stems trail out across the water from its roothold on the bank.

**Knapweed** and **yarrow** are two very common plants in all types of grassland and waste ground. Knapweed flowers grow in a tight head of short purple florets, although some south-western varieties have a showy ring of large florets on the outside of the flowerhead to attract insects. Butterflies, moths and flies are all frequent visitors to these flowers. Knapweed was once used to treat bruises and wounds but this traditional use is more

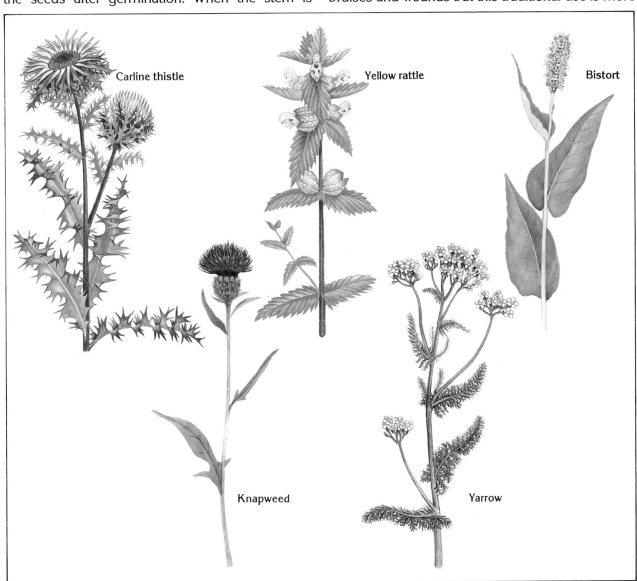

Carline thistle

Yellow rattle

Bistort

Knapweed

Yarrow

shaken the seeds rattle inside the bladders and this has given the plant its common name. For the same reason it was also known as 'money in the purse'.

**Bistort**, a plant of damp grasslands, has two distinct forms. The tall, upright, land-growing form is common in wet meadows, where it may once have

often attributed to the yarrow, as its alternative common names imply. Bloodwort, knight's milfoil and soldier's woundwort all commemorate yarrow as the herb that was applied to wounds sustained on the battlefield. The green leaves were also chewed as a toothache cure.

**Centaury** takes its name from Chiron the centaur, the magical half-man, half-horse of ancient Greek mythology. It was used for healing and the treatment of wounds. Centaury is a plant of dry grasslands, especially in chalk and limestone country, but it is also found on the dry, sunny borders of woodlands and the short turf on sand-dunes near the sea. Although widespread in England it is rare in Scotland and is found there mainly around the coast.

Coastal sand-dunes are also a favourable habitat for **dove's foot cranesbill**. Here it grows in a dwarf form, stunted by the sea, its tiny pink flowers peeking out from beneath its soft, hairy leaves. In fields and waste ground it is taller and more robust.

The small, bunched flowers of the **white, or Dutch, clover** can be found in almost every rich grassland habitat in Britain. It spreads by means of long, creeping runners and it has nodules on its roots containing bacteria that make nitrogen. When the plant dies back for the winter, the nodules break down and the nitrogen is released into the soil.

**Ox-eye daisy** is another common grassland flower, varying from 60cm (2ft) tall to a mere 15cm (6in) or so in poor habitats. It is a ready coloniser of newly-turned ground, soon appearing on new road embankments and disturbed roadsides. Dog daisy or moon daisy are its older country names. In Europe it was hung in the rafters of houses to ward off lightning but in Britain its use was more practical – it was strewn on the beaten earth floors of medieval cottages to drive away fleas.

The yellow, star-like flowers of the **common agrimony** are carried on tall, graceful spikes that have given the plant the country name of 'church steeples'. Cockle-bur is another of its names, a reference to its small seeds covered in hooked hairs that cling to clothing and animal hair. A related species of agrimony has pleasantly-scented flowers. The common agrimony has only scented leaves, which smell of apricots when crushed. It is a common plant on roadsides and hedgebanks throughout the British Isles.

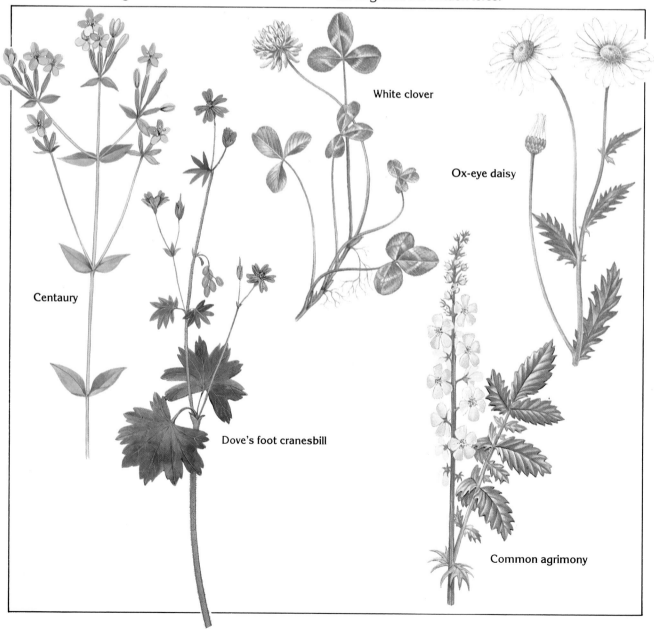

White clover

Ox-eye daisy

Centaury

Dove's foot cranesbill

Common agrimony

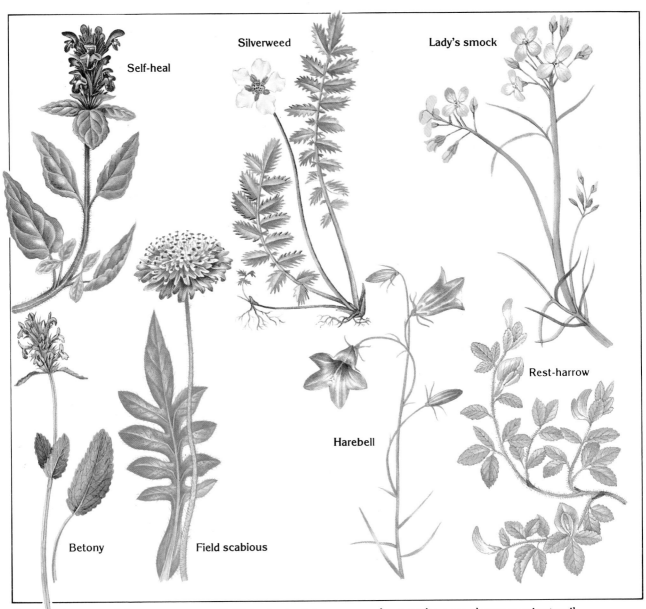

Self-heal

Silverweed

Lady's smock

Betony

Field scabious

Harebell

Rest-harrow

**Self-heal** is one of the commonest British plants. It is found throughout the length and breadth of the country in all types of grassy habitats and will grow in mountain country up to 800m (over 2000ft) above sea level. Its flowers, usually a purple-violet colour, but sometimes pink or white, are borne in a compact, square cluster.

Although not quite as common, **silverweed** is found all over the British Isles, especially where the ground is heavy clay. Its soft, shining, silver leaves were used by the Romans as a kind of insole in their wooden sandals to relieve their aching feet.

Wetter pastures and roadsides are the habitat of **lady's smock** and **betony**. Lady's smock is also known as cuckoo flower as it appears at the same time as the cuckoo arrives and ceases flowering when the cuckoos begin their migration back to Africa. Its clusters of distinctive pink and lilac flowers enliven roadsides and pastures and its seed pods are the food of the pretty orange tip butterfly. Betony also grows in heathland and scrub and is common around ruined monastic buildings where it was once grown by monks as a charm against evil.

In drier meadows, roadsides and waste places the pale-blue to violet blossoms of the **field scabious** brighten up the dusty landscape. The name scabious is a corruption of 'scabies', a reference to the plant's use as a herb to cure skin disorders. The flowers have the peculiar property of turning green if touched by a lighted cigarette.

The **harebell** is the bluebell of Scotland, and certainly the northern flowers are taller and of a deeper blue than those growing in the south. It grows in open, chalky grasslands, on sandy soils and in dune pastures throughout Britain, but it is absent from the south-west.

The **rest-harrow**, although common in the south and east, has a largely coastal distribution over the rest of the country. On dune grasslands it grows as a low, creeping plant with vicious, partly-hidden spines. Elsewhere it forms a thick, tough mat which in the days before the tractor would bring horse-drawn ploughs and harrows to a halt – literally 'arresting the harrow' as the name implies.

Daffodils are possibly the most talked about, written about and admired of all our field and meadow plants. The **wild daffodil** is a small, more delicate plant than the cultivated variety and grows in damp meadows and woodlands and along riversides. It has a patchy distribution, occurring over most parts of England and Wales but it is absent from Scotland. Where it does grow it can be very abundant, the nodding blooms carpeting acres of ground in one of nature's most glorious floral displays. Pollination is usually carried out by early-flying bumble-bees which visit the yellow trumpets in the spring.

A meadow yellow with buttercups is also a spectacular sight, nowadays sadly uncommon because of the habitual use of herbicides. The **meadow buttercup** is the commonest and tallest species, growing everywhere in damp grassland and on roadsides – even on mountain tops! The juice of all buttercups is acrid and poisonous and can cause rashes or skin blistering in some people. Buttercups are also poisonous to stock. In the meadows their bitter taste deters most animals but if fed accidentally to stock they can cause serious problems. The **bulbous buttercup** is the earliest flowering of the buttercups and prefers drier habitats including sand-dune pastures. It is easily recognised by the downcurved sepals beneath the flower.

**Bird's-foot trefoil** can be found growing alongside the bulbous buttercup in dune pastures by the sea. It is also common in drier meadows, especially in chalky or limy districts. The yellow flowers of this low-growing but sometimes bushy plant are often shot through with orange, the contrast of the yellow and orange flowers side by side earning it the name of 'eggs and bacon'. Bird's-foot trefoil has more than seventy common names, most of them referring to fingers and claws, shoes and fairies.

Late summer and autumn is the time for the tall flowering spikes of the yellow **toadflax**. It occurs in almost any type of grassy habitat on sandy, gravelly and chalky soils. Although widely distributed it is rare in north-west Scotland and Ireland. The bright yellow flowers have a long spur and a prominent lip supposedly shaped like a toad's mouth.

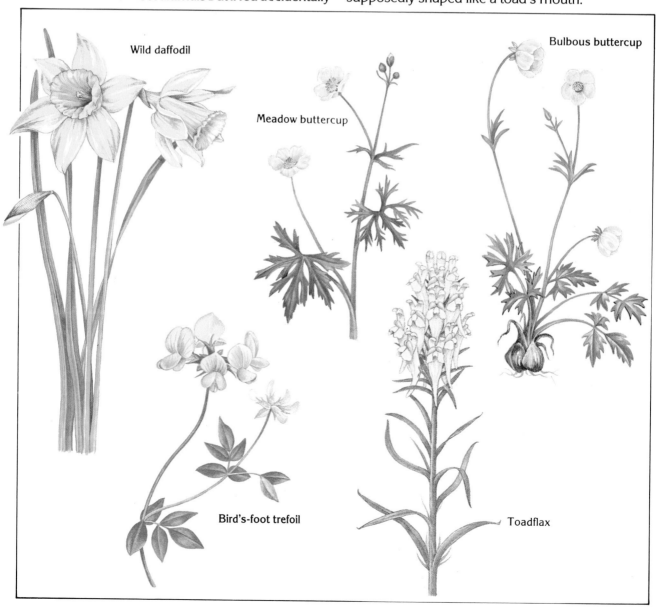

Wild daffodil

Meadow buttercup

Bulbous buttercup

Bird's-foot trefoil

Toadflax

# FUNGI of FIELD and MEADOW

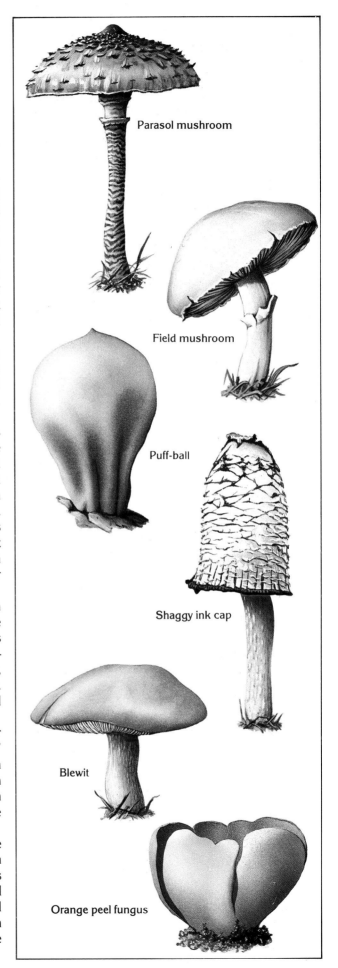

Parasol mushroom

Field mushroom

Puff-ball

Shaggy ink cap

Blewit

Orange peel fungus

---

*NEVER eat a toadstool or a mushroom unless it has been positively identified.*

---

The **parasol mushroom** is one of the largest and most noticeable fungi found growing in pastures. It can stand up to 38cm (15in) tall and its cap can measure up to 30cm (12in) across. Although it is found in pastures, it has a strong association with woodland, growing only along the edges of pastures fringed with woods and also occurring in grassy glades within the woodland. It often appears on ant hills, and has a particular liking for pastures grazed by horses.

The **field mushroom** is the one we buy from the greengrocer and it is now grown commercially on a vast scale. In the wild it appears in late summer and autumn after summer rains damp the still-warm soil. It is common in all pastureland throughout Britain.

The **puff-balls** are a widespread group of species found in grassland and pastures, though some occur on tree stumps in woods. They appear from July to October and are whitish at first but soon turn a dingy brown. They have a thick double skin which becomes slack and opens at the top when ripe. Falling raindrops expel clouds of the brown spores which are then carried away on the wind. The giant puff-ball found growing among long grass can reach the size of a football. It may appear earlier in the year than the other species, from May to October.

The **shaggy ink cap**, or 'lawyer's wig', is a common fungus growing in groups on lawns, roadside grasslands and rubbish heaps. When young it looks like a lawyer's wig but as it ages it slowly dissolves – deliquesces – from the base upwards into a black, inky fluid which in the past was actually used as ink. It is an edible species, only eaten when young and firm.

**Blewits**, named after the bluish-lilac colour of their stems, are plentiful in fields and pastures. 'Blue-leg' is another common name. They appear rather late in the year, during October and November, growing in crowded rings. Their caps are a greyish-brown colour but their spores, carried on white or pale brown gills, are a dull red.

The cup fungi are among the most attractive of the fungi. There are a number of species, many with bright colours, and they grow in a variety of habitats – from dead leaves and garden lawns to roots and dead wood. The **orange peel fungus** illustrated grows on lawns and roadsides and is a dull-orange in colour. Their cup-like shapes have earned them the names of 'elf cups' or 'pixie cups'.

# PLANTS of WOOD, SCRUB and HEDGE

*In autumn the berries of black bryony and the papery 'cones' of hops brighten the hedgerows and scrub as the last of the summer flowers linger amongst the ferns.*

More species of plants grow in woodlands and hedgerows than in any other habitat. This is not surprising in a country that is part of the great European temperate forest belt. The trees that dominate a woodland create the special conditions within it, but it is mainly the soil and the climate that decide just where each species of tree will grow and which plants will grow in the woodlands. In the lowlands pedunculate oak — the English oak — dominates the woods. In the west and north the pedunculate oak gives way to its relative, the sessile oak. On dry, chalky soils the beech is supreme, while in the waterlogged soils of fens and marshes the alder is the only tree hardy enough to survive. Ash woods grow on limestone and Scots pines thrive on the cold, wet hillsides in the north as well as on the warm, dry, sandy heaths of the south.

Left to themselves woodlands naturally develop a characteristic layered structure. The top layer is the canopy, typically 18 to 21 metres (60 to 70ft) high, where the crowns of the trees reach out to meet each other, casting the ground below into shade. Beneath the canopy is the shrub layer. Depending on the amount of shade, this will either contain a few weak shrubs and spindly saplings or it will be thick with strongly-growing bushes and vigorous young trees. Blocks of scrubland and ribbons of hedgerow are simply the woodland shrub layer freed from competition and the shade of canopy trees. Next comes the field layer, a mixture of grass, bramble and herbs, and finally the ground layer, a thin band of litter and moss, apparently insignificant yet vital for returning nutrients to the soil for the well-being of the whole wood.

Each different type of woodland and each different type of soil has its own characteristic field layer: green, lush and varied on the heavy soils of lowland oak woods, sparse under the dense shade of chalkland beech woods. Many woodland plants flower early in the year to catch the full light of the sun before the leaves on the trees unfurl. Without question, spring is the time of a woodland's greatest glory and at this time hedgerows too burst into blossom and become spangled with wild flowers.

In the spring each year throughout the British Isles the five-petalled white flowers of the **wood sorrel** carpet our woodland floors. It is often abundant and dominant, especially under oak and beech, and is often one of the only flowers found growing on the floor of lightly-planted conifer woods. The bright green leaves are shamrock-shaped, the root leaves folding down in dull weather, earning the plant the name of 'sleeping clover'. The leaves have a pleasant, sharp, mouth-watering taste and it has been cultivated as a salad plant and sauce herb since the Middle Ages. Wood sorrel can also be found growing on fallen logs and as an epiphyte on the mossy branches of trees.

The beautiful, solitary, drooping, white flowers of the **wood anemone** are one of the delights of the woodland in spring. They are almost as common as the wood sorrel but they flower earlier. They are related to the buttercups and like them are poisonous, but they have a delicate, sweet scent. They grow in woodlands and hedgerows in all but acid or waterlogged soils and can be found in sheltered gullies and on cliff ledges quite high up in the mountains of Scotland and Wales.

Where there is some lime in the soil **enchanter's nightshade** will grow profusely under all but the very densest of shade. It spreads by creeping, underground runners and it can become a troublesome garden weed if it is established in shady shrubberies. Despite its name it is not related to the true nightshades and it has no magical or 'enchanting' properties, the common name being invented by medieval herbalists. The fruits of enchanter's nightshade are club-shaped, easily detached and covered with hooked bristles that catch on clothing and fur.

**Yellow archangel** is a plant of woodland rides and clearings and is usually only abundant after woodland clearance or coppicing. It is common in southern England and the Midlands on heavy soils but becomes rarer towards the north and in Scotland. The yellow flowers grow in whorls around the stem. When crushed, the leaves give off an unpleasant smell which helps to deter plant-eating animals and insects.

The common **wild strawberry** of woodland, scrub and hedgerow is the original strawberry. The cultivated version with its very large fruits is a hybrid between two North American species. What the wild strawberry lacks in size it gains in sweetness, delicacy and the pleasure of gathering one of the best wild foods. It grows throughout Britain, although it is less common in Scotland, and can be found at heights of over 700m (2000ft). Wild strawberry spreads by means of both the tiny seeds on the outside of its berries and by long runners that reach out all round the plant and take root at their tips. The name strawberry comes from the practice of putting straw round the plants to prevent the berries being covered in mud in wet weather.

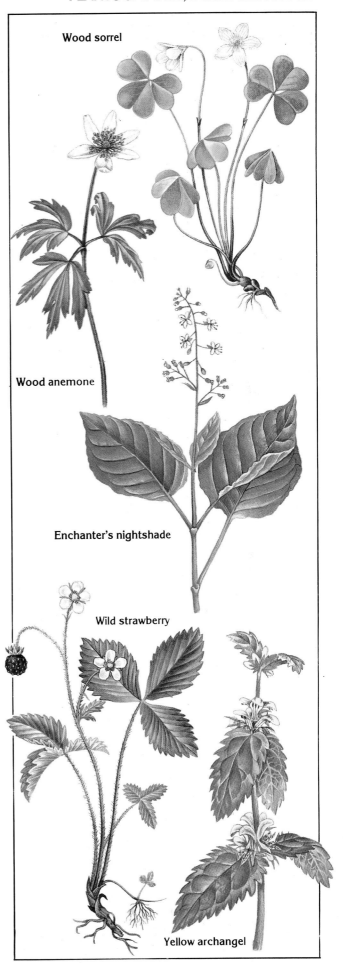

Wood sorrel

Wood anemone

Enchanter's nightshade

Wild strawberry

Yellow archangel

113

**Primroses**, from the Latin *prima rosa*, 'first rose', are regarded as the heralds of spring, and are perhaps the best-loved and most picked of all our wild flowers. They grow everywhere in Britain, in woodlands and hedges and even in grassy places next to the sea. The delicately-scented flowers emerge from March to May in most places, but in the south-west they regularly flower from around Christmas time and fill the winter hedgebanks with colour. Primroses are also very hardy, growing in mountain gullies at heights over 700m (2000ft). There are two types of primrose flower, pin-eyed and thrum-eyed. Pin-eyed flowers have a long style with a green knob that reaches the mouth of the corolla tube; in these flowers the pollen-bearing stamens lie at the bottom of the tube. In the thrum-eyed flowers the position is reversed, the style sitting below the cluster of stamens around the corolla tube. It was Charles Darwin who discovered that these differences were a device to ensure that only long-tongued bees and moths were able to transfer the pollen of the primrose and thus secure proper cross-fertilisation of the flowers.

The beautiful starry white flowers of **ramsons** are an unfailing attraction for the ignorant flower picker, but once picked the act is quickly regretted. Ramsons are the wild garlic of damp, shady woods and when picked or crushed they give off an overpowering scent of garlic. Their scent is so strong that their presence in a wood can be detected some distance away. In favourable habitats they grow by the thousand, often in the company of bluebells, covering the woodland floor with a white carpet of flowers. Cattle are fond of wild garlic and will break into woods to get at it, but unfortunately it taints their milk, making it unfit for sale although not unfit to drink despite its garlic flavour!

**St John's wort** grows in woods, hedges and on grassy banks over most of Britain but it is rare or absent from most of Scotland. Its wonderful golden flowers can be seen from July through to September. The common or perforate St John's wort has translucent glands in its leaves that look like pin-pricks when held up to the light and indeed an old country belief has it that the Devil, jealous of the plant's association with St John, pricked holes in the plant in a frenzy of hate.

The blue spires of **bugle** are common on the edges of woodlands and in damp woodland rides. It spreads by short underground runners and sometimes forms extensive patches. In early summer the flowers have a very strong attraction for pearl-bordered fritillary butterflies which may cluster round the plants in large numbers.

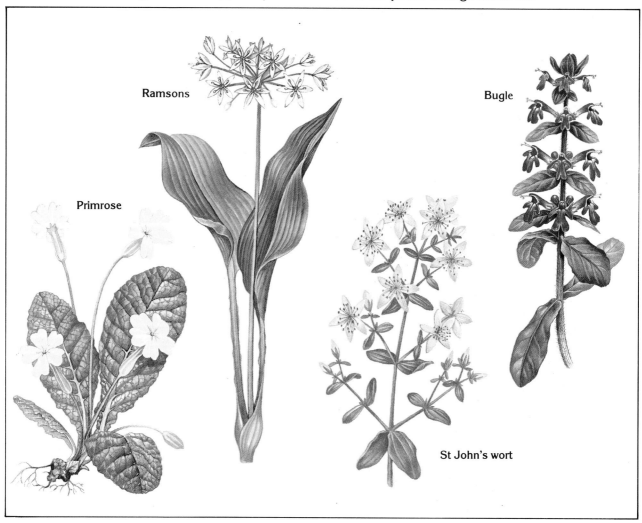

Ramsons

Bugle

Primrose

St John's wort

If primroses are regarded as the most popular flowers of the spring, then **bluebells** must be a close second. In light, acid soils where they dominate the woodland floor they grow in breathtaking profusion, a haze of brilliant blue, giving off a powerful, heady and delightful scent. They are most common in ancient oak woods but also grow on hedge banks and occasionally in pastures where these were formerly woodland. Near the sea, bluebells are common in the salt-drenched grasslands on the cliffs. Picking the flowers does no harm, but they can be damaged by trampling the leaves and bluebells can quickly disappear from small woodlands with easy access and heavy use. The bluebell shares the country name of 'crow-toes' with the early purple orchid and certainly the two often grow together.

The **early purple orchid** is a plant of coppiced woodlands, roadside verges and sea cliffs. It is common in shady woodlands where it grows a much longer and deeper-purple spike than those plants in more open habitats. The tubers of this lovely orchid were once used to make a much-prized drink called 'salop' and in the Middle East they are still eaten. They contain a substance called bassorine which provides more nutritious matter than any other plant. It is said that 28g (1oz) of bassorine is sufficient to sustain a man for a whole day. The rich purple flowers smell strongly of tomcats.

**Dog's mercury** is another plant common in shady woodlands. On chalk or lime-rich soils it will carpet the woodland floor and exclude any other species. It is especially common under beech trees, a dark habitat in which few wild flowers can survive. Dog's mercury is successful here because it grows, flowers and sets seed before the leaves of the trees have fully emerged to blot out the light. Oddly, dog's mercury can also be found among shady mountain rocks at heights up to 1200m (4000ft), a strange habitat for what is essentially a woodland plant. It is virulently poisonous to stock, especially cattle, and has an unpleasant smell.

**Ground ivy** is found almost everywhere, in grassland and waste places as well as in woodland. Although common, it is usually dominant only in recently-coppiced oak woods where its creeping habit allows it to take full advantage of the new flood of light before grasses and other herbs overwhelm it. The bruised leaves of ground ivy give off a strong and distinctive smell. In the past it was also known as alehoof, in part because of the shape of its leaves and also because it was used to flavour and clarify ale in the days before the use of hops.

**Wood avens** is a plant of damp, shady places, woodlands, scrub and hedge banks and it can at times be a troublesome garden weed. Its root gives off a strong smell of cloves and was used as a moth repellent. Traditionally it was also hung around the house to ward off evil spirits. The Romans valued it highly as a remedy against malaria and used it in the same way as quinine was later used.

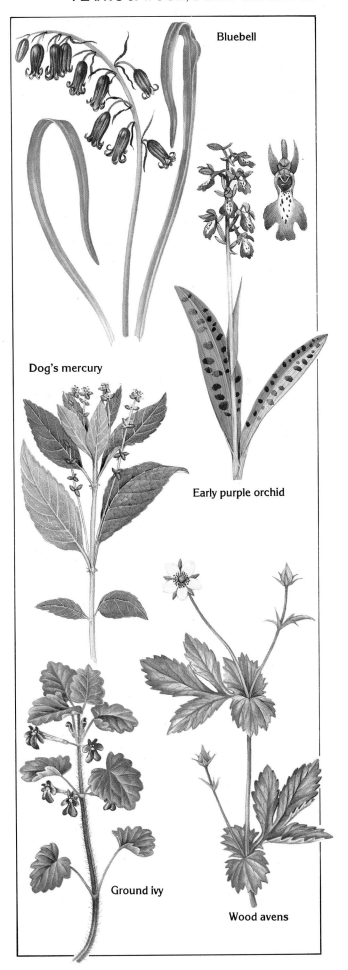

Bluebell

Dog's mercury

Early purple orchid

Ground ivy

Wood avens

The large green hood of the **cuckoo pint** is one of the strangest and most striking of springtime flowers to be found in shady hedgerows. The hood, or sheath, encloses a thick, fleshy stem at the base of which are the male and female flowers. The sheath narrows around these flowers and forms a chamber from which comes a smell of rotting manure, which is very attractive to small flies. Once the flies crawl inside the chamber they are trapped by a mass of downward-pointing hairs at the chamber's entrance and they have to remain there, dusted with pollen, until the sheath withers and they are released. They then fly off to the next cuckoo pint to repeat the process and fertilise the flowers as they fly from plant to plant. In late summer the cuckoo pint's bright red, glossy berries peep out from the bottom of every hedgerow, a tempting but deadly harvest. The berries are very poisonous and another of the plant's common names, adder's meat, was given because it was believed that the adder ate the berries to get its poison.

The **foxglove** of hedgerows and woodland clearings is also a poisonous plant. It contains digitalin, a poison that affects the heart. 'Deadmen's bells' and 'deadmen's thimbles', two of its other names, graphically describe its poisonous and dangerous qualities. Yet it is also regarded as the plant of fairies, elves and magic and is attractive enough to have been brought into cottage gardens for show. Foxes were supposed to wear the flower bells as gloves and their magic properties enabled the foxes to creep up silently on chickens or away from pursuing humans. The flowers are pollinated by bumble-bees which busily work from flower to flower throughout the summer.

The milky juice of the **wood spurge**, like that of all the spurges, is poisonous and an irritant, causing blisters and rashes in some people. Wood spurge is a tall, limp-leaved plant crowned with a striking cluster of yellow-green, saucer-like flowers. It is a common plant of woodlands and hedgerows in southern England but is rare or absent from most of the north.

**Hedge woundwort** is one of the most common hedgerow plants in Britain. It is a tall-growing plant with soft, furry leaves and beetroot-coloured flowers. When crushed, the leaves give off a foul smell said to be like the smell of rotting flesh. Surprisingly though, woundwort leaves were used for dressing wounds, hence the name. Perhaps it was thought that if a medicine smelt or tasted horrible it must be doing you good! In recent years it has been discovered that a volatile oil extracted from the leaves does indeed have antiseptic properties.

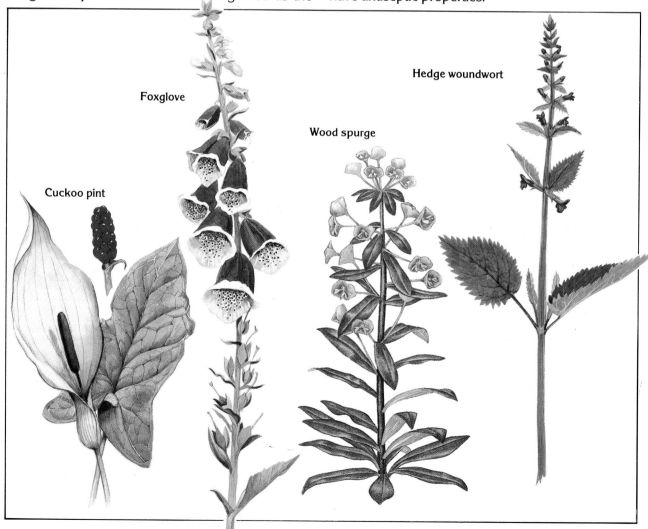

Foxglove

Hedge woundwort

Wood spurge

Cuckoo pint

Honeysuckle, hop and black bryony are three of the commonest climbing plants in Britain. **Honeysuckle** grows everywhere, in woods, hedges and scrub, climbing over trees and bushes but just as often trailing on the woodland floor and forming thick tangles of vegetation. The young stems of honeysuckle grow rapidly, twining anti-clockwise in a tight hold around twigs and branches. They can cause considerable damage to young saplings by constricting the soft outer tissues of their trunks and causing ugly distortions in their growth. The clusters of pale-yellow flowers appear throughout the summer but there are two main flowering periods, one in June and the other in September. The flowers give off a beautiful sweet scent which is strongest at dusk and attracts moths, particularly hawk moths. The nectar in the flowers is at the bottom of the very long flower tubes and can only be reached by long-tongued insects like moths — even honey bees are unable to drink from honeysuckle. By late summer bright red berries clothe the twining stems, attracting berry-eating birds which spread the seeds about the countryside in their droppings.

**Hop** is a common climbing plant in the woods, hedgerows and scrub of the south and east, becoming rarer in the west and north. It may have originated in the woodlands of south-east England but once its use as a bitter flavouring for ale was discovered in the Middle Ages it was widely planted and cultivated. The advantage of hops in brewing is that they enable the ale to be kept longer, a property known since the ninth century. Its widespread use was delayed for centuries, however, by the opposition of 'real-ale purists' amongst ale-brewers! It is the female 'cones' (fruits) with their resinous secretion that are used for brewing.

The long strings of red berries of the **black bryony**, the hedgerow 'necklace', are one of the delights of autumn. Black bryony grows in woods and scrubland but it is most abundant in hedgerows a year or two after they have been trimmed. The long, twining stems with glossy, heart-shaped leaves scramble over bushes to a height of 4m (12ft) or more. The scarlet berries are poisonous and this plant, like the cuckoo pint, goes by the alternative name of adder's meat or snake's meat.

**Twayblade** is one of the commoner orchids, growing beneath dense scrub in wet soils or damp woodlands and shady pastures. In spite of being so common, the plant takes at least fourteen years to reach maturity. It is pollinated by small flies and beetles attracted by nectar secreted in a groove on the central lip of each flower. The pollen is showered explosively over the insect as it lands on the flower.

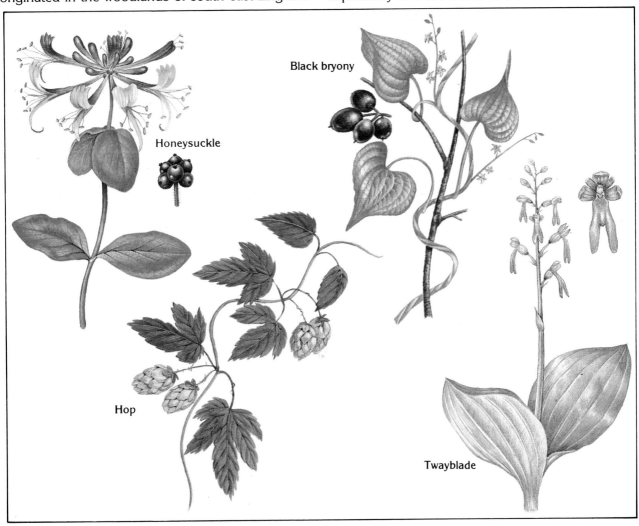

Black bryony

Honeysuckle

Hop

Twayblade

Roses seem always to have been one of man's favourite flowers. They were certainly one of the first plants to be cultivated for pleasure rather than because of the need for food. The native **dog rose** grows all over Britain in woodlands, hedges and scrub and has been adopted, perhaps not surprisingly, as England's national flower. The term 'dog' may be a corruption of 'dagger', referring to its sharp thorns, or it may have simply been a way to distinguish it from what were thought to be the more superior cultivated roses. The large flowers of the dog rose vary from white to deep pink and give way to bright red berries, called hips. The plant scrambles over bushes and clings to branches with the aid of its curved and cruelly-sharp thorns. Rose petals can be eaten in salads, and religious rosaries originally consisted of strings of rose petals rolled into balls. Inside the hips the hard seeds are bedded into a layer of fine, hair-like fibres that were used by children as the original 'itching powder'. These can cause a dangerous irritation of the stomach and gut if swallowed. When making rose-hip syrup – which is very rich in vitamin C – the hairs must be very carefully strained off.

The **dog violet** gained its tag of 'dog' because it was dismissed as being inferior to the less common scented violet. But what finer sight can there be than a hedgebank in spring covered in dog violets, stitchwort and cuckoo flower? It grows in woods and hedges and also in sand-dunes and on heaths throughout Britain. The **greater stitchwort**, its companion on western hedgebanks, is also common and abundant, although it does not grow in acid soils.

Ferns were among the earliest of plants to evolve and they still retain many of their primitive features. They have no flowers and produce no seeds. Instead, dust-like spores are produced beneath the leaves. There are female eggs and male sperms among the spores and fertilisation can only take place in water, the mobile sperm swimming around to find an egg. The lack of flowers or an obvious means of reproduction was thought to endow ferns with magical properties. A **male fern** root carved into the shape of a hand was said to confer invisibility on the person who carried it! All ferns are commoner in the west where there is greater rainfall and higher humidity. Male fern is common in woodlands, hedgerows and roadsides and **hart's tongue** will also grow on walls and rocks.

The sedges are related to grasses and **pendulous sedge** is the largest of the woodland species. It is a very striking plant that grows in large tussocks from which long tassels of flowers emerge in summer.

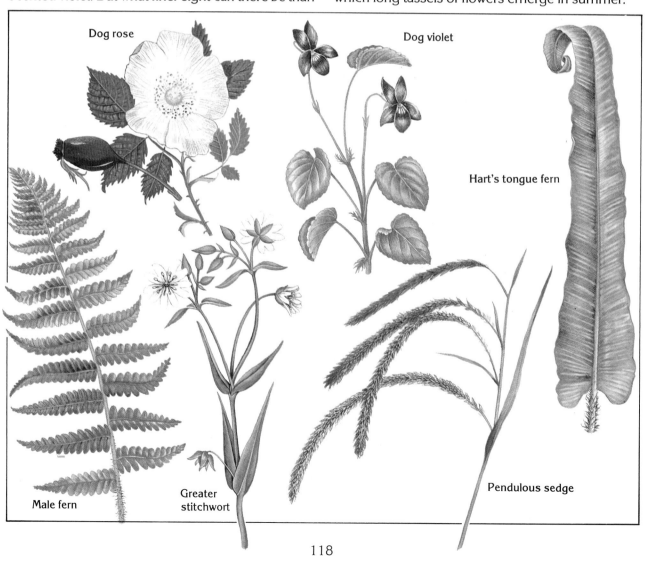

Dog rose

Dog violet

Hart's tongue fern

Male fern

Greater stitchwort

Pendulous sedge

In March, before the buds on the trees have begun to burst, the golden-yellow flowers of the **lesser celandine** carpet the floor of damp woodlands all over Britain. Hedge banks, pastures, sea cliffs and stream banks also come alive with the bright stars of this common spring flower. In the sun the flowers open wide but in dull weather they close, revealing the yellow-green sepals beneath the petals. However, the flowers are said not to open before nine and they always close by five, whatever the weather. Lesser celandine sets few fertile seeds in our cold springs and instead relies on producing small tubers (which have been compared to grains of wheat) above the root stems. These are easily washed off and distributed by rain. This was the favourite plant of the poet Wordsworth and its blossoms were carved on his tomb.

**Moschatel** is also a common, although often overlooked, spring flower of damp, heavy, oak woodlands. It also grows in hedge banks and among mountain rocks up to 1200m (4000ft) above sea level. The curious flower has five faces, four arranged in a square with the fifth on top, facing the sky. For this reason it is also known as 'town hall clock'. It rarely sets seed in Britain, spreading instead by means of creeping underground stems. When it does fruit, the seeds, looking rather like berries, droop on long, limp stems. Toward evening in damp weather the whole plant gives off a faint smell of musk but the smell disappears if the plant is bruised.

Spring is also the time of flowering for the **red campion**. There can be few finer sights than the massed flowers of red campion mixed with bluebells and primroses beneath the soft, light greens of springtime leaves in damp western woodlands. Each plant is either male or female and the red campion readily hybridises with a close relative, the white campion of grasslands, to produce another pink form.

The vetches as a group flower from the spring right through the summer. The **bush vetch** is one of the commonest, growing on roadsides and hedge banks all over Britain. It grows up to 1m (3ft) tall, anchoring itself to other plants with fine, coiling tendrils at the ends of its leaf-stalks. The seeds are carried in long seed pods which become black when they dry out and burst open in the warm sunshine with a faintly audible crack.

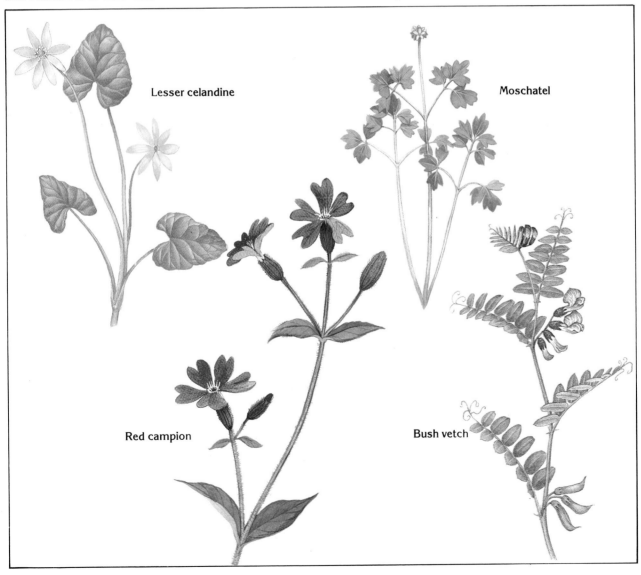

Lesser celandine

Moschatel

Red campion

Bush vetch

Ivy and traveller's joy are two persistent, woody climbers that may live for a very long time. **Ivy** can live for more than a century, its main trunks becoming thick and shaggy, like ropes. The clinging roots along the ivy's stem are used only for support. They do not penetrate walls or the bark of trees to find nourishment. In its early stages, ivy creeps across the woodland floor until it meets a tree trunk, then it rapidly climbs the trunk, in time reaching as high as 30m (100ft) into the crown of the tree. In the early, creeping stage ivy bears the familiar lobed leaf, but when it reaches into the crown it sprouts oval, unlobed leaves and in the autumn produces clusters of greenish-yellow flowers attractive to a host of autumn flies and late-season butterflies.

**Traveller's joy** is common but found only on soils containing chalk or lime. Its twining stems can grow up to 30m (100ft), scrambling over trees and bushes in thickets and on woodland margins. At times, its rope-like stems hang in festoons, like lianas in the South American jungle. Once established, it can live for over sixty years. Its alternative name, 'old man's beard', refers to the feathery plumes of its seeds which are carried by the wind. Other names are 'boy's bacca' and 'gypsy's bacca' because lengths of the dried stem were smoked like cigars by gypsies.

**Bramble** is a scrambling rather than climbing plant, common in woods, scrubland, hedgerows, neglected fields and on waste ground. The name bramble comes from the Old English 'bremble' or 'brembly', meaning prickly. The more modern name of blackberry is a reference to its succulent autumn berries. Blackberries are probably the most sought-after wild crop in Britain; they are easy to pick, grow in profusion and make delicious jams, jellies and pie fillings. The berries are also avidly taken by birds who spread the tiny seeds across the countryside in their droppings. Country tradition has it that blackberries should not be picked after 10th October. This the day when the Devil was cast out of heaven by St Michael and fell into a bramble bush. Ever since then on the same day he is said to curse the berries, making them foul and unpalatable and bringing bad luck to any person who picks them.

**Bittersweet** berries are poisonous, hence its other common name, woody nightshade, after the very poisonous but unrelated deadly nightshade. It is common in hedges in England but rare elsewhere. It has a scrambling, woody growth, sometimes reaching 1.8m (6ft) in height. All parts of the plant are poisonous, but not dangerously so, tasting bitter at first but leaving a distinctly sweet aftertaste. Bittersweet also grows on shingle beaches on the seashore where it has a low-growing, creeping habit.

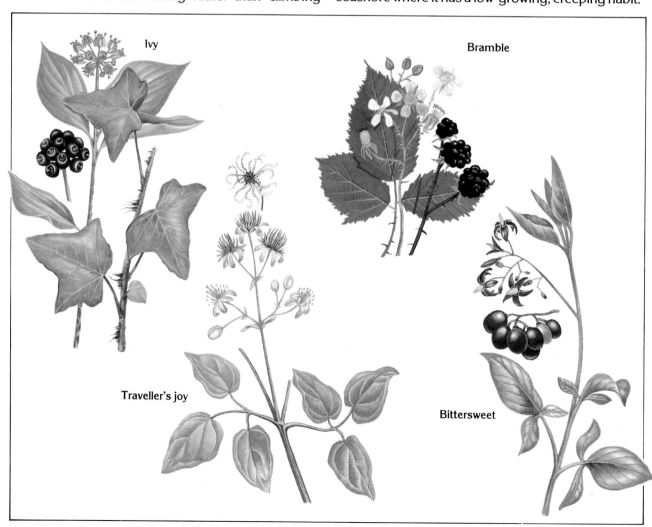

Ivy

Bramble

Traveller's joy

Bittersweet

# FUNGI of WOOD, SCRUB and HEDGE

Sickener

Fly agaric

Chanterelle

Stinkhorn

Birch bracket

Cep

---

*Woodlands contain a number of more unusual and interesting fungi and they also contain the most deadly poisonous. **NEVER** eat a toadstool or a mushroom unless it has been positively identified.*

---

The **sickener** is a large, attractive fungus that grows in all types of woodland but it has a preference for conifers. There are a number of related species with red, yellow or black caps that appear from July to October. It is poisonous and causes nausea.

Similar in appearance to the sickener is the **fly agaric**, but this fungus can be distinguished by the white scales on its cap, the remains of the covering on the fungus at its small, 'button' stage. Its name comes from the old practice of placing broken pieces of fly agaric in a dish of milk to attract and kill flies. Woodlands, especially conifer and birch woods, and bracken are its favoured habitats, and the fungus usually appears in the autumn.

The **chanterelle** is an unusual funnel-shaped species with deep grooves on its underside. It grows in all types of deciduous woodland and in grassy places in pine woods. It can be found throughout the summer and into the autumn.

**Stinkhorns** are the most unmistakable of the fungi, not only because of their shape but because of their strong, unpleasant smell of rotting flesh. The smell is there to attract flies to the sooty-green, spore-bearing slime on the cap. The flies feed on the slime and pick up spores on their feet and bodies, which very effectively disperses them over the countryside. The slime is very soon gone, leaving behind a honeycomb mesh on the cap of the fungus. Stinkhorns are common in all types of woodlands, and even in shrubby gardens, appearing over a long season from May to November.

Fungi grow on trees, both living and dead, as well as on the woodland floor and one of the commonest and most conspicuous species is the **birch bracket**, or birch polypore. The birch bracket lives on dead or dying trees and its fruit bodies appear singly or in tiers on standing trees or fallen logs. They are hard and woody and remain on the tree for months, the previous year's fruit body often remaining alongside the current year's growth.

The **cep**, or 'penny bun', is a short, squat fungus of all types of woodland, although it has a preference for coniferous woods on sandy soil. It grows up to 20cm (8in) wide and has a slippery cap when it is wet. It can be found throughout the summer and well into the autumn.

# PLANTS of HEATHLAND and MOORLAND

*Heathers dominate the moorland landscape, turning whole hillsides purple in late summer when they are in flower. Bilberries are an important food for many moorland birds.*

Heaths and moors develop on thin, poor, acid soils where there is little nourishment to support a varied community of plants. At first glance heathland and moorland seem to be similar habitats, often containing the same plants and sharing a similar bleak and windswept appearance. They are, however, distinctly different. Heathlands develop on dry, well-drained, sandy or gravelly soils in the south while moorlands develop on the cold, waterlogged soils found on the uplands of the north and west.

Heathland can be found in all the southern counties from the Lizard Peninsula in Cornwall to the vast tracts of the Breckland in Suffolk, but the greatest areas of heath are concentrated in the Home Counties near London and around the New Forest in Hampshire. Heather, or ling, which flowers in great purple sheets in late summer, is the dominant plant. With it grows bracken, gorse and wavy hair-grass. The commonest grass in the west is the flying bent, so called because its dry, straw-coloured stems break off and fly in the winter winds.

Heather dominates moorland too, but where the soil is cold and water-logged it gives way to cross-leaved heath, wavy hair-grass and purple moor grass. On Exmoor where the land is boggy there are great areas of deer grass, an uncommon plant elsewhere in such quantities. The cold, wet conditions on moorland prevent the breakdown of plant remains. Instead they gradually build up as thick layers of dark brown or black peat which increases the general wetness of the soil.

Where it is abundant, heather is managed by rotational burning. Old heather becomes woody and leggy, casting a deep shade on the ground and preventing the sun from warming the soil. The old shoots provide very little food for sheep or red grouse, both economically important species on these wild lands. Traditionally heaths and moors are burnt on a rotation of seven to twenty years to remove all dead wood and rejuvenate the heather. After a burn the heather puts out young, tender shoots which are greedily taken by grouse and sheep. The removal of dead vegetation also encourages other plants to flower.

Gorse and broom are the two glories of British heathlands. Both flower with a mass of blossom that turns whole hillsides yellow and fills the air with heady scent. **Gorse** is the first to flower, usually in March but sooner in frost-free western districts. The pea-like flowers, with their rich scent of coconut, produce black seed pods which split explosively in warm sunshine, scattering the seeds some distance away. The folk belief that gorse flowers all year round is not quite true. There are two other species of gorse and these come successively into flower as the others die back. The wood of gorse burns well and with an intense heat. It was once regularly harvested to be burnt in bakers' ovens.

Whereas gorse is prickly with sharp, curved spines, **broom** has long, straight, supple stems that grow up to 2m (6ft) in length. The stems used to be gathered to make brooms and brushes but there were some precautions to be observed because:

If you sweep the house with blossomed broom in May
You are sure to sweep the head of the house away.

The flowers give off a strong scent of peaches and although they contain no nectar they are visited by bees for their pollen.

**Bilberry**, or whortleberry, often grows in company with gorse or broom but prefers damper, peaty soils. It is widespread in Britain in woodlands, heaths and moors and is tolerant of both exposure and shade. At higher altitudes it is often the dominant plant but lower down, although abundant, it is often concealed by the heavy growth of heather. The blue berries are popular for pies and jams. On grouse moors the berries and young shoots of bilberries are an important item in the red grouse's diet.

**Crowberry**, a much less widely distributed plant than bilberry, is found on the moors of Scotland and northern England. In south-west England it grows in places on Exmoor and Dartmoor, but only as a very rare plant. It can also grow in the drier parts of very wet and peaty blanket bogs, sometimes becoming the dominant species. The black berries, which appear in August, are edible, but quite tasteless – fit only for crows, as its name suggests.

The tiny yellow flowers of **tormentil** can be found on every heath and moor up to 1000m (3000ft), especially where the soil is acid. It is a low-growing, creeping and trailing plant which bears its flowers on long stalks, lifting them above the leaves. Tormentil used to be boiled in milk and used for the treatment of, and to ease the 'torment' of, colic.

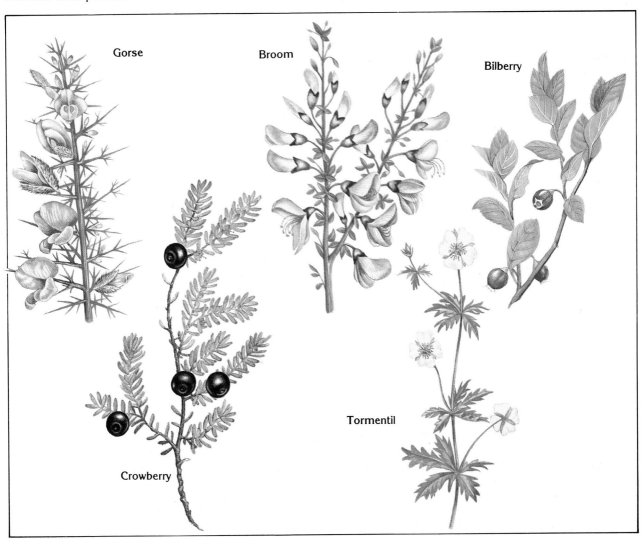

Gorse

Broom

Bilberry

Crowberry

Tormentil

In the south and east the heather and gorse of coastal heaths are parasitised by **dodder**, a plant completely lacking in chlorophyll that trails over its host with a mass of red, thread-like stems. Dodder obtains all its nourishment from its host plant, sometimes killing it in the process. In July the threads are covered in scented, pinkish-white flowers.

Of the heathers found in upland moors and lowland heaths the **ling**, or common heather, is the most frequent and plentiful. On wet or dry soils, provided they are acid, ling will cover acres of hillside and heath, flowering in a purple haze in the autumn. Bees are very fond of the nectar produced by ling and beekeepers move hives out on to the moors to take advantage of the flowering crop.

**Bell heather** is common on drier heaths and is found in suitable habitats throughout Britain. The dark-purple flowers are carried in a nodding cluster at the top of the stem. **Cross-leaved heath** with its pale, almost pink flowers is commoner on wet parts of heaths. Its leaves are downy and greyish, with the margins rolled inwards.

The mountains and wet, grassy roadsides of the uplands of Scotland and northern England are the habitat of the **melancholy thistle**. Although it has toothed leaves, it lacks the spines of other thistles. It grows in patches, spreading by means of creeping underground stems. The soft, drooping leaves have felted white undersides. An extract of this thistle taken in wine was reputed to 'expel superfluous melancholy out of the body and make a man as merry as a cricket'.

**Sheep's sorrel** grows abundantly on the stony, acid soils of heaths, forming low clusters, and its seeds make a deep-red mist of colour late in the summer. The leaves contain oxalic acid and have a sharp but not unpleasant flavour. Common sorrel, a larger relative of grassy places but occasionally found on heaths, is cultivated as a salad plant on the Continent, a tradition stretching back to the Middle Ages when many more wild plants were eaten.

**Clubmoss** is more closely related to ferns than to mosses. It grows throughout Britain but is most abundant on the wet, peaty heather moors and high mountainous regions of Scotland and the north of England, growing near the summits of even the highest peaks. Clubmoss reproduces chiefly by leaf-like buds which fall off the parent plant and grow to form new plants. Powdered clubmoss was used to coat pills in order to stop them sticking together, and it has such a water-repellent power that a hand powdered with clubmoss can be dipped in water without becoming wet.

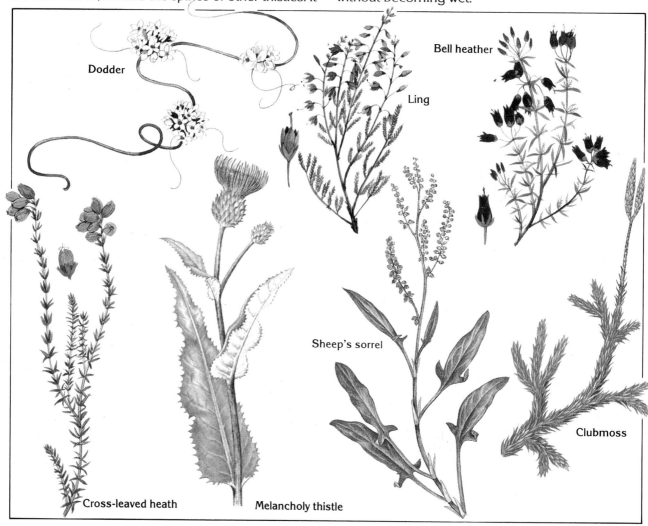

Dodder

Bell heather

Ling

Sheep's sorrel

Clubmoss

Cross-leaved heath

Melancholy thistle

# PLANTS of BOG, FEN and MARSH

*The dense beds of common reed hide all kinds of wetland plants. Water mint grows near the ditch edge and, in open areas, tall marsh orchids, kingcups and willows can be found.*

Bogland develops in areas with very high rainfall and is typically associated with stretches of moorland and heath. Small bogs form in waterlogged hollows or in poorly drained valleys. In areas where the rainfall is exceptionally high, bogs will cover enormous areas of countryside. In Ireland, for example, bogland covers as much as one-seventh of the countryside. These blanket bogs, as they are known, can also be found in the Highlands of Scotland, in Wales, the Pennines and on Dartmoor. The plants of blanket bogs are similar to those found on moorland but the wetter, more active parts of the bog are dominated by the soft, spongy, fast-growing sphagnum mosses.

Fenlands, like bogs, start their lives as a layer of peat on waterlogged ground. They form in slow-draining lowlands where there is plenty of lime to keep the water sweet, which allows the proper breakdown of organic remains. Dense and extensive stands of reeds and other tall waterside plants grow out of the still water. Willows and alder grow along drainage channels and rare and unusual floating plants grow in open water. The greatest fenlands in England were located in East Anglia around the Wash, but since the seventeenth century most of these have been drained and now only a few small nature reserves preserve all that is left of the fenland habitat.

Marshes differ from bogs and fens in that they contain no peat. They usually develop on waterlogged ground at the edges of ponds and lakes or beside slow-flowing lowland rivers. Flooding in marshes is usually seasonal and the extent and timing of flooding creates great differences in vegetation between different areas of marshland. Rushes, sedges and sometimes extensive beds of reeds cover most areas of marshland, and among them grow a great profusion of increasingly rare and threatened flowering plants. Marsh marigolds, or kingcups, grow early in spring, followed by the marsh violet and, in early summer, by the marsh orchid.

Some of our most attractive and unusual plants grow in the wet, swampy conditions of marshes and bogs. One of the tallest and most prolific is the **great willowherb**. It grows up to 2m (6ft) tall in marshy places and wet ditches. The long, softly-hairy leaves resemble those of the willow, as its name suggests, but an older name, 'codlins and cream', has a more intriguing origin. The great willowherb flowers resemble those of the codlin apple tree — large and deep pink with a white centre, and its fluffy white seeds that billow out in the wind from the plant's long seed pods look like cream.

The seeds of **cotton grass** also have long, fluffy hairs to aid their dispersal in the windswept, acid bogs where this attractive plant grows. There are several drooping, fluffy flower heads on each stem and in favourable habitats they speckle the bogs and fens like giant snowflakes. Cotton grass is a common plant in the north and west but is becoming very rare in the south because of drainage.

**Bog asphodel** too is a western and northern species. its golden, star-like flowers, borne on long spikes, are one of the delights of the bogs and moors where it grows. In the autumn the whole plant, stems and flowers, turns a peachy orange. It used to be believed that sheep and cattle eating the flowers would develop foot-rot but it was the permanently wet land where it grew that caused the problem, not the plant. The flowers of bog asphodel yield a golden-yellow dye that was used by Lancashire girls to dye their hair.

**Lousewort** got its strange name from the belief that it produced lice which infested cattle and sheep grazing in the wet, acid pastures where it grew. Its other name, 'red rattle', comes from the rattling sound made by the ripe seeds in the small flower bladder when the plant is shaken.

Commonest of the forget-me-nots is the **water forget-me-not**, found near water in marshes, pools and ditches. It is a straggly plant with a long, coiled flower stem that resembles a scorpion's sting, hence its old name of 'scorpion grass'. The name forget-me-not is supposed to have been given to the flower after a knight, walking by a river bank with his lady, bent down to pick the flowers, fell into the water and was swept away. As the current caught him he threw the flower on to the bank, calling, 'Forget me not'.

In sphagnum bogs and wet, peaty areas the tiny red rosettes of the carnivorous **sundew** spread out like spoons on the ground. The leaves are covered in hairs tipped with glistening drops of sticky fluid — the dew that defies even the fiercest sun — which trap unwary insects. The struggles of an insect cause the leaf to curl in and over it, holding the creature fast until it decomposes and it is absorbed as food by the plant.

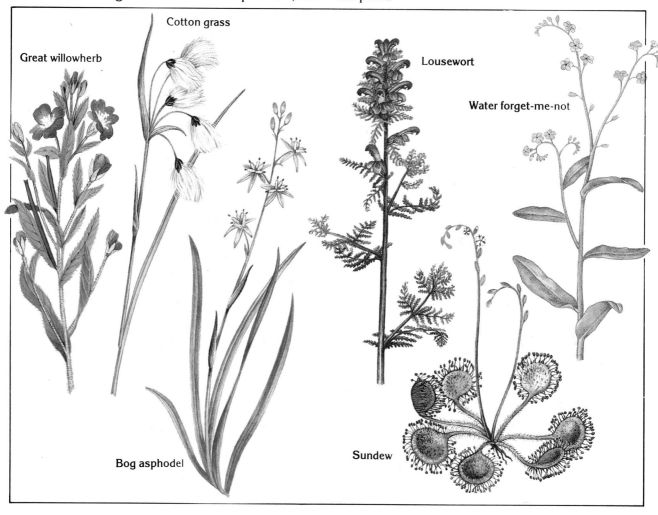

Great willowherb

Cotton grass

Bog asphodel

Lousewort

Water forget-me-not

Sundew

Like the sundew, the **butterwort** is a carnivorous plant. It is found over wet rocks and in peaty bogs in northern England and Scotland but it also occurs in scattered moorland localities in the west. The broad, lance-shaped leaves curl inwards to trap insects which walk across them. The carnivorous habit of these bog plants is probably related to the lack of nutrients and nitrogen in the soil. Plants able to supplement their food supply with the bodies of dead insects must have a great advantage in these difficult conditions. The single violet-coloured flower is carried on a long stem in May and June.

**Moorland,** or **round leaved, crowfoot** is one of the earliest flowers to be found in boggy moorland pools. Its tiny, white, buttercup-like flowers sometimes form spectacular sheets of blossom on the water's surface and it can be found as early as February, though it flowers mainly in spring and early summer.

There are few orchids in peaty bogland but a number of species grow in marshes and fens. Two widespread species are the marsh helleborine and the early marsh orchid. The **marsh helleborine** is undoubtedly one of the most attractive of the orchids, with large, showy, pinkish-white blooms carried on long stems. It has an extensive creeping underground rhizome from which may spring hundreds of plants in quite a small area of fen, dune or marsh. Pollination is carried out by species of solitary wasp. The plant literally sticks a pollen sac to the head of a visiting wasp, which is transferred to the stigma of the next flower the wasp visits. The **early marsh orchid** occurs with a number of sub-species

in almost any wet, marshy habitat, the colours of the flowers varying from pink to a deep magenta in sand-dune forms.

On acid soils throughout the British Isles, except in the east, the **golden saxifrage** covers streamsides and marshy, wet places with sheets of golden flowers and bright green foliage. The bright yellow flowers that appear in April and May have no true petals but have instead bright yellow sepals.

The **marsh marigold**, or kingcup, is a common but declining species of fens and marshes. Land drainage is robbing it of habitats and depriving us of one of the showiest of the marshland flowers. It has large, buttercup-like flowers and big, kidney-shaped leaves. It often grows in standing water.

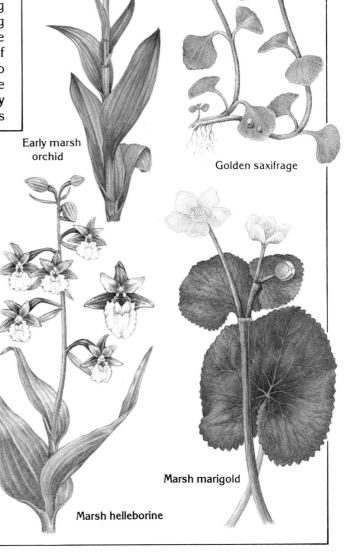

Early marsh orchid

Golden saxifrage

Butterwort

Moorland crowfoot

Marsh marigold

Marsh helleborine

**Bogbean** grows in the wetter parts of marshes, often in standing water. The dark-green leaves are similar to those of young broad beans and were used for flavouring beer in the north country, where the plant was known as 'bog hop'. They were also dried to make tea to relieve fevers and headaches. The spike of pink and white flowers appears in May and June.

**Water mint** will also grow in the shallow standing water of ditches and marshes but it is also widespread in damp woods and on streamsides. The leaves are rough and hairy and give off a strong smell of mint. Some plants are tinged dark-purple. It grows up to 60cm (2ft) tall with whorls of pinkish-mauve flowers appearing in July. In medicine it is known to be good for the digestion, and this may have been the origin of the mint sauce we still eat with our meat today.

The **gipsywort** of lowland marshes and ditches resembles water mint but it is a taller plant, with deeply-toothed leaves and bunches of white flowers along the stems. The plant yields a strong, fast black dye with which gypsies were reputed to stain their skins, for what reason we do not know! The dye was used to colour cloth.

In bogs and wet, peaty heaths the tiny **bog pimpernel** scrambles across the ground and between the thick vegetation. Its beautiful, delicate, funnel-shaped flowers have a series of fine lines running out from their centres. These are 'bee guides' which lead bees directly to the nectar in the flower. It is a widespread, although not common, plant in the west and north.

Perhaps the most conspicuous, if not the commonest, of all marshland plants, is the **meadowsweet**. It occurs all over Britain in marshlands, wet meadows, riversides and on roadsides. Its feathery plumes have a strong, sweet scent, totally different from the more bitter scent of its leaves. The dried plant has a smell of new-mown hay and in Elizabethan times it was often strewn on floors, releasing its scent as it was crushed underfoot. Medicinally, its leaves have the same properties as aspirin. Added to mead as a flavouring, it was considered to be a fine cure for the 'ague', the British form of malaria, and for this reason the plant was called 'meadwort' – 'meadowsweet' is a modern corruption of this name. Despite its widespread use during medieval times, meadowsweet has acquired an association with death. It was considered unlucky to bring it into the house – its presence was believed to induce a deep trance-like sleep from which the sleeper might not awake.

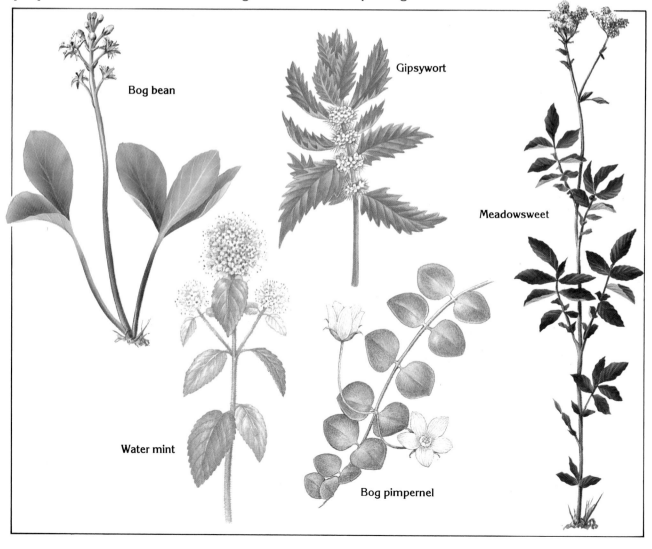

Bog bean

Gipsywort

Meadowsweet

Water mint

Bog pimpernel

# PLANTS of PONDS, LAKES and RIVERS

*Reeds, rushes and irises grow thickly at the edges of rivers and lakes, and in slow-flowing waters the leaves of water crowfoot and pond lilies carpet the water's surface.*

Ponds are an abundant and pleasant feature of our countryside. Natural ponds form in old cut-off river channels, in hollows and in areas of subsidence. Farm ponds, originally dug to provide water for stock, are today often neglected, filled in or used as convenient rubbish tips. The newly-awakened interest in creating garden ponds for pleasure and ornament has in some ways made up for their loss in the countryside, but many of the old ponds still left are of the utmost importance for rare and unusual species.

Woodland ponds, usually shaded and full of decaying leaves, have only a sparse plant population. Only algae and the tough little starwort survive here. Open ponds in full sunlight are thronged with plant and animal life. Some plants have their roots in mud and their leaves floating on the surface, others grow freely in the water itself and in others the leaves and flowers emerge out of the mud and water in thick stands.

Lakes are much larger than ponds and are usually deeper too. Natural lakes have developed in the great

hollows gouged out by the glaciers of the Ice Age or in valleys dammed by vast quantities of soil and shingle dumped by the melting ice cap. Some lakes have been formed in the deep holes created by gravel extraction and even the huge lakes of the Norfolk Broads are the flooded pits of former peat workings. In deeper lakes aquatic vegetation is found mainly around the shallower margins near the shore. Most of the species that grow in ponds can be found here but there are also species more suited to deeper water conditions and species with long stems and floating leaves that can grow out into open water. Only in shallow lakes can the rich mixture of aquatic plants spread out from the margins to colonise the open water.

Few plants can take root in the rushing torrents of upland streams and it is not until the rivers reach the lowlands and begin to slow down that many plants appear. Here you will find pond and lake species, but there are also those that can adapt their growth to suit the speed of flow. Many others, mainly marshland plants, crowd along the river banks.

Dense clumps of the dark-green, sword-like leaves of **yellow iris** stand beside streams and spread across marshy meadows all over Britain. The vivid yellow flowers that appear in May are soon gone, each flower in succession withering after a few days to produce large, long, circular pods in which the round, flat seeds are stacked. Roasted, these seeds make a very good coffee substitute. 'Daggers' and 'skegg' – referring to the leaves – are two other names for this plant. A skegg was a short, stabbing sword. The thick, tough creeping rhizomes yield a very fast black dye which was often used in the manufacture of ink.

Although it was only introduced into Britain in the last century, the **Himalayan balsam** has spread to virtually all parts of the country and is often abundant in wet ground alongside rivers and streams. It is a distinctive, very tall plant with red stems and large, dark-green leaves edged with red 'teeth'. The hanging, pinkish-purple flowers look quite exotic beside the less conspicuous plants of our trickling streams. The ripe seed pods burst at the slightest touch and have earned the plant the name of 'jumping jack'.

Ditches, ponds and the wet, marshy edges of rivers and streams are the habitat of **brooklime**, a member of the speedwell family. The bright blue flowers – sometimes they are pink – are carried on long spikes and the whole plant has a trailing habit, taking root wherever the stem touches the water or soft mud. Its young leaves and tops are rich in vitamin C and can be eaten as a salad.

Unlike other cinquefoils, the **marsh cinquefoil** is an upright plant which grows to a height of 45cm (18in) in fens, marshes and on moorland. Its flower is a rich red-purple. It is a commoner plant in the west and north than in the south.

**Water lobelia** is also a northern and western plant, growing in acid, upland waters where few other plants are able to grow. It prefers the shallow margins of lakes and pools where it can gain shelter from wind and, on larger lakes, escape the damaging effects of waves. The rosette of strap-like leaves grows under water. Water lobelia is usually rooted among stones and new plants will arise from long, creeping stolons.

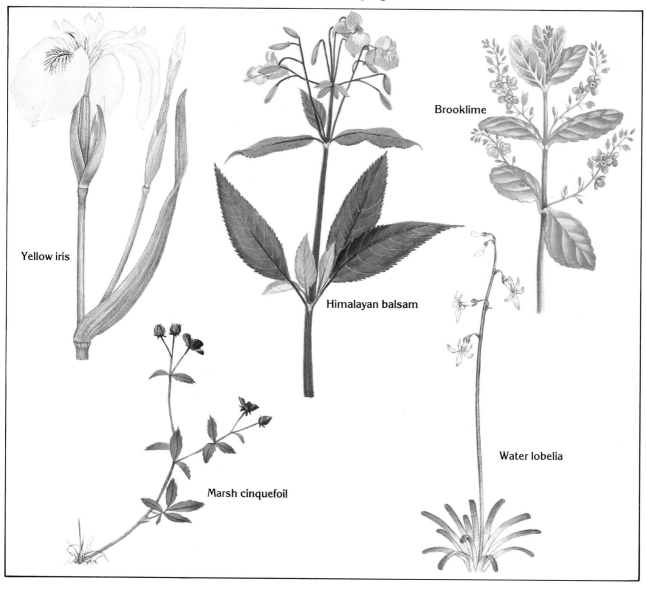

Yellow iris

Brooklime

Himalayan balsam

Marsh cinquefoil

Water lobelia

Submerged aquatic plants are mainly plants of shallow, open water, but they can be found where the water is too deep or the bottom too stony for most emergent plants, or where emergents have been cleared away by man or by a flood. They also grow in newly-created lakes where there has been little time for colonisation. Light is important to them and many of them are able to continue to grow in the water even if they are broken off from their root-hold in the mud.

**Hornwort** is a fast-growing and rapidly-colonising species. It grows in ponds, lakes, dikes and streams and will even penetrate brackish water in coastal areas. A shade-tolerant species, it can grow in streams and water bodies overhung by trees or thick vegetation. It is a common plant in the south-east but rather rare and local elsewhere in the country.

**Water milfoil** is another rapid coloniser of new stretches of open, still water. Two species are common. Spiked water milfoil is a plant of the south and east, especially in lime-rich waters, while alternate-leaved milfoil grows in acid waters in the north and west. Their leaves are finely divided and feathery and the stems are easily broken off. Taken out of the water, the leaves completely collapse. Only

the flower spikes appear above the water. There are male and female flowers on the same spike and they are pollinated by the wind.

Less than a century after its introduction from North America in 1842, **Canadian pondweed** spread to almost all parts of Britain. Its colonisation was both dramatic and costly – it multiplied so rapidly that whole reaches of rivers and other waterways were choked with it, interfering with navigation and earning it the name of 'drain devil' on the Thames. The stems may reach lengths of up to 3m (10ft). There are separate male and female plants, although the male plant is very rare in Britain. The female plant does not often flower but when it does it produces a tiny, purplish floating flower on a long stem. Nowadays Canadian pondweed has become less rampant and it is not as troublesome as it used to be. It is also now a popular aquarium plant.

**Water starwort** grows in shallow water and in wet, muddy patches by ponds, lakes and streams. On land and floating on the surface of the water the leaves are large and spoon-shaped, but those growing under water are long and narrow. It is a very common plant, growing in wet places up to 1000m (3000ft) above sea level.

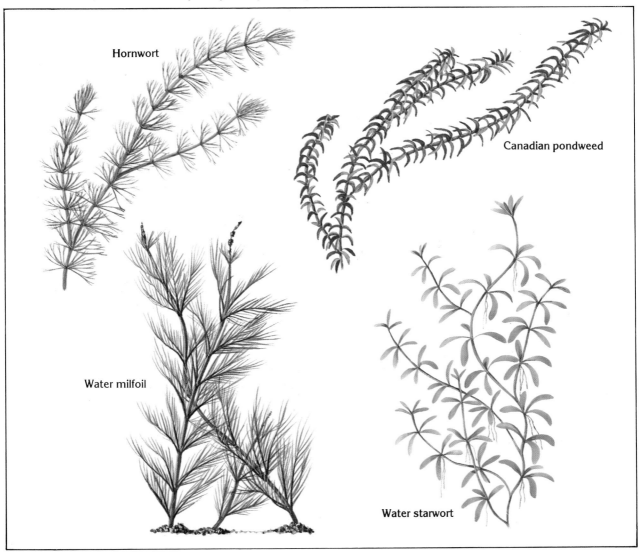

Hornwort

Canadian pondweed

Water milfoil

Water starwort

Plants with floating leaves can colonise open expanses of water free from the competition of the thick tangles of vegetation that generally crowd the waterside shore. **White water lily** grows in deeper water than most aquatic plants can tolerate. Rooted in the bottom mud of lakes, ponds and slow rivers, mostly in the north and west, it sends up leaves to the surface on the ends of long stems. The flowers and leaves float because their tissues are spongy and full of air cells that give them buoyancy. Because of its beautiful, scented white flowers the white water lily is cultivated and widely planted. During the evening the flowers close, sometimes sinking below the surface overnight.

Most of the pondweeds – *Potamogeton* species – are submerged plants with no aerial leaves. **Broad-leaved pondweed**, however, does have large, elongated, oval leaves that float over the surface of the water. It is found in lakes and slow-flowing rivers and streams, often growing out from the shallow margins. Reproduction in pondweeds is chiefly through fragmentation – buds developed on the stems and roots in summer drop off the plant as it dies back in the winter and they take root in the spring. Seeds are produced on a flower spike that protrudes above the water. The flowers are pollinated by insects.

**Water crowfoot**, like many other members of the crowfoot family, has both floating and submerged leaves, each of distinctly different form. The floating leaves are lobed and deeply cut, while the submerged leaves are finely divided. It is a common plant of ponds, ditches and lakesides, growing out into the water from a root-hold on the bank.

**Duckweeds** are a common group of tiny plants that float on the surface of ponds and lakes and in pockets of still water on rivers. They reproduce very rapidly by vegetative budding, new plants constantly forming and separating from the old ones. In a surprisingly short space of time the whole surface of a pond can be covered with duckweed in this way. Budding ceases towards the winter and the plants lie dormant, often sinking to the bottom in shallow water. Flowers of duckweed are extremely small and are very rarely produced – if they are it is in very warm, shallow water fully exposed to the sun. Common duckweed is the commonest species. A larger species, great duckweed grows in fenland ditches and fat duckweed, which has swollen leaves beneath, is sometimes abundant in the lowlands.

A number of aquatic plants have either submerged or emergent leaves according to the conditions in which they grow. In swiftly-flowing water **arrowhead** grows a crop of strap-like submerged and floating leaves and does not flower. In slower-flowing water and in canals, however, it pushes a bunch of large, arrowhead-shaped leaves above the water's surface. This is the flowering form. Separate male and female flowers are borne on the same plant. The female flowers have no petals; the male flowers have three white petals with a purple blotch at the base. The Chinese and Japanese cultivate this plant for its edible tubers which are blue, speckled with yellow spots.

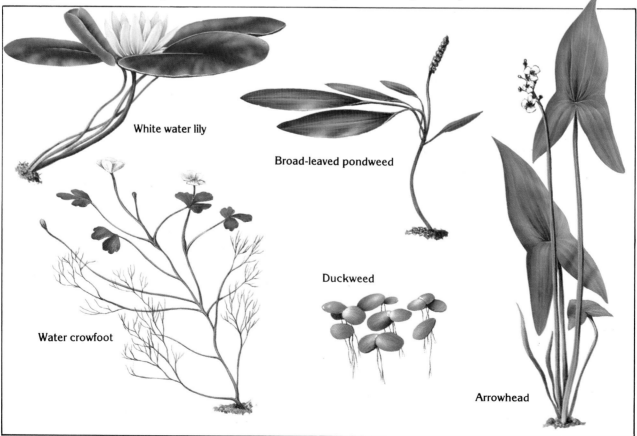

White water lily

Broad-leaved pondweed

Water crowfoot

Duckweed

Arrowhead

Among the best-known water plants are the 'emergents' of lakes and rivers. They are plants with roots in mud below the water and long, usually broad leaves that emerge above the water. **Great reedmace**, the 'bulrush' or 'cat's tail', is perhaps the best-known of these water plants and is popular with flower arrangers. Although great reedmace is generally known as bulrush this name is properly given to a completely different plant, the tall-growing rush used in basket making. Great reedmace is common in lakes and ponds, spreading by means of a creeping rhizome and it can spread over a very large area, sometimes forming a root mat that floats out over the water. The familiar long, furry, dark-brown spikes are the developing seed heads. They appear in June and July, but the seeds are not shed until February when the winter winds tease out the fluffy seeds and carry them away.

**Bur-reed** is common in ponds, ditches and marshes but it is also often plentiful in slow-moving lowland rivers. It grows over 1m (4ft) tall and has round, separate, burr-like flowers on long stems. The compact, round seed heads break up in the autumn, releasing small, floating, boat-shaped seeds which are avidly eaten by ducks. In swifter-flowing waters, bur-reed has long, floating, strap-like leaves.

The clusters of rose-pink flowers of the **flowering rush** are so beautiful that it has long been cultivated as a garden plant. It is a widespread but local plant occurring commonly in southern England but only rarely in the north and Wales. Ponds, dikes and slow-moving waterways are its habitat but it is never very abundant. It is not a rush and the name 'flowering rush' was probably given to it because its long, narrow leaves look like those of true rushes.

The big, broad leaves of **water plantain** are unmistakable when seen growing in shallow water in ponds, ditches and canals. It also grows in slow-flowing rivers, on mud banks shallowly covered by water. It is not a plantain, despite the resemblance of its leaves to the common rat's tail plantain. The umbels of white flowers growing up to 90cm (3ft) in height are carried on a long spike growing out of the centre of the plant. It spreads by means of seeds and corm-like tubers which lie dormant in the mud until spring.

The **lesser spearwort**, one of the most attractive if somewhat easily overlooked of the buttercups, is found in wet, marshy places throughout Britain, often growing among the community of waterside plants, from where it has earned its alternative name of 'water buttercup'.

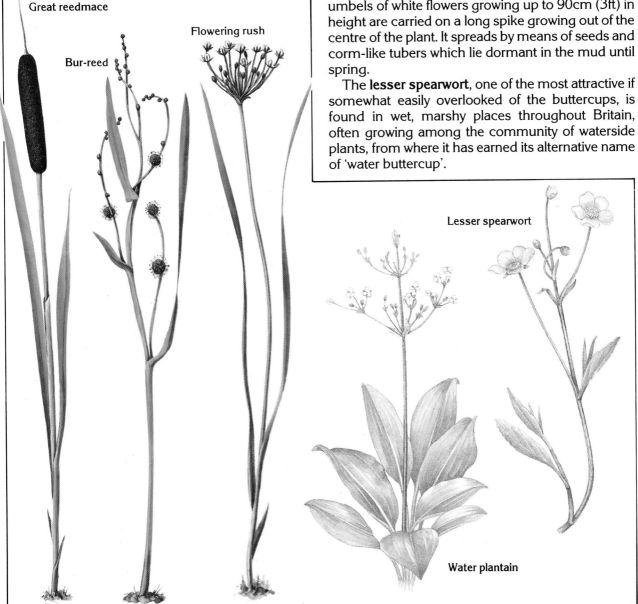

Great reedmace

Bur-reed

Flowering rush

Lesser spearwort

Water plantain

# PLANTS of the SEA COAST

*In early summer the salt-drenched sea cliffs are a mass of colour. Yellow flowers of kidney vetch grow among mats of thrift, and rock samphire clings to crumbling cliffs, growing in tiny pockets of soil. On sandy shores the large flowers of sea bindweed are a pretty sight.*

Britain's coastline is one of the most varied and spectacular in the world. Our group of islands is geologically very diverse and where sea and land meet there are landscapes of cliff, flat marshland and sand-dune. Hard rocks form massive, sometimes sheer cliffs that resist the pounding waves while soft rocks and clay crumble or slip constantly on to the shore. On some coasts massive shingle banks protect great areas of regularly-flooded salt-marsh and often associated with them are dry, shifting sand-dunes. In summer the coast may be idyllic, with gentle seas lapping the beach and warm breezes blowing, but in winter the sea can be transformed into a roaring mass of breakers that tear at the shore. Icy, salt-laden winds blow straight off the open ocean, blasting the shore and stunting trees. Each year these terrible winds dump over 50 kg (1 cwt) of salt on every acre of land around the coast, a load too toxic for many plants to withstand.

Salt and wind then are the main factors that decide which species of plant can grow on the coast. Sheltered coasts, protected from the wind, may harbour lush woodlands with a full range of common plants, but on exposed coasts the vegetation is low-growing and distorted. The most successful coastal plants have evolved some means of combating the salt. Most of them are succulents, having thick, fleshy leaves in which they store water to prevent the damaging effects of salt. Some of them have in addition a fine covering of silvery hair that reduces water loss and the amount of water that the plant needs to suck up through its roots is decreased. Other species are hard and spiny, like cacti, keeping their precious fresh water locked up tight within their stems.

The more interesting species of coastal plants grow on the inhospitable and unstable shingle banks and shifting sand-dunes scattered around our shoreline. Sheltered cliffs are clothed in a rich community of plants but crumbling cliffs support few plants, although the species that grow there are sometimes rare or unusual. The Lundy cabbage, for instance, grows only on the cliffs of Lundy Island in the Bristol Channel and nowhere else in the world.

134

Many of the plants on the coast have thick, fleshy leaves to combat the effects of salt and many of them are edible. The **sea beet**, a tall, straggling plant, is the direct ancestor of the cultivated beet. It is also the ancestor of sugar beet, chard, mangold and spinach – a rare accomplishment for a plant often overlooked as a common weed of seashores, shingle banks and salt-marshes. It was first brought into cultivation 2,000 years ago in the Middle East, where its thin, spindly taproot was developed into the thick beetroot we grow today. The wild sea beet's root may not be edible but its other common name, sea spinach, tells us that its fleshy leaves can be picked, cooked and eaten as spinach. The small leaves on the growing shoot of the plant make a delicious, if salty, addition to salads.

**Rock samphire** too is an edible plant much valued in the past but almost unheard-of today. It is a common cliffside plant of the south and east, growing on rocks and shingle and sometimes in sand. It is squat and bushy, growing up to 30cm (1ft) tall, with thick, fleshy, edible leaves. In medieval times the leaves were pickled and sold on street markets as 'crest marine'; it was collected and sent to market right up to the nineteenth century. Eaten raw as a salad the leaves have a biting, sulphurous taste, but it is best known as a pickle. The name samphire is a corruption of 'St Pierre' – St Peter's plant from Peter the rock, referring to the places where it grows. St Peter was also a fisherman and the plant was the fishermen's talisman.

**Sea campion**, although praised as a wholesome edible plant by herbalists, was never eaten as a vegetable. It grows commonly and abundantly throughout the British Isles on sea cliffs and shingle and it can also be found over 700m (2000ft) up on mountains inland. It is low-growing, forming a mat of small, oval, waxy leaves with a distinct whitish or silvery sheen. The white flowers sit inside large bladders and the plant is often regarded merely as a seaside form of the bladder campion which is widespread in inland places.

The fleshy, kidney-shaped leaves of the **sea bindweed** are insignificant in comparison to its large, showy, pink and white trumpets of flowers. The flowers close up at night into a tight spiral and open wide in the daytime. The leaves form a loose rosette from a creeping rootstock on dune pastures and these roots help to bind the sand in the fragile sand-dune habitat. It is common on the coast of the south, west and most of the south-east, but is absent from northern Scotland. Because of disturbance, erosion and the trampling feet of holidaymakers it is, unfortunately, decreasing in many places.

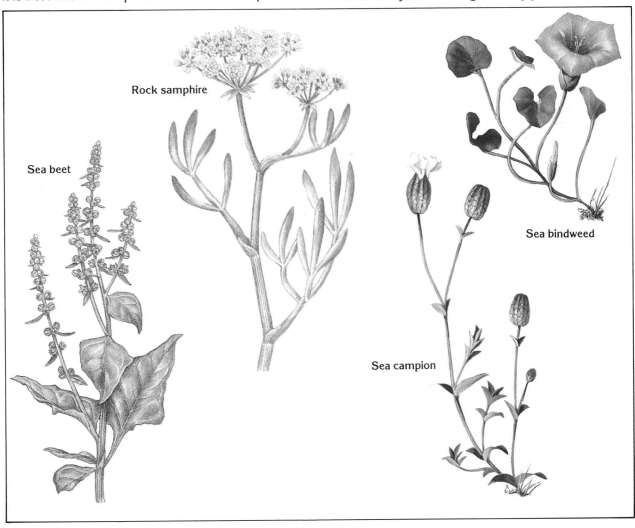

Rock samphire

Sea beet

Sea bindweed

Sea campion

**Alexanders** was introduced into Britain by the Romans as a pot herb. All parts of the plant are edible. The leaves were eaten in white sauce, the soft stems were cooked like asparagus, the roots were eaten as a substitute for parsnip and the flowers were added as a garnish to salads. It is said to have a delicate, aromatic flavour. Almost invariably it grows by the sea, in grassy places on cliffs, in hedge banks and on roadsides. Inland colonies may have originated in kitchen and herb gardens as the plant was widely cultivated in the past, especially by monks. A tall plant, growing up to 1.5m (5ft) high, it has large umbels of yellow flowers that make a colourful and sometimes spectacular sight in coastal areas in the spring. It is said to be named after Alexander the Great.

**Scots lovage** is found only around the Scottish coast where it is common and abundant. Its bright green, leathery leaves were eaten to prevent scurvy although it has a strong, yeasty flavour. It was often added to soups and casseroles to fill them out when meat was in short supply. A common alternative name for this plant is 'sea parsley'.

The resemblance of the leaves of **burnet rose** to the leaves of the commonly-cultivated salad burnet gave the rose its name. In Wales it is called the 'burrow rose' after its habit of growing in the coastal sand-dunes known locally as burrows. Burnet rose is a low-growing plant with stems covered in a mass of slender spines. The scented white flowers of early summer with their yellow centres are soon gone and are followed in August by unusual purple-black hips. It is widespread on sea cliffs, heaths and in sand-dunes which contain lime.

**Thrift**, or sea pink, is one of the commonest of all coastal plants. On sea cliffs any pocket of soil is quickly colonised and the plant sends down a deep taproot to hold it on to the rocks and to seek out water and nutrients. The masses of pink flowers in summer mingle with the yellow of kidney vetch and the white of sea campion to make a fine wild flower display. It was brought into cultivation long ago and a number of colour forms have been bred from the original wild stock. In places it is the dominant plant, ousting even the grasses. Its dense rosettes of thin, grass-like leaves form a spongy cushion over the cliff tops. Thrift is also common on the upper parts of salt-marshes where it may form dense and dominating stands. Where it grows thickly on the salt-marsh it causes large quantities of mud to be deposited quite rapidly and the level of the salt-marsh quickly grows. In the mountains of Scotland, Ireland and Wales it may grow at heights of up to 1000m (3000ft), being found even on the summits.

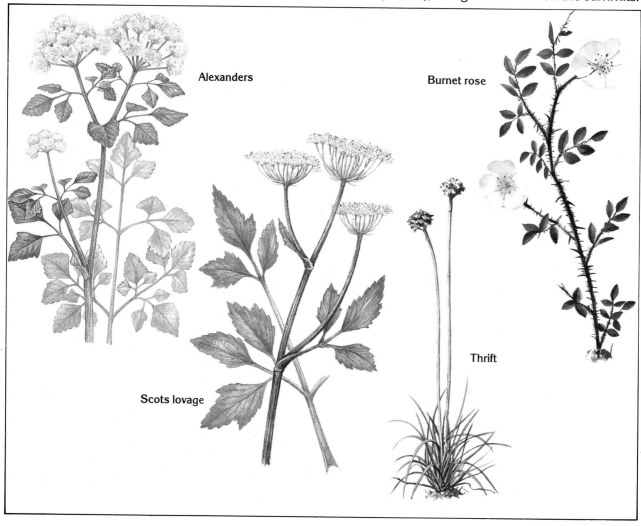

Alexanders

Burnet rose

Scots lovage

Thrift

Although **kidney vetch** is a common inland plant in the British Isles, especially on chalky or limy soils, it is at its best on coastal cliffs. It is a common companion of thrift and together the two plants make a pretty summer display. The large bunches of flowers are usually bright yellow but on the coast, particularly in the south-west, a variety of different coloured flowers may grow on the same plant — white, cream and crimson are frequent colours. The seed pods are quite small, carrying only one seed to each pod. In herbal medicine it was used, like many other downy and hairy plants, as a compress to staunch bleeding from wounds.

The **spring squill**, or vernal squill, is an uncommon plant of grassy cliff tops in south-west England, Wales and the northern tip of Scotland. Its bright blue flowers peeking through the grass are one of the unexpected delights of the places where it grows. A member of the lily family, it has long, narrow, twisting dark-green leaves that remain among the grass for much of the year.

**English stonecrop** is another plant found chiefly on the west coast of Britain. It is a succulent plant growing up to 8cm (3in) tall on rocks and thin, poor grassland. It is especially plentiful on granite rocks or sandy soil and will grow at heights of over 1000m (3000ft) above sea level. The succulent leaves store water to enable the plant to continue growing on parched rocks during dry summer weather.

There are three common species of scurvy grass growing around the coast of Britain. **Common scurvy grass** is the most abundant, though it is absent from most of the south-eastern coast. It is a species of drier salt-marshes and grassy coastal cliffs but it is often found inland, perhaps as original escapes from herb and 'physic' gardens. The plant is rich in vitamin C and was taken as a winter tonic and to combat scurvy from very early times. The dried herb or a bottled distillation of the plant was carried aboard ship to combat the effects of scurvy brought on by the lack of fresh fruit and vegetables on long sea voyages. Scurvy grass has a hot, somewhat unpleasant taste that was disguised by the addition of herbs and spices added to the tonic brew. In the seventeenth century there was a fad for taking a scurvy grass drink first thing in the morning, but with the arrival of the much pleasanter-tasting citrus fruits from newly-opened trade routes it was ousted as an important source of vitamin C. English scurvy grass is a more pleasant-tasting but less common plant of salt-marshes. It is difficult to grow so never gained the popularity of the common scurvy grass.

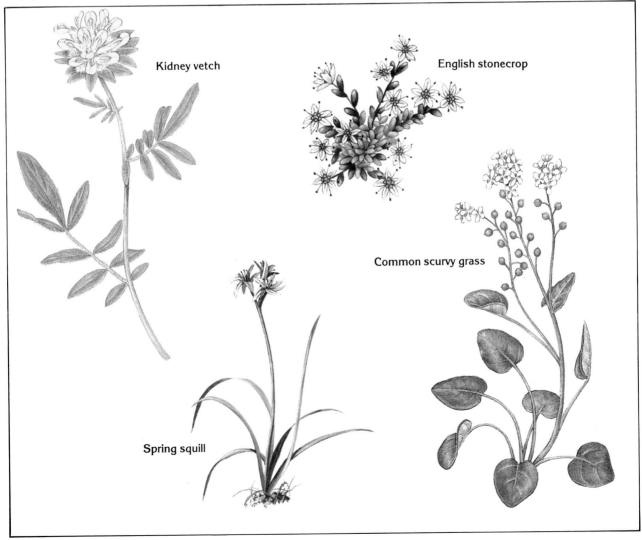

Kidney vetch

English stonecrop

Common scurvy grass

Spring squill

# TREES

Trees are the tallest living things on earth. The giant coast redwood trees of California, USA, can grow to heights of over 100m (350ft) and two other American conifers, the Wellingtonia and the Douglas fir, may reach heights of 90m (300ft). Trees are also the longest-lived things on earth. The common yew is believed to attain an age of 2,000 years, but the record for longevity goes to the bristle-cone pine, a native of the Rocky Mountains in North America. This small, bushy conifer seldom reaches more than 12m (40ft) in height and the oldest individuals, stunted and misshapen, are up to 4,500 years old and still growing!

Only very low temperatures and very low rainfall restrict the growth of trees. If man had not interfered, continuous tracts of forest would cover more than a third of the surface of the land. In the cold northerly latitudes, stretching in a band from Alaska in the New World to Siberia in the Old World, is an almost unbroken belt of conifer forest. Conifers are often referred to as softwoods because their wood is less hard than that of the deciduous, broadleaved trees that dominate the warmer lands to the south. Conifers bear their winged seeds in protective cones and their leaves are long, thin and evergreen, remaining on the tree for two years or more. The broadleaved forests of warmer, lower latitudes are less extensive in range and in many countries, including Britain, the forests have been cut down to make way for agriculture. Broadleaved trees have flat leaves that grow in a variety of shapes. These leaves are less hardy than the resinous leaves of conifers and are shed in the autumn when the tree 'rests' to avoid the winter's cold. The alternative name for broadleaved trees – deciduous trees – refers to this annual shedding of the leaves.

For trees to attain their great size they need support and nourishment for the continually expanding and top-heavy leaf canopy. Wood is the substance that holds them upright and this, together with a vast, spreading network of underground roots, helps trees to resist virtually all conditions except the most violent of storms. Wood starts life as a layer of living cells beneath a protective cover of bark. Its function is to transport water up to the leaves and to bring back sugar from the leaves to feed the roots. Each year the living layer of wood beneath the bark expands outwards to serve the growing leaf canopy but, at the same time, each year the innermost layers of wood die and become hard, strong and unyielding, so providing the perfect support for the spreading leaf canopy. The leaves make food for the tree by a process known as photosynthesis. Carbon dioxide absorbed by the leaves is turned into sugar by the action of sunlight on a substance called chlorophyll, the green pigment found in leaves.

Man has always had an interest in trees, mainly because of the usefulness of wood as a building material and as a fuel, but the seeds of trees can be useful too. Seeds, nuts and fruits are a major part of every human community's diet. Fruit especially has evolved to be palatable. The soft, sweet flesh of the fruit surrounds a hard, indigestible seed. The seeds are discarded by man, or pass through the digestive tracts of animals and birds, and in this way become dispersed over a very wide area.

cross-section through a tree trunk

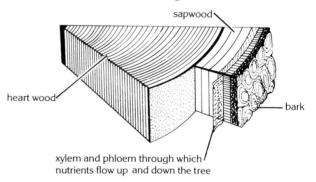

sapwood

heart wood

bark

xylem and phloem through which nutrients flow up and down the tree

## TREE FACTS AND FEATS

**OLDEST TREE**

| | |
|---|---|
| *Great Britain* | The Fontingall yew in Scotland is estimated to be 2,500 years old and is still growing. |
| *World* | A bristlecone pine in the White Mountains of California, USA, is 4,600 years old and still growing. |

**TALLEST TREE**

| | |
|---|---|
| *Great Britain* | A grand fir at Strathclyde, Scotland, is 57.3m (188ft) tall. |
| *World* | The tallest conifer is a coast redwood in California, USA, which is 110.3m (362ft) tall. The tallest broadleaf is a eucalyptus in Tasmania which is 99m (325ft) tall. |

**LARGEST FOREST**

| | |
|---|---|
| *Great Britain* | The Kielder Forest in northern England is 29,273ha (72,336 acres) in extent. |
| *World* | The vast coniferous forest of northern Russia covers 1,100 million hectares (2,700 million acres) – 25 per cent of the world's forested area. |

**MOST LEAVES**

| | |
|---|---|
| | A large oak has about 250,000 leaves but a cypress tree may have as many as 40-50 million leaves. |

# TREES of TOWN and CITY

Green fields and wildlife vanish from the landscape as man expands his cities, yet it seems that man cannot do without trees. They are planted by roads and in churchyards for their shade and greenery, in suburban gardens for their colour and shape and in groups in parks and squares as a substitute for the woodlands that were swept away by development. But urban trees have special problems – the dust-laden, polluted air and the impoverished soil which has been crushed by machinery and covered in concrete and stone.

The most successful town tree in Britain is the **London plane**. It is a hardy, fast-growing tree with a huge, spreading crown and it is very long-lived; the first trees planted in Britain are now over 300 years old. Of all the trees, this is the one most tolerant of air pollution. Its grey bark peels off constantly to reveal fresh yellow bark beneath which prevents the vital breathing pores on the trunk from becoming clogged with grime.

After the London plane, the best known town tree must be the **horse chestnut**, which was introduced into Britain in the mid-1600s from eastern Europe and is familiar to every schoolboy as the 'conker tree'. It grows into a tall tree with a spreading crown. Despite its eventual huge size the horse chestnut is short-lived, often breaking up after only 150 years.

An abundant tree in churchyards, parks and roadside avenues is the **common lime**. It grows tall but is an untidy tree, the smooth, grey, finely-fissured trunk sprouting dense masses of twigs from its base and from the bole. Another disadvantage is the enormous amount of unpleasant sticky honeydew rained down from the tree by millions of sap-sucking aphids which live on its leaves.

The evergreen **yew** has been associated with man and his religions for thousands of years. The Victorians grew it in hedges, trimming it into a variety of ornamental shapes and it was widely planted in the grounds of large town houses. Unpruned it grows into a broad, conical tree and can be very long-lived. Specimens up to a thousand years old are known. The foliage and seeds are poisonous but the flesh of the fruit is not and both seeds and flesh are eaten by birds without harm.

Another common evergreen tree is the **Lawson's cypress**, yet it was not introduced into this country until the mid-nineteenth century. Tall and narrow with fern-like foliage, it is a hardy, fast-growing tree. It is often planted in gardens or grown as an evergreen hedge and dozens of varieties in many shapes and colours have been bred.

London plane

Horse chestnut

Common lime

Yew

Lawson's cypress

# TREES of BROADLEAVED WOODLAND

The broadleaved woodlands of Britain are a mixture of the native trees that colonised Britain after the last Ice Age and foreign trees deliberately introduced much later for timber and ornament. Some trees, though native and widespread throughout the British Isles, previously had a restricted distribution due to soil conditions, climate and competition from other species. The **beech** is one of these. Now widespread and in many parts of the west and north the dominant forest tree, it was until man's intervention common only on chalk soils in the south. In favourable soils it grows tall with spreading horizontal branches, thick with leaves that cast a heavy shade in summer, preventing the growth of plants beneath. Long, smooth, grey trunks and a deep carpet of orange-brown leaves underfoot are typical of beech woods. The beech is a long-lived tree, surviving for 200 years or more before breaking up.

Without doubt, though, the dominant and most widely distributed trees in Britain are the oaks, which are equally at home in the fertile lowlands and the thin, poor soils of the uplands. There are two species in Britain – the **pedunculate oak** (the so-called 'English oak') and the sessile or durmast oak. Pedunculate oak has short-stalked leaves and bears its acorns on a stalk, while sessile oak has leaves with long stalks and acorns growing close to the twigs. In open country the pedunculate oak is a spreading tree with low branches, often reaching a great age, especially when pollarded. In woodland it is more upright, its grey, fissured trunk frequently bearing large, sprouting burrs.

**Ash** is a frequent companion of the oak, particularly where there is a little lime in the soil. In limestone areas woods composed completely of ash may form, with a mass of flowers growing beneath the light, open canopy. Ash is often the last tree to come into leaf and the first to lose its leaves in the autumn. All that remain are the bunches of winged seeds on bare twigs and the velvety black buds of the next year's leaves already visible. The seeds are known as 'keys', supposedly because they resemble bunches of keys, but in fact 'key' is a corruption of 'kit', the name of a medieval stringed finstrument with a bulbous end and a wide, flat neck. Ash is a short-lived tree, usually breaking up after only 120 years. In wet places it is often disfigured by cankers and burrs.

The birch is also a short-lived tree, breaking up after as little as fifty to sixty years in the south but it sometimes remains healthy for over 150 years in Scotland. It is a hardy tree of acid heaths, moors and sandy woodlands and grows further north than anv other European tree. The **silver birch** with its graceful, drooping branches and shining silver bark is truly worthy of its name 'Lady of the Woods'. Its relative the downy birch is not so striking. It is a more upright tree of wet woodland and moors, with a bronze, peeling bark in its early years of growth.

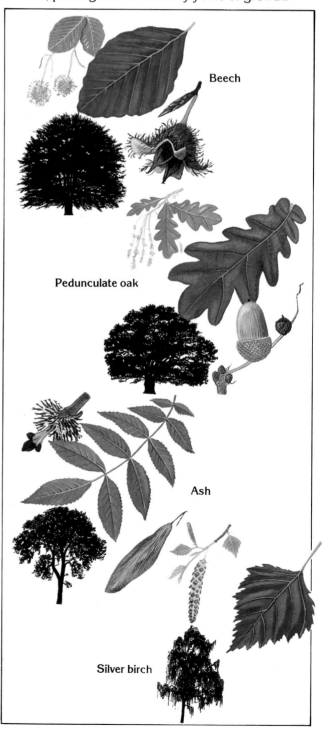

Beech

Pedunculate oak

Ash

Silver birch

The wild cherry and hornbeam are two examples of trees which once had a restricted distribution but which are now quite widespread. The **wild cherry** or **gean** is a small tree of chalky soils. Its bark is smooth, shiny and reddish-brown and peels off in horizontal strips. In spring the tree bursts into a mass of delicate white blossom that, unfortunately, rarely lasts more than a week. The tree's autumn colour is quite striking, the leaves turning to shades of brilliant orange and crimson. Because of its beauty, wild cherry has been widely planted in parks and gardens as well as in woodlands over much of Britain.

**Hornbeam** was once mainly a tree of the south-east where it grew in association with oak. In the nineteenth century landowners planted it extensively for timber and it can now be found in most parts of Britain. Superficially it resembles a beech tree but it can be distinguished from the beech by the deep fluting on its bark and the serrated edges of its leaves. Its winged seeds hanging in clusters are also totally different from beech nuts which are encased in spiny shells.

Sycamore and sweet chestnut were probably introduced by the Romans, although sycamore was not widely planted until the Middle Ages. Both trees have naturalised well in Britain, especially the **sycamore** which is a remarkably hardy and invasive tree. It seeds freely, forming dense thickets of fast-growing saplings which are difficult to eradicate and against which the seedlings of other trees find it difficult to compete. Given favourable circumstances sycamore is able to completely oust the existing tree species of an established woodland in only a few decades. It is extensively planted not only because of its attractive foliage but also because it is resistant to wind damage and air pollution. It is usually the only abundant self-seeded tree in towns and inner cities. In unpolluted air its leaves become covered with black blotches of tar spot fungus.

**Sweet chestnut** is abundant on light soils in southern England where it was originally planted as a coppice tree, yielding long poles which were cut and split for fence pales. It is also much favoured as a park tree where, freed from competition, it grows a widely-spreading crown with irregular, twisting branches. In old trees the heavy ridges of bark tend to grow as a long, continuous spiral into the canopy of the tree. The long catkins of sweet chestnut give way to prickly seed cases containing the edible nuts. Only in good summers do the nuts grow large enough to make collecting them worthwhile. The sweet chestnut is a very long-lived tree and, although they lose crowns and limbs, specimens up to 600 years old are known.

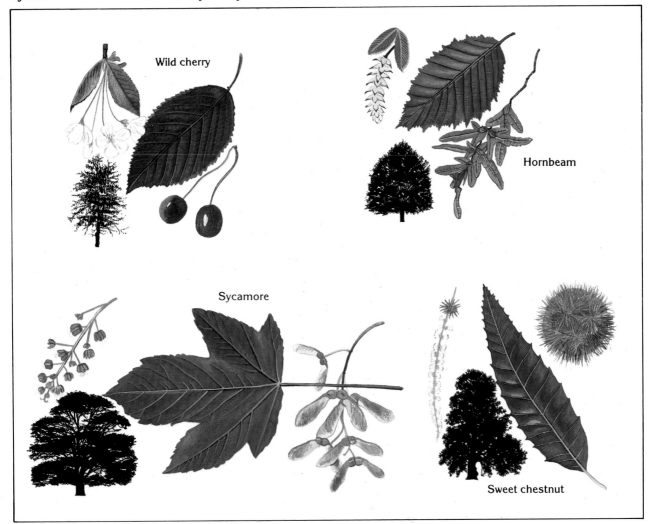

Wild cherry

Hornbeam

Sycamore

Sweet chestnut

# TREES of CONIFEROUS WOODLAND

Since the end of the First World War enormous areas of coniferous forest have been planted on upland moors and hillsides. Most of the larger plantations have been created by the Forestry Commission as part of a national programme to reduce Britain's dependence on foreign timber. Many small plots, however, are the result of private endeavour and this has often meant the replacement of broadleaved woodland by the fast-growing exotic conifer. The only natural conifer forest in Britain is the Caledonian Forest in the central Scottish Highlands which is composed of the native Scots pine.

The **Scots pine** has also become naturalised in southern England where it grows abundantly on lowland heaths. It is used less often as a forestry tree nowadays but it is still very common. Young Scots pines have a conical shape but older trees are gaunt and flat-topped with distinct orange bark in the upper branches. It is a long-lived tree, surviving up to 250 years in the Scottish Highlands.

The **Norway spruce** was introduced into Britain from Europe as long ago as the Middle Ages. It is a common plantation tree but is best known as the traditional Christmas tree. The Christmas tree custom was brought to us from Germany in 1844 by Prince Albert, Consort of Queen Victoria, and thousands of acres are now given over to the production of trees for the Christmas market. Norway spruce is fast-growing, with a conic form and very long, papery cones. The needles are borne on stiff, peg-like stalks, a characteristic of spruces.

The **Sitka spruce** was introduced into Britain from the west coast of North America in 1831. Since then it has become the major coniferous forest tree in Britain, particularly in the west with its wetter climate. Hundreds of millions of Sitka spruce have been planted and it has even been tried as a replacement for Norway spruce as a Christmas tree. Unfortunately, its stiff needles are too sharp to make it really suitable for this purpose. Sitka spruce is tolerant of poor, wet soils and is extremely fast-growing, often putting on a second spurt of growth in late summer. The needles are arranged in a whorl around the twigs and have two blue-white bands underneath, sometimes giving the tree a blue-grey appearance when seen from a distance.

**Larches** are unusual among conifers in that they are deciduous, shedding their leaves in the autumn. Their winter buds are carried on straw-coloured twigs. In spring the bright green leaves unfurl in tufts, and the trees are covered in tiny pink flowers known as 'larch roses'. Larches are fast-growing trees, conic at first but soon broadening with age and developing massive drooping branches. The distinctive cones may remain on the tree for ten years or more. As well as being grown for timber, larches are used as natural firebreaks and as landscape trees, softening the harshness of dark-green conifer plantations.

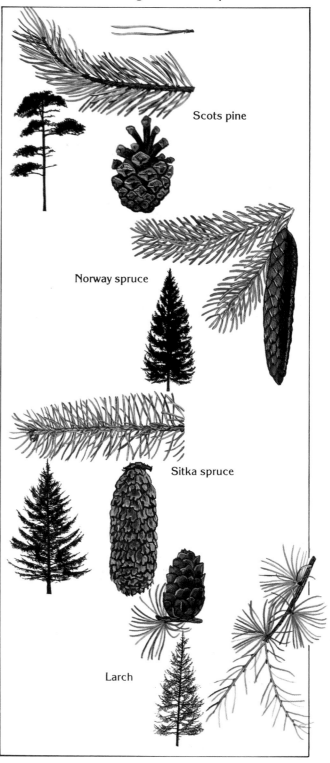

Scots pine

Norway spruce

Sitka spruce

Larch

# TREES and BUSHES of WETLAND

The wetland and riverside trees of our countryside today are only a poor reminder of the vast tangle of forest that once grew along every river in the land. Man has tamed the rivers in order to cultivate pasture on land that was previously woodland swamp.

**Alder** was a dominant tree in those ancient riverine woods. There are nodules containing nitrogen-fixing bacteria along the entire length of the alder's root system, a boon in constantly waterlogged soil lacking in nitrogen. This, and the possession of a very deep tap-root, have contributed to the alder's success. It's root system anchors the tree well on the riverbank and reduces erosion. Most water authorities now plant alder as part of watercourse protection schemes.

Willows too were common in those ancient woods and commonest of all in southern England was the **crack willow**, so called because its twigs break off cleanly with an audible snap. Conical in growth when young, if left to grow freely it develops a broad, domed crown. Most crack willows have been pollarded, however, and sport a bushy crown of long, straight poles. In the past pollards provided sticks – withys – for basket making. Sadly, pollards are now being left to grow out, their trunks often splitting from the weight of the massive unlopped poles. Pollarded willows can survive for a hundred years or more.

The **white poplar** was probably introduced into Britain from central Europe. It is seen beside rivers or in parks, the leaves appearing silver in the wind, but it grows as a semi-wild tree only in swampy fenland woodlands. Older trees have a characteristic lean, usually away from the prevailing wind. There are separate male and female trees, the females shedding white, fluffy down, but most regrowth is from root suckers.

Of the bush willows the **goat** or **pussy willow** is probably the commonest. It grows in damp woods, amongst scrub and in marshes; it is also quick to colonise derelict land. Open-grown trees are bushy but in woodland this willow very often grows as a small tree. The broad, wrinkled, downy leaves have a pronounced twist to their tips and male and female catkins are borne on separate trees. The female catkins are green and it is the yellow male catkins that are familiar to us as "pussy willow".

The **Guelder rose**, a small, leggy bush, is not common but can be found throughout Britain in damp hedgerows, wet woodland and fens. From May to July it produces curious flat umbels of flowers. The large white outer flowers, although sterile, are intended to attract insects. Inside this showy ring are the small, nectar-bearing flowers that eventually form a bunch of drooping translucent red berries.

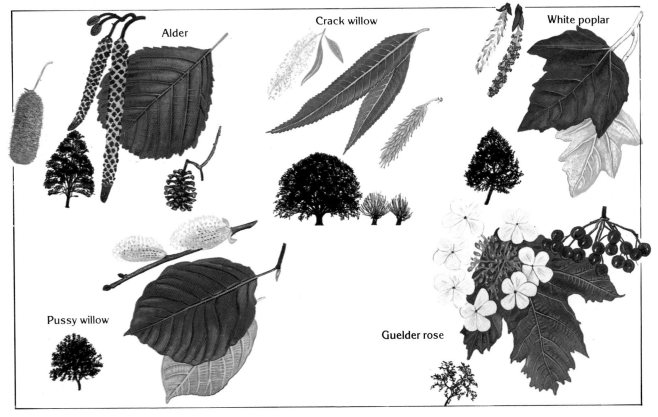

Alder

Crack willow

White poplar

Pussy willow

Guelder rose

# TREES and BUSHES of HEDGEROW and SCRUB

Hedgerows are historically a very recent addition to the British landscape. The Saxons were the first people to use hedges to mark their boundaries and to pen in their stock, but the hundreds of thousands of miles of hedgerow in the countryside today are largely the result of eighteenth-century planting. These narrow bands of shrubs and bushes have been a haven for wildlife over the centuries as woodlands have been felled and scrubland cleared.

**Hawthorn** is the commonest and most widely planted hedgerow shrub. It is so easily established that it is also known as quickthorn, growing rapidly to form a spiny, stock-proof hedge. In May and June it is covered in masses of white blossom which later produce a crop of red berries – haws – which are avidly eaten by birds, mice and voles. Common hawthorn berries have only one seed but the Midland hawthorn, primarily a woodland shrub, has two or more to each berry and a less deeply indented leaf.

Within a surprisingly short space of time a planted hedgerow is invaded by a variety of other species. **Elder** is often the first of the newcomers. It likes disturbed ground rich in nitrogen and is common around rabbit warrens, badger sets and under starling roosts, where the deep layers of accumulated droppings are lethal to most other species. The masses of white blossom in early summer yield a prolific crop of purple berries in the autumn.

Other shrubs were deliberately planted in hedgerows for their value as food for man or his stock. The **crab apple**, a low-growing, spiny tree was planted for the crop of sour apples, used in jam- and cider-making. Strangely enough, the evergreen, spiny-leaved **holly** was planted in some areas as a winter fodder crop. When the leaves are crushed the spines are rendered harmless and they make a nutritious feed. The waxiness of the holly leaves helps resist cold and prevents water loss and the leaves remain on the tree for three to four years. Berries are borne only on female trees.

The **field maple** can be found in hedgerows over most of the country but it does best on soils containing some lime. Its leaves turn a rich butter yellow in the autumn and it has winged seeds similar to those of the sycamore.

The **rowan** occurs occasionally in hedgerows, mainly in the west and north. It grows abundantly on hills in dry woods and as scrub in rocky country. Its ability to survive in upland areas coupled with the resemblance of its leaves to those of the ash has earned it the alternative name of mountain ash.

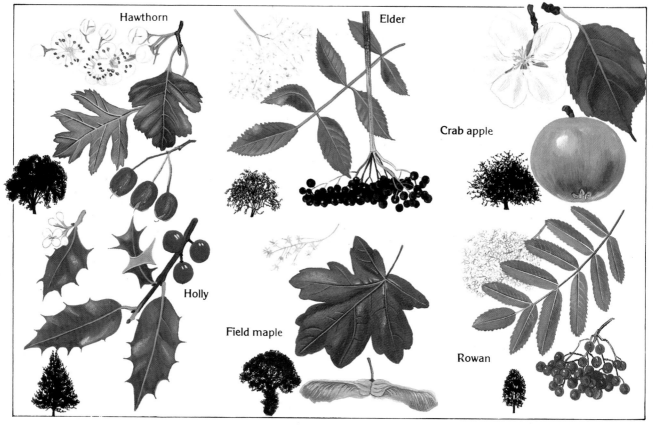

Hawthorn

Elder

Crab apple

Holly

Field maple

Rowan

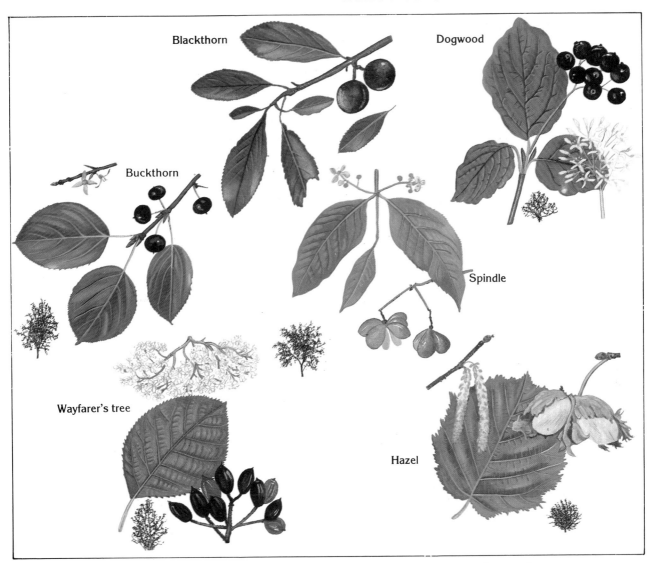

After the hawthorn, **blackthorn** is possibly the commonest hedgerow shrub, especially on heavier soils. Once established it can persist indefinitely, spreading from suckers and forming dense, impenetrable, thorny thickets. Blackthorn is the ancestor of the domestic plum but its tough, blue-black fruit – sloes – are bitter and astringent to taste. The hard wood of the stems makes fine walking sticks and polishes to a handsome black finish.

**Dogwood** also forms thickets but it is not so widespread or quite so persistent as blackthorn. It grows best in soil containing lime and on chalk downland it can be a serious nuisance, its vigorous suckers readily invading ungrazed pasture. In winter the bare stems take on a striking reddish hue which makes the plant stand out in any hedgerow. Dogwood stems are tough and hard and were at one time used as meat skewers. The small clusters of black berries ripen in October and are eaten by birds.

Buckthorn, spindle and the wayfarer's tree are also lime-loving shrubs which although widely distributed are not often abundant. **Buckthorn** is a dense, thorny bush with tiny green flowers, male and female flowers being carried on separate trees. Its name was 'buck's horn tree' because of the resemblance of the

flower-bearing spurs to deer antlers.

The **spindle** gets its name from its past use as a spindle – a hand-held stick used to spin wool. Spindle wood was favoured because it was tough and would not splinter if broken. It was also used by gypsies to make pegs and skewers. Young twigs are green and square and older stems are greyish and smooth-barked. The fruit capsule of the spindle is a striking coral pink; this splits to reveal four bright orange seeds which are very attractive to birds.

The **wayfarer's tree** grows only on the chalk of southern England. It was given its common name by Gerard, the sixteenth-century botanist and traveller, when he discovered it as he wandered the old drove roads over the chalk downs. The downiness of the leaves and the hairs on the young twigs help prevent water loss – an important attribute for a plant growing on dry, rocky soil.

As much a woodland tree as a hedgerow bush, the **hazel** can be found all over the British Isles. It grows readily after cutting and was favoured as a coppice shrub under oaks and other forest trees as it is tolerant of some shade. If it is coppiced or regularly trimmed back in a hedge hazel will survive for hundreds of years.

# WHERE TO FIND FLOWERS, TREES and SHRUBS

One major problem with plant hunting is that you have to be prepared to travel. Many of our most fascinating plants are found only in isolated and often inhospitable places and lots of plants will grow only in certain soils, which are not always present near the places where we live. However, for the beginner there is plenty to see and discover in the local countryside and in local parks and gardens. To find more unusual plants in your area visit old quarries, mineral workings or road cuttings where plants might grow on exposed rocks of a different type from those around you. On holiday too don't neglect the sand-dunes, sea cliffs and marshes of the seaside and a visit to relatives in a different part of the country can be more fun if there are good plant sites nearby.

## PLANT SITES

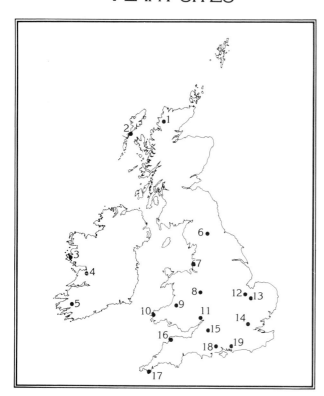

### 1. Inchnadamph, Sutherland and Inverpolly, Ross-shire

Both sites are National Nature Reserves. Inchnadamph is an area of limestone rich in rare plants. Inverpolly is a wild mountain area of sandstone, gneiss and limestone with a fascinating mountain flora and relict woodland of birch and hazel. There is an information centre at Knockan.

Arctic-alpine species include alpine lady's mantle, alpine willow herb, bearberry, crowberry, dwarf birch and wild azalea.

### 2. The Outer Hebrides

A marvellous collection of islands with unique flora growing on limy sand-dunes known as machair. Lochmaddy on North Uist is a well-known centre for exploring the islands, their fresh and sea water lochs, and moorlands. Some unusual North American plants occur on the islands.

### 3. The Connemara Mountains

An area with a very wet climate which has led to the development of extensive blanket bogs. A number of Arctic and alpine species of plants can be found growing near sea level here. Heaths are locally abundant and a speciality: Irish heath, St Dabeoc's heath, Mackay's heath, Cornish heath and Dorset heath.

### 4. The Burren, County Clare

An area of limestone flora unique in Europe. Extensive areas of limestone 'pavement' and an extraordinary range of both Arctic and Mediterranean species of plants. May and June are the best months, when there are carpets of bloody cranesbill, many rare orchids, mountain avens and hoary rock rose.

### 5. The Killarney Oakwoods, County Kerry

Typical sessile oak woods with holly and strawberry tree. Atlantic ferns and mosses are a speciality.

### 6. Upper Teesdale, Cumbria and Durham

Contains two National Nature Reserves: Moor House, Cumbria and Upper Teesdale, Durham. An area of moorland, alpine meadow, lowland hay meadow, steep valley woodland and waterfalls. Botanically outstanding. Includes several species of lady's mantle that grow nowhere else in Britain, also Teesdale sandwort and Teesdale violet.

### 7. Ainsdale, Lancashire

A National Nature Reserve. A particularly rich area of sand-dunes with rare species of plants and amphibians, and an interesting variety of birds. Plants include dune helleborine, marsh helleborine, and green-flowered helleborine beneath pines.

## 8. Chartley Moss, Staffordshire

A National Nature Reserve. A sphagnum moss 'quaking' bog – a floating moss community 15m (50ft) deep which formed thousands of years ago. As well as the bog communities there are stands of Scots pine growing on the peat.

## 9. Cars Tregaron, Dyfed

A National Nature Reserve. An actively growing raised bog with moss beds and carr vegetation. One of the finest bogs in England and Wales.

## 10. St David's Head, Dyfed

Part of Pembrokeshire Coast National Park. Site of some tremendous displays of cliff and seaside flora, at its best in spring and early summer. Thrift, spring squill, primrose, bluebell, kidney vetch, scurvy grass, sea campion and gorse.

## 11. Forest of Dean, Gloucestershire

A National Forest Park. Forested since time immemorial. Very interesting oak woodlands but has native large-leaved lime in the Wye Valley and the sweet chestnut growing at Flaxley is probably native.

## 12. Woodwalton Fen, Cambridgeshire

A National Nature Reserve. Some of the finest remaining fen flora in East Anglia. Contains among many interesting species a very rare woodrush, fen violet and marsh sow-thistle.

## 13. Wicken Fen, Cambridgeshire

A National Trust Reserve. Exceptionally good fenland reserve containing many rare species including marsh fern, milk parsley and saw-sedge which grows over large areas.

## 14. Epping Forest, Greater London and Essex

An extensive area of open common, heathland and woodland that stretches from London into the Essex countryside. As a common, most of Epping Forest is accessible to the public. Very fine stands of native oak/hornbeam woodland.

## 15. North Meadow, Wiltshire

A National Nature Reserve. An area of hay meadow held in common but managed in a manner prescribed by law. A rich community of wild flowers.

## 16. Braunton Burrows, North Devon

A National Nature Reserve and International Biosphere Reserve. One of the most outstanding botanical sites in southern England. A large sand-dune system supporting many rare and protected species. Clustered club-rush, water germander, French toadflax, sharp rush, sea stock and a large number of orchids.

## 17. The Lizard, Cornwall

National Trust. A unique flora containing Cornish heath, rare clovers and rushes, sand quillwort, rupture-wort and prostrate forms of broom and dyer's greenweed. There are many other unusual species nearby including a prostrate form of asparagus at Kynance Cove.

## 18. The New Forest, Hampshire

A huge area of semi-natural woodland, heath and bog, containing many notable and rare species. Pale butterwort, greater sundew, bog orchid, wild gladiolus, the native species of lungwort and coral necklace are all specialities of the New Forest.

## 19. Kingley Vale, Sussex

A National Nature Reserve. One of the finest yew woods in Europe.

# BOTANIC GARDENS AND COLLECTIONS

Abbotsbury, Dorset
A very fine collection of exotic and native trees and shrubs. An arboretum with large numbers of sub-tropical species.

Bedgebury, Kent
The National Pinetum of the Royal Botanic Gardens, Kew. A very fine and extensive collection of conifers.

Bodnant, Gwynedd
National Trust. The finest garden in Wales.

Culzean Castle, Strathclyde
National Trust for Scotland. A very good collection of native and exotic trees and shrubs.

Penjarrick, Cornwall
A very good collection of sub-tropical trees and shrubs.

The Royal Botanic Gardens
Kew, London and Edinburgh
Two of the finest botanic gardens in Britain. Extensive glasshouse, greenhouses, exhibitions and libraries.

Stourhead, Wiltshire
National Trust. Very good gardens and a fine arboretum.

Westonbirt, Gloucestershire
One of the best arboretums in England.

# THE SEASHORE

As an island, Britain is endowed with a shoreline of marvellous variety. Landscapes of dizzying sheer cliffs alternate with sheltered bays and wild, flat coastal plains. In the west our shores are pounded by the full force of ocean waves while in the east the coast is exposed to the withering blasts of icy winter winds that blow from the desolate plains of central Europe. Britain has six thousand miles of coastline but only six hundred thousand acres of seashore – very little when compared with the enormous acreages of other habitats found on land. This narrow ribbon around our coasts was created by the sea and the creatures that live there depend for their existence on the certainty of the daily rise and fall of the tide.

## THE TIDES

Tides, the regular twice-daily movement of the sea up and down the shore, are caused by the gravitational pull of the sun and moon. The moon, being closer to the earth, exerts the greatest influence. As it passes round the earth it pulls the sea beneath it into a pronounced 'bulge'. On the opposite side of the earth a similar bulge is created by strange and complex gravitational forces. As the moon circles the earth – every 24 hours and 50 minutes – it sweeps the two bulges of water along with it, causing the daily rise and fall of the tides. When the sun is at right angles to the moon it exerts its own pull and lessens the height of the bulges. Tides at this time are known a 'neap tides'. These tides rise and fall less than half the distance of their opposites, the 'spring tides', which occur when the

sun and moon line up together to exert a very great pull and cause extra large bulges. In some parts of the British Isles spring tides may rise and fall as much as 12m (40ft).

Once or twice a year some spring tides uncover much more of the shore than normal and expose the creatures that live there to the hostile world of the open air. All shore life must be able to survive out of water or within the protection of shallow pools left by the retreating sea, if only for short periods of time; their level of tolerance determines just where on the shore certain creatures will be found. Seashore-dwelling animals and plants have to be tough because exposure to the air also means exposure to sun, wind, rain and cold – elements unknown in the little-changing world of the sea.

## TYPES of SEASHORE

There are two main types of shore on our coasts – rocky and sandy. Rocky shores are undoubtedly the richer habitat, providing hollows, crevices and broad platforms where shore plants can attach themselves and where shore creatures can find security. Shifting beach sands, by contrast, are inhospitable places for life. The sand provides no attachment for plants and because of this lack of plants there are few herbivores and consequently many fewer predators than there would be in other habitats.

Seashores can be divided into three distinct zones depending on the amount of time each part of the shore remains uncovered by the tide: the *upper shore*, a region the sea may not reach for days or weeks on end; the *middle shore*, a region covered and uncovered every day by the tide; and the *lower shore*, a region uncovered for only an hour or two each day or perhaps only once or twice a month in some places.

Rocky shores show the strongest zoning and it was probably here, in the upper regions of rocky seashores, that millions of years ago life first learned to live on land and set in motion the long, slow process of evolution that finally led to man himself. On the upper shore life has evolved which is neither fully terrestrial nor fully marine. Typical of these animals is the small periwinkle. By day it hides in cracks in rocks, emerging at night to feed on algae and lichens. Like the land snails it is tolerant of quite dry conditions but unlike them it needs the moisture from drenching salt sea-sprays, and must wait for stormy spring tides before it can liberate its spawn into the sea. Upper shore seaweeds combat the drought conditions with a thick wax coating on their fronds which slows down the loss of water.

On neap tides the sun and the moon pull against each other.

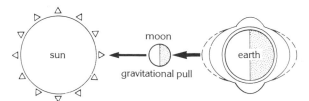

On spring tides the sun and moon pull together.

How the sun and the moon affect the tide.

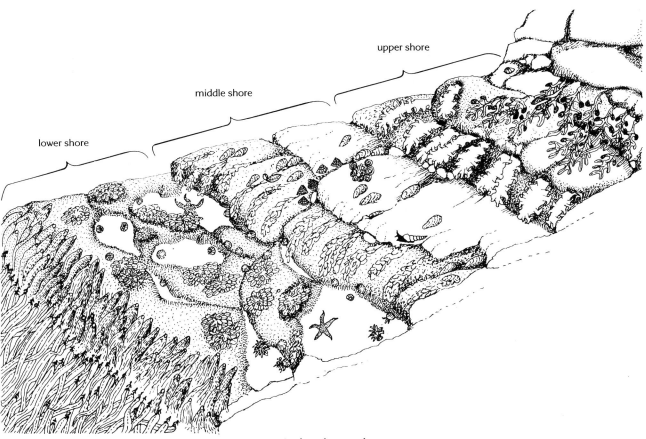

upper shore

middle shore

lower shore

a typical rocky seashore

Channelled wrack, the most tolerant of the upper-shore seaweeds has a groove on the underside of each frond which helps retain water and keeps the plant alive even when it has become so hard and brittle as to appear lifeless.

The middle shore is the most interesting region. Here life must not only be tolerant of prolonged exposure to the air, it must also be able to withstand the constant battering of the foaming breakers that smash on to the shore. Storm waves can exert a force of over 25 tonnes to the square metre, enough to tear seaweeds from the rocks, rip boulders from the shore and smash man's sea defences like matchwood. Where wave activity is fierce, barnacles and mussels coat the rocks, the barnacles held fast by their natural 'cement' and the mussels by their anchoring byssus threads. On more sheltered coasts thick carpets of seaweed are able to cover the shore and seashore creatures seek shelter beneath their moist fronds. On the middle shore molluscs have rounded shells so they can roll with the waves without damage; they have operculums – horny plates that seal the opening to their shells to prevent their drying out and they cluster in rock pools where there is life-giving sea water. Yet rock pools, although a haven for seashore life, are difficult habitats in which to survive. Water temperatures may vary from freezing point in winter to very warm in summer. Summer breezes may dry out a pool completely or concentrate the salt to a much higher level than normal for seawater. Rain, on the other hand, may

dilute the water in pools so that the salt concentration is very much reduced. Not surprisingly, nearly all the successful plants and animals of the middle shore are very hardy and tolerate a wide range of conditions. More delicate species are confined to deep pools where conditions are less demanding or are found on the lower shore where they are uncovered only briefly each day.

## SEASHORE FACTS AND FEATS

**LARGEST ANIMAL**

| | |
|---|---|
| *World* | The ribbon worm of the North Sea. A specimen 54m (180ft) was washed ashore in Scotland in 1864. |

**LARGEST STARFISH**

| | |
|---|---|
| *Great Britain* | A spiny starfish collected in Scotland measured 76.2cm (2ft 6in) across. |
| *World* | A brisingid starfish collected from the Gulf of Mexico measured 138cm (54.33in) across. |

**HIGHEST TIDE**

| | |
|---|---|
| *Great Britain* | At Beachley on the River Severn the tide can rise and fall 15.9m (52 ft 2in). |
| *World* | In the Bay of Fundy, Nova Scotia, Canada, the tide can rise and fall 16.3m (53ft 6in). |

**HIGHEST WAVE**

| | |
|---|---|
| *World* | In the middle of a hurricane during a voyage across the Pacific Ocean a vessel recorded a wave 34m (112ft) high from trough to crest. |

# LIFE on ROCKY SHORES

*Rocky shores are the best seashore habitats. Seaweeds and molluscs cover the rocks and fish, shrimps, starfish and many other animals live in the rock pools, hiding under seaweed and stones or jammed into tiny crevices.*

Rocky shores are the most rewarding and absorbing of the seashore habitats. They combine the pleasure of being by the sea with the thrill of exploring an unfamiliar world – a world released by the sea for only a few hours each day. Whether made up of broad, flat platforms or jutting pinnacles of rock, each rocky shore has its own characteristic life. Flat rock platforms are often covered with moist beds of seaweed under which creatures hide from the sun. Rugged shores where waves foam and crash are too violent for seaweeds – instead the rocks are encrusted with barnacles and mussels cemented tightly to the rocks. Most rocky shores have shallow pools and deep, shaded clefts which harbour creatures normally found much lower down on the shore. Very deep pools are fringed with seaweeds rarely exposed on the shore and beneath their fronds hide fishes, crabs, starfish and even lobsters, trapped by the retreating tide. At first a rock pool may appear quiet, with few signs of life, but patience and stillness

will be rewarded as the creatures of the pool gradually come out of hiding.

Deep clefts in the rocks and the areas beneath overhangs are other rich hiding places for marine life. Often damp, shaded and humid, and protected from the worst of the weather, they bring lower-shore creatures up into the middle shore where they can be examined without the haste forced on the observer by a rapidly-returning tide. In these shady places can be found the rarer sea anemones, sponges, sea-squirts and cowrie shells, while in the cool water at the base of clefts may be found starfish and sea urchins. The white, limy tubes of tube-worms line the rocks and various fan worms with their beautiful crowns of tentacles are common among the mud and sand caught in cracks in the rocks. The most interesting seashore species can be found on the lowest part of the shore during those very few days in the year when the tide retreats much further out than normal.

150

On rocky shores crashing waves foam over jagged outcrops and swirl into deep pools, and plants and animals have to be tough to withstand the battering force of the surging waves. Most dwellers on rocky shores have adopted devices to avoid being torn from the rocks or washed away by the sea.

After a brief free-living larval stage **barnacles** attach themselves firmly to rocks, surviving on even the most furiously-pounded shores. Barnacles live their entire lives lying on their backs. Cemented upside-down they enclose themselves in a protective armour and seal their upper sides with a set of movable plates. When the tide comes in the plates are opened and the animal's legs emerge, sweeping back and forth in the water to draw in the minute plankton brought by the sea. As the tide ebbs the plates are tightly closed, protecting the barnacles within from desiccation and enabling them to live high up on the shore where few other sea creatures can survive.

On shores where wave pounding is less severe **mussels** grow alongside the barnacles and they too

circular feeding forays, scraping off the t' algae and young seaweed growing on always returning to exactly the same plac foray. On the middle and lower shore yc find small depressions on the rocks v have worn away the stone in ma' base'.

The familiar **bladder wrac** paired air sacs covers me mass of shiny brown front plant buoyancy as the tic creatures live among its wavir its cool, damp mass of vegete out.

The **rough periwinkle** is abu seaweeds of the middle shore. L shell colours may be white, yellow, Its relative the **small periwinkle** can l higher up on the shore, packed into cre the reach of normal tides and it is a clas    example of a sea creature making the transition to land life. It can withstand desiccation almost as well as a land

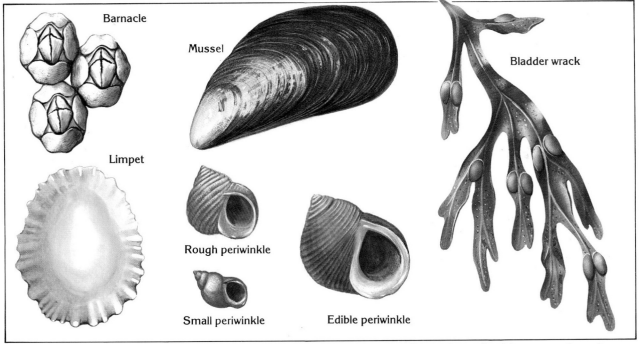

Barnacle

Mussel

Bladder wrack

Limpet

Rough periwinkle

Small periwinkle

Edible periwinkle

are anchored to the rocks. They grow in dense, blue-black masses attached to rocks, stones and each other by sticky byssus threads secreted by a special gland. Though often quite small on the shore, mussels reach a large size in the rich, sheltered waters of estuaries and there they are collected to be eaten by man. Mussels are bivalve filter feeders living mainly on the middle shore. Under water the shells part and siphons draw in and expel sea-water from which plankton is extracted by a sieve of mucus.

The powerful suction of a large muscular foot and a low, cone-shaped shell which offers little resistance to the waves helps prevent **limpets** from being washed off the rocks. At the slightest touch they clamp on to the rock so tightly that they are difficult to remove without damage. Limpets make short,

snail but it still needs to shed its spawn into the sea during winter storms and very high tides. The rough periwinkle broods its young within its body and gives birth to live young during the summer. Both periwinkles are plant feeders, the rough periwinkle eating algae and young seaweed, the small periwinkle feeding on the lichens of the upper shore.

Another of the common shore periwinkles, and the largest, is the **edible periwinkle**. Its shell is black, occasionally brown or red, with a finely-sculptured surface. It is abundant on the middle and lower shore among seaweeds, rocks and rock pools. Unlike limpets or barnacles which resist the pounding waves, periwinkles simply allow the sea to take them and they roll about the shore unharmed in their tough, rounded shells.

# LIFE on ROCKY SHORES

Where fresh water trickles over the rocks **sea lettuce** grows on the upper shore and in pools. Quite shapeless out of water, once submerged it spreads out as a bright-green, paper-thin fan. Among the fronds of sea lettuce and beneath the dense growth of other rock pool seaweeds hides the **common shrimp**. It is a versatile creature that can tolerate a wide range of salinities, hides under stones or buries itself in sand and can change colour to some extent to match its surroundings. Omnivorous, it eats green seaweeds and small crustaceans which it collects with pincers on its front legs. The common shrimp is quite hardy and can survive for brief periods out of water if stranded.

In the same rock pools the delicate and beautiful sea anemones can be found. Commonest on the lower and middle shore is the **beadlet anemone**. Red is its usual colour but it may be covered in green spots or be entirely green or brown. The ring of gently-waving tentacles possesses batteries of stinging, paralysing threads which are thrown around passing prey such as the common shrimp. Captured animals are drawn into the body cavity by the tentacles and digested.

Two other inhabitants of rock pools – starfish and sea urchins – although very different in appearance are, in fact, closely related. **Starfish** roam widely over rocks and pools on the lower shore, moving by means of thousands of extensible, flexible tube-feet distributed under the five 'arms'. The tube feet operate by means of hydraulic pressure and as well as being useful for movement they have a strong grip and can exert a very considerable force – enough to prise open bivalve molluscs which the starfish eats. The arms of the starfish are easily broken off but are quickly regrown. This ability is important, as it helps it to escape from predators and also could prevent it from getting trapped under rocks and stones.

**Sea urchins** have a similar system of tube-feet which they use to move around and to search for food. The spines on a sea urchin are more useful for protection but they do help in movement too. One common rock pool species wedges itself into crevices and uses its tube-feet to cover itself in a camouflage of seaweed. Sea urchins are mainly herbivorous, feeding on seaweed, although they occasionally eat animal matter.

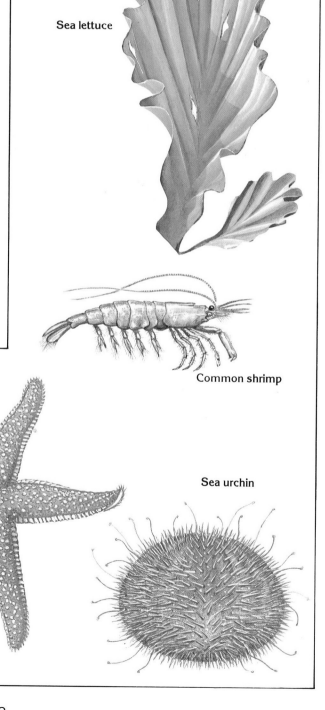

Sea lettuce

Common shrimp

Sea urchin

Beadlet anemone

Starfish

Creatures that cannot survive for long periods out of water live low down on the shore where the sea leaves the rocks uncovered for only a short time. **Tangles** is typical of the seaweeds that live at the water's edge, exposed only on the lowest of tides when the fronds hang limply from erect stems. Off-shore they form dense underwater forests.

Several topshells occur on the shore, easily recognised by the worn tips of their shells which reveal the mother-of-pearl beneath. The **painted topshell** lives on the lower shore and is the species that gives the group its name. Brightly-coloured and sharply-pointed like an old fashioned spinning top, topshells graze, like most shore molluscs, on the film of vegetation which grows on rocks. Topshells have primitive gills easily clogged by sand and silt, so must live in a rocky environment.

An unusual group of molluscs that generally live low on the shore are the **chitons**. These are small and flat with a shell of eight articulated plates and they resemble woodlice in appearance. Chitons cling like limpets to rocks but the movable plates of the shell enable them to shape themselves to fit any bumps and hollows in the surface. If they are knocked off they will curl up like woodlice.

The **edible crab** ventures only on to the lower shore, seeking protection under rocks and seaweeds. This pinkish-red crab can reach weights of up to 4.5kg (10lb) but those on the shore rarely reach any great size. The black-tipped pincers of this crab are very well developed and can give a nasty nip.

Fishes living on a rocky shore must be able to withstand the buffeting of waves and the swirl of water through deep gulleys. The **goby**, commonest of the shore fishes, avoids being washed away by clinging to rocks with pelvic fins modified into a simple sucker. This small fish can be found in rock pools or is seen swimming in shoals in shallow off-shore waters. It has protruding eyes, a sharp-spined dorsal fin and colouring that blends beautifully with the rocks and seaweeds of the shore. The male goby entices a female to lay her eggs under a stone or in an empty sea shell and he then guards them until they hatch, fanning them with his fins to keep them supplied with oxygen.

The **blenny** or **shanny**, another common shore fish, can also be found under stones or in rock pools. Larger than the goby, it has a dorsal fin the length of its back, no scales and a soft, slimy body. It can survive for long periods out of water and is often found wedged in rock crevices or under seaweeds. The blenny feeds on barnacles and small bivalves which it bites off rocks with its hard, toothed jaws.

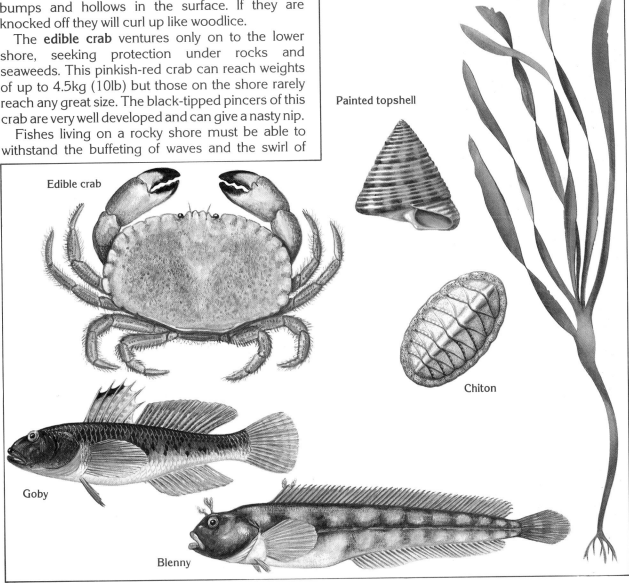

Tangles

Painted topshell

Chiton

Edible crab

Goby

Blenny

# LIFE on SANDY SHORES

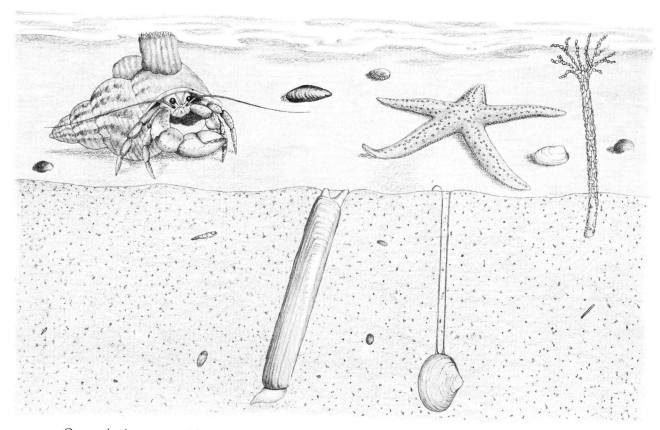

*On sandy shores most life, such as razorshells, cockles and sand masons, is found below the sand.
Hermit crabs can be found at the water's edge and starfish are often washed up by storm tides.*

The great expanses of sand that collect in bays and natural harbours are a difficult habitat for seashore life. The sea keeps the sand constantly in motion so shore-dwelling life cannot fix itself to a solid base; in bad winters stormy seas may strip whole beaches bare of their sand to reveal rock and clay beneath. Very little organic matter is trapped in sand to nourish the creatures that live there so most sand-living animals use it only for protection; they filter their food from seawater or scavenge for edible debris washed in by the tide.

At the top of the beach, reached only by the highest of tides, the sand becomes dry and in sunshine can become very hot. To survive here sand-dwellers must burrow deep down to reach the life-saving moisture. After a high tide the holes of sand-hoppers pepper the sand and they remain deep in their burrows until the return of the next high tide, days or possibly even weeks later. Lower down on the shore filter-feeding animals such as the sea potato – a type of sea urchin – and the razorshell conceal themselves in the sand and siphon organisms from the sea as the tide advances over them. On most sandy shores they are hard to find and they have to be searched for when the tide is at its lowest.

Between the tides sandy beaches may be short of life, but off-shore, where the beach is permanently covered by water, many creatures live in the sand. Often the only sign of their presence is when they, their shells or their bodies are washed up on to the shore. After rough seas a search of the tide line will reveal a wide range of creatures.

Camouflage is important for many of the animals on sandy shores. Most of them have a sandy, speckled colouring or, like some shrimps, can change their colour to match their background. Burrowing crabs and shrimps may be common in shallow pools left by the tide. Disturb them and they dash off, only to 'disappear' as they stop and ease themselves into the sand, relying on their colouring to hide them.

At the very top of sandy beaches, washed only by the high spring tides of winter, is a narrow strip of free-draining sand too salty and infertile for most land plants to grow in. This is the habitat of two hardy, succulent seashore plants, the prickly saltwort and the sea rocket. Resistant to drought and salt these plants often grow in masses along an entire shoreline. The **prickly saltwort**, usually partly buried in sand, grows into a bush 30-60cm (1-2ft) high. It has long, thin, cylindrical leaves each tipped with a sharp spine. In the past this plant was collected, dried and burnt over a pit, releasing an alkaline substance that was used in the making of washing soda. The **sea rocket** is a fast-growing plant with pretty pink flowers that make a fine display when growing in profusion on the seashore. Its large, oval seed capsules break off from their stems and are dispersed by the sea, the seeds remaining completely unaffected by their immersion in salt water.

Above the tide line sand may blow off the beach to make great banks of sand-dunes. Here only one plant, **marram grass**, grows in any quantity, dominating the landscape with its masses of tall, waving tussocks and literally holding the dunes together. Marram roots probe deeply to collect all the moisture available in this arid habitat and the plants counter the swamping effect of the ever-shifting sand by simply sending up new shoots and roots which grow through it. So effective is marram grass in stabilising moving sand that it has been planted on thousands of acres of shifting dunes all over Britain.

**Sand sedge** is another common creeping plant of sand-dunes with the power to bind sand, but it cannot tolerate being buried as can marram grass. Its rhizomes travel just beneath the surface in straight lines several feet long. Every 15cm (6in) or so a small tuft of leaves sprouts from the root and these in turn send out runners, resulting in a criss-cross pattern of growth across the sand.

The **sea holly** grows away from the edge of the shore but close enough to be drenched by the salt sea spray. It is a small, bushy plant with blue-green stems and leaves and beautiful powder-blue, dome-shaped flowers. The stiff leaves have a series of holly-like spines around their edges, from which the plant gets its name.

Sand sedge

Prickly saltwort

Marram grass

Sea holly

Sea rocket

155

Sandy shores are a poor habitat. There is very little for animals to feed on and the constantly shifting sand makes it difficult for them to build permanent homes. Most sandy shore life is found below water level but many creatures venture on to the shore, mostly at the low tide mark.

**Hermit crabs** can often be found inside sea shells, tumbling along in the waves at low tide. They are more closely related to shrimps and prawns than to crabs and they live in shells to protect their soft, vulnerable bodies. Young hermit crabs use a variety of small shells but larger specimens always use the empty shells of the common whelk. They transfer to larger shells as they grow, carefully testing the new shell for size before swiftly making the change. If threatened the hermit crab withdraws tightly into its shell and blocks the entrance with its large claw.

The **common whelk**, whose shell the hermit crab uses, is a scavenging animal that rarely ventures on to the shore but its large, empty shells are commonly washed up on the beach along with its strange, sponge-like egg masses. Each capsule in the egg mass contains several hundred eggs but only a dozen or so eventually emerge, as the first whelks to hatch eat the rest of the eggs.

Another easily recognised shell regularly washed up on the beach belongs to the **razorshell**. Razorshells live off-shore, or at the very lowest levels of the tide, burrowing vertically into the sand. Both ends of their tubular shells are open. From the top protrude two siphons which draw in and expel seawater, which the razorshell sieves for food, while from the other end emerges the muscular foot with which it digs rapidly and deeply into the sand.

**Sand masons**, pink worms with a crown of waving tentacles, also burrow deeply, building themselves a protective tube of sand grains cemented together with mucus. The tube may be 30cm (1ft) long but only the top 25mm (1in) or so projects on to the beach. A lacework of sand grains protects the tentacles which are used to catch food.

Much less commonly seen on the shore are **brittle stars**, an off-shore species of starfish that can occur in enormous numbers in coastal waters with sand or gravel beds. They are carnivorous, feeding on small sea creatures, and they move with rapid, jerky movements, readily shedding any of their five 'arms' to escape predators. New arms regrow rapidly.

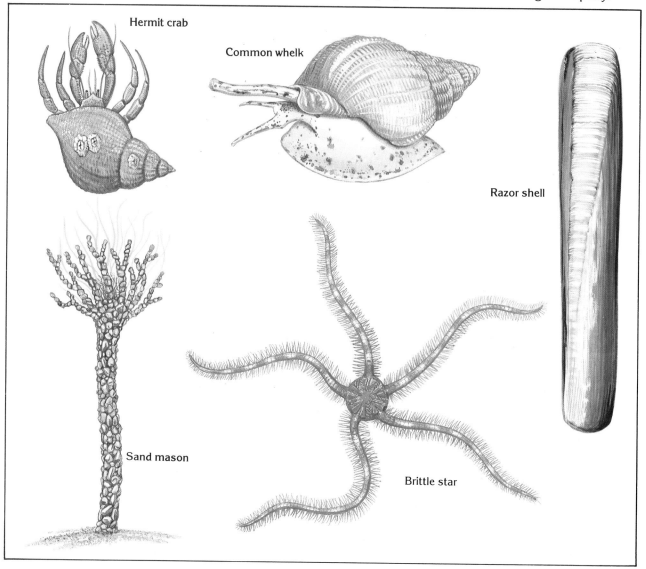

Hermit crab

Common whelk

Razor shell

Sand mason

Brittle star

# LIFE of MUDDY SHORES

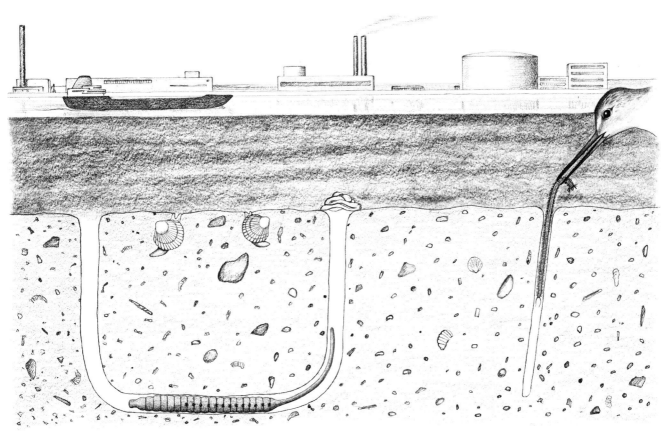

*Like sandy shores, life in muddy seashore habitats is found mostly beneath the surface. Look for the marks lugworms leave on the surface of the mud when they feed, but if you want to see the animals themselves you will have to dig them out with a spade.*

Not surprisingly, the muddy shores of estuaries are a neglected habitat. The mud is heavy and sticky and at times mud-flats can be dangerous, trapping the unwary walker. It is, however, a rich world. Organic matter brought down by rivers enriches the mud which teems with unseen life. On the surface of the mud there are countless millions of tiny snails feeding on bacteria and organic debris. Beneath stones and weed the tiny young of shore crabs seek shelter from predators. Most life in mud-flats lives buried in the mud, emerging to scavenge and feed only under the protective cover of the tide.

Mud-dwellers feed either on the organic particles in the mud itself or filter food from the swirling waters of the tide. On the surface their presence may be revealed only by a pock-marking of holes or a 'cast' of mud, but turning over just a spadeful of mud will show how astonishingly abundant they are. There will be straight burrows containing ragworms and thousands of U-shaped burrows containing the minute crustaceans *corophium* that crawl out of their tubes to pick up their food from the surface of

the mud with lobster-like claws. Deeper still will be found the peppery furrow shell, a shellfish that 'hoovers' mud from the surface with a very long siphon. Cockles lie near the surface, extending their siphons when the tide comes in to filter plankton from the water. Lower down the estuary shore among muddy gravels live the filter-feeding carpet shells and gaper shells. Where the gravel is not too coarse peacock worms build tubes up to 30cm (1ft) deep in the gravel, clustering together in thousands where the habitat is suitable.

Because of the shelter and safe anchorage that estuaries offer to shipping, most of them house major sea ports. With them come industry, the reclamation of the mud-flats and pollution. Barrages, huge dams across the mouths of estuaries, are another threat. They create very large freshwater lakes which eliminate the tidal flow and the regular floods of salt water that mud-life needs to survive, and they also cover the feeding grounds of the vast numbers of waders that come to estuaries in the winter months.

The bright green algae **enteromorpha** (there is no common English name) is one of the first plants to colonise the mud of salt-marshes. Thin and tubular, it grows up to 45cm (18in) in length and is inflated by pockets of gas which give it buoyancy when the tide comes in. Like all the other salt-marsh plants, enteromorpha slows the tidal currents and causes the water to drop its load of sediment, bringing about a gradual rise in the level of the mud.

As the mud-flats begin to rise they are colonised by glasswort, a native succulent, or spartina grass, a rampant and quick-spreading grass. **Glasswort** looks rather like a miniature tree cactus and grows best in sandy mud. It gets its name from the fact that it used to be gathered and burnt for the alkali it yielded which was used in the making of glass and soap. **Spartina grass**, also called cord grass or rice grass, grows very well on soft, wet mud. This fascinating plant arose from a hybrid of a native species and an introduced North American species. It is very vigorous, colonising and binding mud

where other plants are not able to grow. It has been used successfully in many coastal reclamation schemes and has been planted in estuaries and on muddy seashores all around the British Isles.

As the growing mud-flats become firmer and build higher, sea-blite and sea aster invade the plant sward. **Sea-blite** is a nondescript, dark-green, bushy plant common in most salt-marshes, but the **sea aster** puts on a fine display with its Michaelmas daisy-like flowers. This plant has two flower forms, one with petals and the other without – the latter is generally known as the 'rayless' form. Crosses between the two are common but there are no rayless plants north of Lincolnshire. Sea aster is one of the most important plants in the salt-marsh community. Its bulk causes a rapid rise in the level of mud and its flowers are a rich source of nectar for visiting insects.

**Sea lavender** is another pretty flower of salt-marshes, named after its lavender-coloured tufts of flowers. It grows in muddy salt-marshes all round the coast and is a favourite plant of flower arrangers. The blooms soon wither but their colour persists for many months.

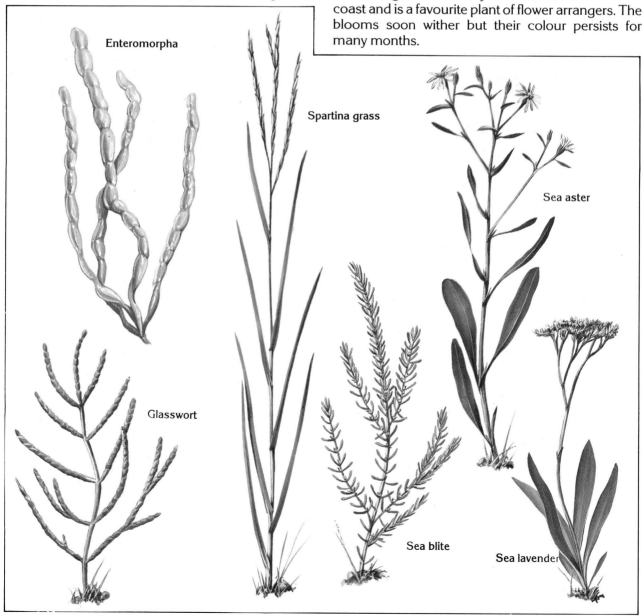

Enteromorpha

Spartina grass

Sea aster

Glasswort

Sea blite

Sea lavender

Most salt-marsh animals burrow into the soft mud to seek protection from predators and to prevent desiccation when the tide ebbs. Some of them hunt for their food but many more filter out the teeming mass of creatures living in the fertile surface layers of mud or the rich, flowing waters of the estuary.

The **lugworm** lives at the bottom of a deep, U-shaped burrow. At one end if this burrow is a shallow depression caused by the worm drawing in mud to swallow, and at the other end is a curled pile of waste products called the 'cast'. Lugworms feed on the bacteria and organic debris contained in the mud and every forty minutes they back up their burrows to eject a cast at the surface. This is when they are most vulnerable to the probing bills of wading birds, but the lugworm is able to shed its tail, which distracts the attacking bird and gives the worm time to escape to the depths of the burrow.

Living deep in the mud makes it difficult to maintain an adequate oxygen supply. Lugworms have haemoglobin, an oxygen-binding pigment, in their blood and ragworms have similar compounds. **Ragworms** usually remain buried in the mud when the tide is out but once covered by water they swim well by means of 'paddles' on each segment or crawl across the surface of the mud in search of small animals to eat. One species of ragworm can reach a length of over 45cm (18in) and specimens of 1m (3ft) long are quite common. A worm that size can deliver a painful bite with its strong jaws.

The bivalve molluscs of muddy shores are all filter feeders, remaining buried in mud and rarely moving. **Cockles** are among the most abundant bivalves, their populations reaching over a million to the acre in suitable places. They lie just below the surface of the mud extending short siphons to draw in and expel seawater from which they extract their food.

**Sand gapers** burrow quite deeply in firm mud, often down to a foot or more, and from their deep stronghold they extend a long siphon to the surface. They are called gapers because their siphons are so large that they prevent complete closure of the shell, which permanently 'gapes'.

Surprisingly, the **shore crab** also buries itself in mud, although it is more often found hiding under seaweed or stones. This hardy crab is common on seashores and in estuaries everywhere in the British Isles. It is tolerant of both seawater and the less salty estuary water and can survive well for long periods in or out of water. The shore crab is a general predator, eating almost anything it can find and it in turn is heavily preyed upon by waders and gulls. Shore crabs' shell patterns are enormously varied.

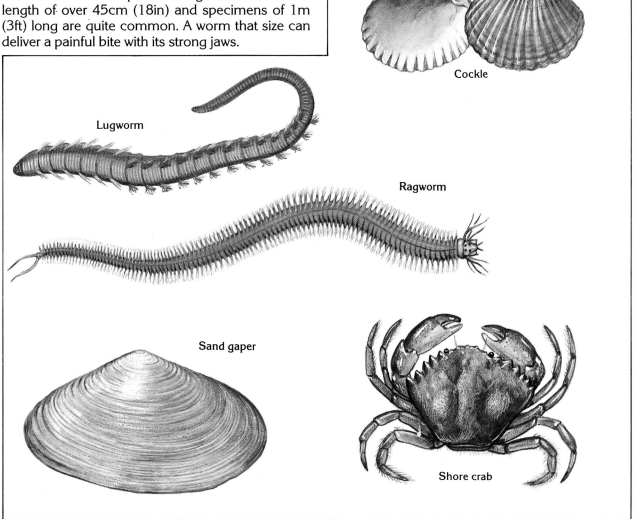

Cockle

Lugworm

Ragworm

Sand gaper

Shore crab

159

# EXPLORING the SEASHORE

The seashore is an exciting place full of unfamiliar sights and sounds and few of us are untouched by the magic of the sea. However, because of its unfamiliarity the seashore can also be a hazardous place with many pitfalls for the unwary landlubber. The tides, sea currents and the special peculiarities of each shore can turn a day of pleasure into a terrible disaster, so before you set out to explore the seashore bear in mind these few cautionary notes:

1. **Always be aware of the tide.** Consult a tide table so that you can decide when is the safest time to visit the shore. If possible, organise your exploration on an outgoing tide – that way you will have much more time to explore and it is a lot safer. Carry a watch so that you know when the tide has turned and you must start to make your way back. On some shores, especially sand and mud-flats, the sea can return with very great speed.

2. **Always tell someone where you are going.** This is a very basic precaution. If you do get into difficulties there is at least one person who knows where you are.

3. **Never venture too far.** Confine your explorations to short stretches of coast at a time. It is all too easy to keep venturing on, forgetting the tide, only to find yourself cut off behind a headland or by a flooded gulley.

## WHAT TO WEAR

Most people exploring the seashore on holiday when the weather is sunny like to wear a swimsuit and they usually get burnt! It may seem an elementary precaution, but always wear a pair of shorts and a tee-shirt at the very minimum until you have got a suntan. Apart from this, the only special clothing you will need are a pair of shoes or wellington boots with good gripping soles for clambering over rocky shores, wellington boots for mud-flats and beach shoes for walking on sandy shores. **Never** wear good leather shoes because seawater ruins leather and rots stitching.

## BASIC EQUIPMENT

It is not necessary to take *any* equipment with you on a seashore exploration – searching and looking can be a rewarding pastime in itself. But a few simple items carried in your pocket or knapsack can make your exploration that much more interesting and memorable.

A hand lens (x8 or x10), a penknife and a few plastic bags for bringing back specimens are useful on any shore. Dip nets for catching creatures in rock pools and a glass jar or clear plastic sandwich box are useful on rocky coasts. Bulkier equipment is needed only on sandy and muddy shores – a spade or trowel for digging and a sieve for sifting animals out of the sand.

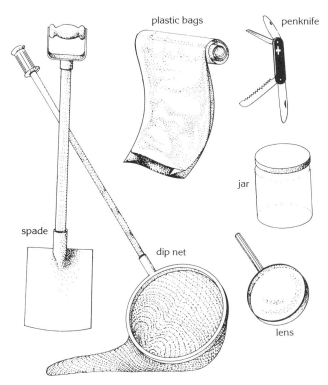

useful equipment for exploring the seashore

## TECHNIQUES
### ROCKY SHORES

The commoner seaweeds and animals on rocky shores are attached to prominent rocks and are easy to find. Less common species have to be searched for and it helps to know some of the likely places to look. Rock pools are an obvious place to begin. Sea anemones, seaweeds and molluscs in shallow pools are easily located but creatures in deeper pools with dense fringes of seaweed present more of a problem. Use a dip net to catch fish and crabs and push it into or underneath the seaweed to dislodge any animals hiding in the fronds. Search carefully among boulders, turning over larger ones to reveal any animals which may be hiding beneath them. But always replace any stones you have turned over – remember, they are home for something. The further down the shore you go the more creatures a

Life in a rock pool

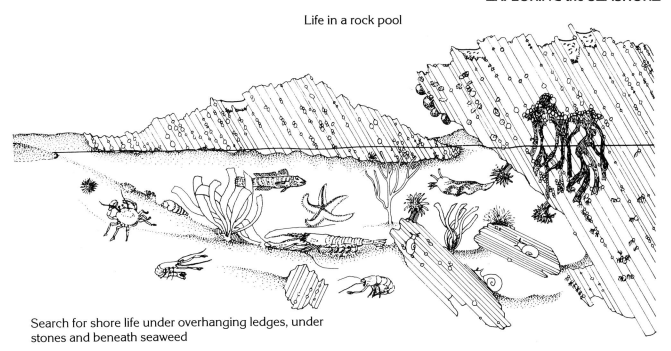

Search for shore life under overhanging ledges, under stones and beneath seaweed

pool is likely to contain.

When it is windy or when the angle of light makes it difficult to see into a pool, float your clear plastic box on the surface. This will cut out all reflections and disturbance and you will be able to look directly through the box into the water. Be patient – when you first arrive at a pool the creatures will go into hiding but if you sit still and wait they will soon reappear.

Search along deep gulleys, especially those with pools of water left in the bottom, for sea urchins, starfish and larger shore fishes. Don't neglect the damp, shaded walls of these gulleys. Examine overhanging ledges and rock crevices for life more typical of the lower shore.

## SANDY SHORES

Most sandy shores support very little life. What there is can most often be found on the lower shore and has to be dug out and sifted from the sand with a sieve. Look for the tell-tale depressions of the burrowing sea-potato or the strange, regular 'scribbling' tracks of burrowing crabs.

The most rewarding pursuit on sandy shores, however, is beachcombing. Off-shore the sand is full of animals; their shells and dead bodies are regularly washed up on to the shore. Walk the strand line of the beach as often as possible, particularly after rough seas. You will soon discover where the best shells are washed ashore or when unusual finds are likely to occur.

## MUDDY SHORES

The life of muddy shores lies buried beneath the surface. To see it, you will have to stamp around in and dig over the sticky mud. Nearly all mud-dwelling creatures leave tell-tale marks on the surface that not only reveal their whereabouts but also tell you exactly which species they are. Lugworms, leave a coiled 'cast' at one end of their U-shaped burrows and a shallow depression at the other. The peppery furrow shell leaves a characteristic 'bird's foot' imprint on the surface, while a number of burrowing creatures leave the mud pin-pricked with holes. Even crabs will burrow into the sides of mud banks. Digging all these creatures out is an easy task and provided you do not mind getting dirty can bring you hours of pleasure.

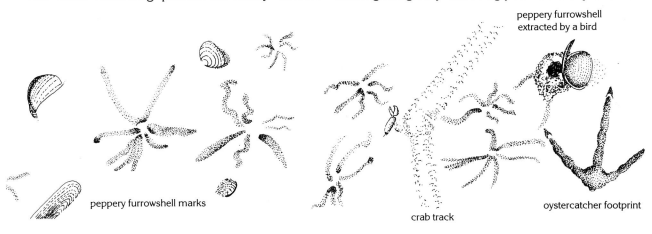

peppery furrowshell marks

crab track

peppery furrowshell extracted by a bird

oystercatcher footprint

161

# PROJECTS

# DOS AND DON'TS

Many of the projects in this book deal with live animals or suggest that you carry out your work in the countryside. As well as being aware of the Country Code there are a few other important points to bear in mind:

- Don't enter private land without permission. The landowner might become very angry if he finds you on his land but if you ask his permission in advance he might be more helpful than you expect.

- If you collect live animals, make them as comfortable as possible and keep them in conditions similar to those of their natural habitat. If they become distressed in any way immediately put them back where you found them.

- Don't take specimens unless there are lots of others around and **NEVER** pick or collect rare specimens no matter how abundant they might seem to be. *Remember*, it is against the law to dig up any plant without the landowner's permission and some rare plants must not be disturbed at all.

- When searching for wild creatures make as little disturbance as possible. Always turn back any stones you overturn, don't break down or trample vegetation and always go quietly in the countryside.

- **NEVER** disturb nesting birds.

# A BIRD TABLE DIARY

A lot has been written about making bird tables and when and what food to put out for birds and we get great pleasure out of seeing the birds close by and watching their activities. Even more pleasure can be gained by keeping a bird table diary.

In your diary note down:

- When each species of bird first arrives and is last seen at the bird table during the year. You will find that some birds will visit the table at any time of the year but others will appear and leave at about the same dates every year. If you keep a regular diary you will be able to predict fairly accurately when a particular species will arrive.

- At what time of day each species arrives at the bird table. Some birds make regular feeding rounds, arriving at feeding stations at approximately the same time each day. This information will be helpful if you want to put out special food or make a particular study of certain birds.

- What food each species eats and at what time of year.

Once you start a diary you will soon begin to learn a lot more about the birds that visit your bird table. Why not go further and make charts and graphs to show in detail the information you have collected?

# BIRD COUNT

A similar diary can be kept in order to make a bird count survey. For this you should choose a route that passes through lots of different habitats and keep a diary of which birds you see and how many of them you see in each habitat. Walk your route at least once or twice a week for a year. Make a note of the time of day and the state of the weather. Turn your figures into a graph or bar chart. You may be surprised at the results.

The diary will give you a clear picture of the bird populations in your area. You will soon discover which habitats the birds prefer at each time of year and you will be able to see how the weather affects bird movements. Frosty weather, for instance, may bring in many new birds to your area and cause others to fly off. You may find that common birds fluctuate considerably in numbers. You may be able to discover the reasons for these movements and other changes once you regularly undertake a bird count survey. You can expand the scope of the count to suit yourself if you find other interesting questions arising from your survey.

# FEATHER POWER

Birds' feathers are made so that the vanes lock together on the wings' downbeat, presenting resistance to the air and keeping the bird in flight. On the upbeat they unlock to let air rush through so that the bird can easily lift its wings. To see how a feather works, find a large flight feather and wave it in the air, changing its position on each pass. Then try these two experiments.

## A FEATHER WINDMILL

Attach a piece of cork to a stick with a long pin and push three similarly-sized flight feathers into the cork, spaced evenly apart. All the feathers must be placed at the same angle – on a slight skew is best. Hold the stick into the wind. Turn the feathers to different angles and note how fast the windmill turns and *which* way it turns. Can you work out why the angle of the feather makes such a big difference?

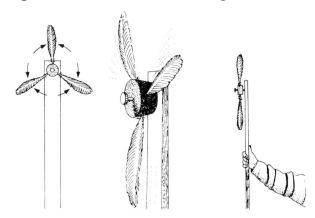

## A FEATHER GLIDER

Make a fuselage of balsa wood and fix a paper-clip to the nose. Fix feathers on to corks with a groove cut out along the bottom and push the corks on to the fuselage. Push the feathers in at a slight 'V' angle and fix the ones on the tailplane so that they slope slightly backwards. Slide the corks back and forth until your plane flies perfectly. The angle at which the flight feathers are fixed will make an enormous difference to your glider's flight. Try them in different positions.

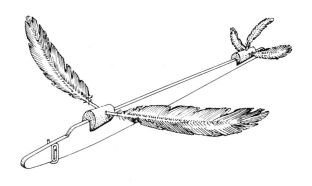

# TREATING SICK AND INJURED BIRDS

Most of us want to try to look after any sick or injured birds we find but it is very difficult and needs a lot of patience to do it successfully. Once in your hands the bird will be completely dependent on you and if you neglect it in any way it will die, possibly a cruel and needless death. So, unless you are very determined and fully prepared to put up with a great deal of mess, hard work and frustration, don't try it. The law actually prohibits the taking or killing of wild birds but it does allow you to care for sick birds so long as they are returned promptly to the wild once they recover. A quick word here about fledglings – people often 'rescue' young birds which have just left the nest, but please don't do this – they are quite mobile and there will be a parent bird around somewhere nearby to feed and protect them.

Most injured birds suffer from shock. They may have been mauled by a cat, or have flown into a window. They will be limp, may be unconscious and will quickly die if left unattended. It is important to get them into a quiet, warm, dark place as soon as possible. Place them in a box lined with tissues (or newspaper if the bird is large) and cover this with a lid. Never use cotton wool or cloth to line the box as this will become entangled with the feet. Put the box in an airing cupboard or similar warm place, or put it on a hot water bottle which has been wrapped in a blanket. This treatment is good for any sick or injured bird. When the bird has revived check it gently for broken wings or legs, but do not try to treat these yourself – take the bird to a vet.

Once the bird has recovered it will soon need feeding. Each bird has its own food preferences – giving it bird seed or bread is definitely not good enough. Give the bird the nearest substitute for its normal diet that you are able to obtain. If it will not feed voluntarily force it to open its beak by gently squeezing on each side of the beak with thumb and forefinger. Push the food in carefully with your fingers. Use an eye dropper for liquids. Encourage the bird to be independent and take its own food as soon as possible. Once you have begun feeding, feed often and at regular times.

You will soon know when your bird has recovered enough to be set free. Its eyes will be bright and it will be alert and active. If it has behaved in a fairly tame way it will probably become suspicious once again and if it has space to move – as in a garage – it will probably try to fly. Release it somewhere where there is plenty of open space so that you can catch it again if there is a problem. Choose a place where there is no chance of the bird being caught by a cat while it is still weak and getting used to being free again.

| TYPE OF BIRD | TYPE OF FOOD |
|---|---|
| FISH EATING AND CARNIVOROUS WATER BIRDS e.g. DIVING DUCKS, GULLS, CORMORANTS (GULL) | STRIPS OF RAW, LEAN BEEF, COD LIVER OIL, BONE MEAL, LARGE EARTHWORMS, FRESH FISH OF A SUITABLE SIZE FROM YOUR FISHMONGER OR FREEZER STORE (MAKE SURE FROZEN FISH ARE FULLY THAWED) |
| OTHER DUCKS AND GEESE (BARNACLE GOOSE) | CHICKEN MEAL AND SMALL AMOUNTS OF MINCED BEEF |
| INSECT EATING BIRDS e.g. SWALLOWS, HOUSE MARTINS, SWIFTS, NIGHTJARS (SWALLOW) | THESE BIRDS ARE THE MOST DIFFICULT OF ALL TO REAR AND CARE FOR. PRE-PACKAGED INSECTILE MIXTURES CAN BE BOUGHT FROM FANCY PET STORES, OTHERWISE FINELY MINCED BEEF, BREAD, MILK AND FLIES ARE THE ONLY SUBSTITUTE. |
| PREDATORY BIRDS e.g. EAGLES, HAWKS, FALCONS (KESTREL) | STRIPS OF RAW, LEAN BEEF, COD LIVER OIL, BONE MEAL, FRESHLY DEAD MICE SMALLER SPECIES, e.g. KESTRELS, OWLS, EAT A LOT OF INSECTS AND WILL TAKE MEAL WORMS AND EVEN EARTHWORMS |
| OTHER BIRDS (GOLDEN PLOVER) | MOST OTHER BIRDS ARE FAIRLY OMNIVOROUS AND WILL EAT A VARIETY OF FOOD INCLUDING WILD BIRD SEEDS, FRUIT AND BREAD. SPECIES THAT TAKE A FAIR PROPORTION OF INSECTS CAN BE FED MINCED BEEF, EARTHWORMS AND MEAL WORMS AS WELL |

TINNED DOG FOOD IS A CHEAP AND ADEQUATE ALTERNATIVE TO RAW BEEF

# MAKING A NEST BOX

cut the pieces of the nest box from a single plank
of unplaned soft wood as shown below. This should
be 20 mm (¾ in.) thick, 15 cm (6 in.) wide and
not less than 140 cm (4ft 6in.) long.

## Bird Box

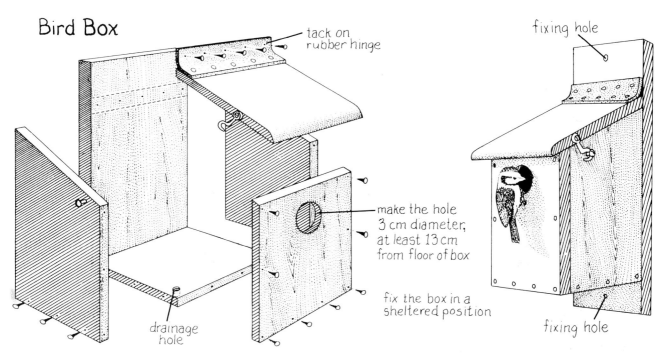

tack on rubber hinge

fixing hole

make the hole
3 cm diameter,
at least 13 cm
from floor of box

fix the box in a
sheltered position

fixing hole

drainage hole

use the construction of the bird box as a model for the other boxes.

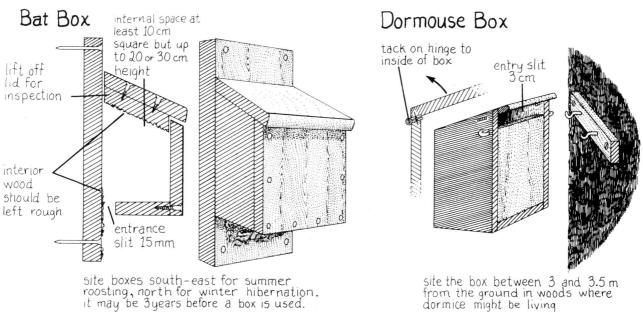

## Bat Box

internal space at
least 10 cm
square but up
to 20 or 30 cm
height

lift off
lid for
inspection

interior
wood
should be
left rough

entrance
slit 15mm

site boxes south-east for summer
roosting, north for winter hibernation.
it may be 3 years before a box is used.

## Dormouse Box

tack on hinge to
inside of box

entry slit
3 cm

site the box between 3 and 3.5 m
from the ground in woods where
dormice might be living

167

# MAKING A MAMMAL FEEDING CAGE

Small mammals such as voles and mice are very shy and can be difficult to watch. One ingenious way of making the watching easier is to build a baited observation cage in your own garden. Site the cage so that you can see it easily from a window of your house. Food – grains, nuts and fruit – is placed on an elevated platform and a small-diameter pipe pushed through the wire of the cage or buried beneath it for the mammals to go in and out. Place your mammal feeding cage in an area of rough grass and trim the grass if it gets too long. Make your food platform so it comes above the grass.

To build your cage you will need the following materials:

- 10 m (33ft) of 5cm x 5cm (2in x 2in) timber.
- Enough wire mesh (mesh size no greater than 1sq cm (½ sq in)) to cover the cage (leave the bottom open).
- Staples to fix the mesh.
- Two door hinges.
- Some timber or plywood offcuts.
- A length of drainage or water pipe.

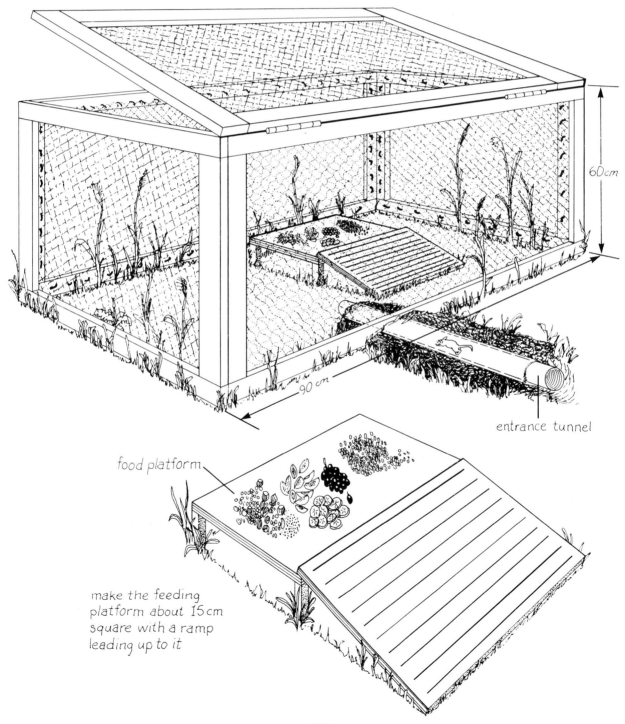

60cm

90 cm

entrance tunnel

food platform

make the feeding platform about 15 cm square with a ramp leading up to it

# A HEDGEHOG HIBERNATION BOX

The friendly hedgehog is a frequent visitor to gardens, where it snuffles about in search of slugs and insects. Putting out bread-and-milk, one of the hedgehog's favourite delicacies, will encourage them to pay regular visits to your garden and you can persuade them to take up more permanent residence by providing them with a winter hibernation box.

This box, designed by the Henry Doubleday Research Association, has proved very successful. Basically, it is a box 30cm x 38cm x 33cm (12in x 15in x 13in), made of untreated timber, with a long entrance tunnel and a ventilation pipe. The entire structure is covered in soil, leaving only the entrance tunnel and the end of the ventilation pipe exposed. It is important to have a small-diameter tunnel to prevent cats from getting into the box. A polythene sheet tacked on to the roof will make the box waterproof. The ventilation pipe is essential to keep the air in the box fresh and to prevent condensation forming. Leave some straw and hay nearby in a dry place for the hedgehog to stuff the box with.

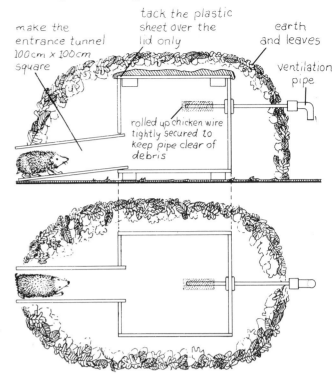

make the entrance tunnel 100cm x 100cm square

tack the plastic sheet over the lid only

earth and leaves

ventilation pipe

rolled up chicken wire tightly secured to keep pipe clear of debris

# MAKING A SKULL COLLECTION

A skull can tell you a lot about the habits of an animal. The teeth especially can give you clues about what the animal eats. Skulls are usually collected from the carcase of a dead animal but may be found already cleaned by scavenging creatures and the elements. Other bones can be cleaned and prepared in the same way as skulls and together they would make a fascinating collection.

## CLEANING AND PREPARING A SKULL

Remove the head of the carcase by making a cut at the neck joint with a sharp knife. This must be done very carefully with small animals or the delicate bones may be crushed and the skull ruined. Carefully clean as much flesh as you can from the skull and then boil the skull in dilute washing soda until it looks clean. Another way of cleaning a skull is to put it near an ant nest and let the ants clean it for you!

After cleaning the skull remove any teeth still attached and glue them back into the sockets. Store delicate skulls in boxes packed with cotton wool.

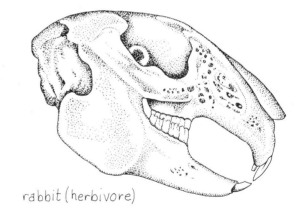

rabbit (herbivore)

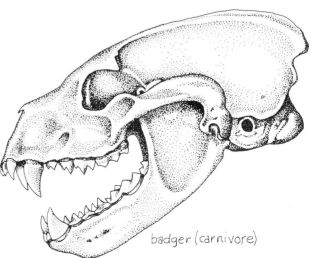

badger (carnivore)

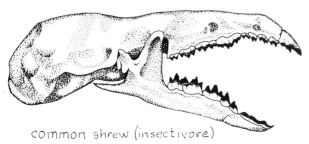

common shrew (insectivore)

# PLASTER-CASTING

Taking plaster casts is a good way of making a permanent record of animal tracks. All you will need to do is to make a small wooden frame about 2.5cm (1in) deep and about 15cm (6in) square. This frame is placed over the animal track and filled with a mixture of wet plaster of paris. Plaster of paris can be bought from a chemist's or hobby shop.

Remove any leaves that obscure the track. Grease the inside of the frame with Vaseline. Press the greased frame gently into the earth around the track. Mix up the plaster of paris with water in a plastic or metal mixing bowl until it is thick but still runny and pour it gently into the frame, smoothing the top level. It will take about twenty to thirty minutes to set. Once it is set, carefully lift up the whole cast and brush off any soil which might be sticking to it. Mark the cast with the date you made it and the name of the animal whose track it is.

# MAKING A HIDE

The best way to observe wildlife is from a hide. Permanent hides, such as those found at nature reserves and bird sanctuaries, are usually quite large and made of wood with shutters which are opened to watch the animals or birds. However, it is quite easy to make yourself a portable hide. Basically this is just an old blanket fixed to two stout but lightweight wooden poles. The blanket, preferably a dull brown or green (daub it with mud if necessary to dull the colour), is tacked to the poles with nails or pinned with a handyman's staple gun. The poles should have sharpened ends – these poles can be bought ready-made from garden centres – so that they can be pushed into soft earth, and to increase stability two guy ropes should be attached to each pole. Cut a viewing slit at a comfortable height. This can be held open by a piece of string or ribbon tied to a large button on the viewer's side of the hide.

This type of hide must be placed so that you have thick vegetaion to your back. Nevertheless it can be quite useful and provided you put it up quietly and unobtrusively and keep still and quiet once you are behind it you may well be lucky enough to observe some of our shyer wildlife.

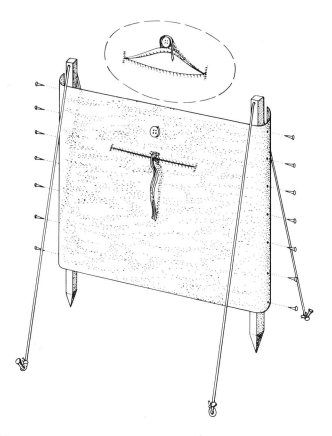

# PLANNING AN INSECT GARDEN

An insect garden is a collection of flowering plants and shrubs attractive to nectar- and pollen-gathering insects. The insects are attracted by the colour and scent of the flowers which promise them food. Moths, butterflies, bees, hoverflies, beetles and even predatory spiders and wasps will settle on the flowers. Among the plants you might also find plant bugs, which feed on plant sap, and woodlice, which eat decaying plant remains.

## WHERE TO PUT YOUR INSECT GARDEN

Your insect garden should be sited preferably in a warm, sunny sheltered plot and near your house, if possible, so that you can easily observe the insects. It can be any size from just a small border to a large shrubbery. If you live near the open countryside or are prepared to let part of your garden grow 'wild' then you will attract a wider variety of species.

## WHAT TO PLANT

For greatest success grow a range of plants which flower at different times of the year. This way there are always flowers available for the insects whenever they call. Some plants can easily be grown from seed and some can be purchased as seedlings or container shrubs. Remember to weed your garden, though. Insects like some weeds but don't let them smother the flowers!

In general, purple and yellow flowers are most attractive to insects. Suggested herbs are Siberian wallflower, sweet william, heather, hemp agrimony, varieties of aubretia, ice plant, yellow alyssum, candytuft, catmint, michaelmas daisy, wallflowers, honesty, sweet rocket, cornflower, thyme. Suggested shrubs are buddleia, lavender, hebe, cotoneaster, mahonia, flowering currant, common privet, ivy.

## PLAN OF A SMALL INSECT GARDEN

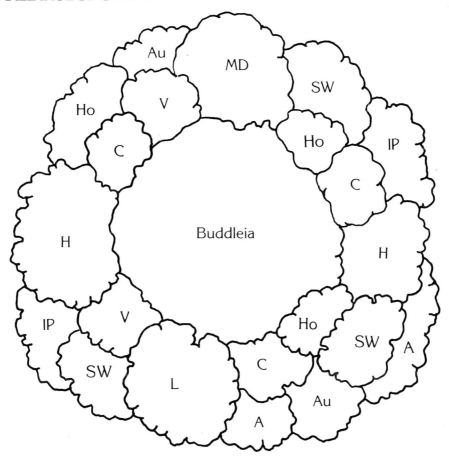

KEY

| Perrennials | | Annuals | |
|---|---|---|---|
| MD | Michaelmas daisies | A | Alyssum |
| L | Lavender | Ho | Honesty |
| H | Heather | SW | Sweet William |
| IP | Ice plant | C | Cornflower |
| V | Veronica (autumn glory) | Au | Aubretia |

# ARTIFICIAL NEST SITES FOR SOLITARY WASPS

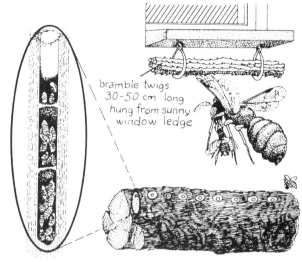

bramble twigs
30-50 cm long
hung from sunny
window ledge

A number of solitary wasps live in suburban gardens and in city parks. Some excavate tunnels in soil or wood, others colonise existing tunnels or make nests in such odd places as keyholes or in holes in the mortar between the bricks of house walls. As well as being quite beautiful, solitary wasps are fascinating to watch as they come and go carrying aphids or caterpillars to fill 'larders' for their young. These wasps use their stings only to paralyse their prey – they will not sting humans.

Some species will readily colonise artificial nests put in warm, sunny, sheltered places. An old log, preferably with the bark removed, can quickly be adapted as a nest site by drilling into it a series of holes 4–7mm (⅛–¼in) in diameter. Bundles of stout, dead bramble twigs may also be used. The wasps will burrow into the twigs and once the nest is established a twig can be split carefully to look at the nest and then resealed with rubber bands so that development of the larvae is not interrupted.

# EXPERIMENTS WITH FLOWERS

Insects are attracted to flowers mainly for the nectar and pollen they produce. Both nectar and pollen are very rich foods made readily available to insects by the flowers and in return the insects carry tiny pollen grains from flower to flower on their bodies, fertilising the plants as they fly about. The variety of colours and shapes of flowers are simply devices to attract more insects and increase the chances of a flower being pollinated. Different insects respond differently to the shapes and colours of flowers. Some species visit all flowers but others visit only certain types of flowers. If you have a garden, or a window box if you live in a city, try the following experiments to see which colours and shapes of flowers are the most attractive to insects.

## INSECT VISITOR DIARY

If you do not have any flowers in the garden buy some from a florist, put them in a vase and leave them outdoors to attract insects. Select a mixed group of flowers with different colours and shapes. If you have a flower garden select as wide a variety of flowers as possible to watch. Watch the flowers at different times of the day and note which insects visit them. Note also which flowers they go to first and if any are ignored, and whether insects visit all the flowers or only some of them. Try to think of reasons why some flowers are more attractive to insects than others. List the commonest insect visitors and the time of day insects arrive.

## ARTIFICIAL FLOWERS

You can take the experiment one stage further by making your own artificial flowers. Mix half a teaspoon of honey with a cupful of water and pour the mixture into a small, narrow container or specimen tube. Tape the container to a thin stick and pin or tape on an artificial flower with a hole in the middle which fits over the mouth of the container. Put your artificial flowers in the garden or window box among real flowers and watch which insects arrive. This is a very good experiment for observing butterflies and bees. Experiment with different shapes and colours (some are suggested below) and compare the results.

If ants are a nuisance, climbing into the containers and chasing away insects, push the stick into a ball of modelling clay or weighted oasis (used for flower arranging – you can buy this from a florist's shop) set in a bowl of water.

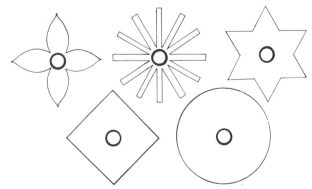

# A POND-LIFE AQUARIUM

Life in a pond is fascinating and diverse and it lends itself very well to being enclosed in a small aquarium. After all, what is a pond but a small, self-contained world enclosed in a pool of water? Pond plants and animals are easy to keep when transferred to an aquarium and they are absorbing to watch. There is always something happening – all sorts of creatures constantly come and go and occasionally animals that normally lie hidden in mud or among weeds will make a surprise appearance.

You can use an aquarium tank made of either glass or plastic. Before filling the tank put a layer of clean gravel on the bottom about 2.5cm (1in) deep and put some soil and stones in one corner in which to plant aquatic weeds. Fill the tank with water, preferably from an unpolluted pond or ditch. If you have to use tap water let it stand in an open bucket for several days to release the chlorine and other chemicals it contains. In order to break the force of the water and prevent it stirring up mud and silt, pour the water gently on to a piece of stiff card placed on the gravel. Stock the aquarium with plants and animals from local ponds and ditches. Tall plants which stick up out of the water can be planted into flower pots to keep them firmly in place. Weight down the submerged plants with a heavy object tied round the stems.

A layer of mud will bring lots of life into the pond and also provide a hiding place or food for mud-dwelling animals. Collect mud from an unpolluted pond or ditch, put it into a bowl and lower it very gently into the water and tip it out, again very gently, over the gravel. Other animals can be collected by dip-netting. Remember always to take care near water – do not lean too far over and risk falling into a pond or deep ditch and take care on muddy or crumbling edges. One other word of caution – your aquarium is very small and has far fewer hiding places than does a natural pond. If you introduce fierce predatory animals such as dragonfly larvae and water beetle larvae they will eat many of the other creatures in it. So will fish. You must decide what is the proper balance for your aquarium pond and choose which predators, if any, you can keep.

Once the pond is stocked you need only to keep the oxygenating plants in check and occasionally wipe the film of algae off the glass. Make sure you keep the water clean and always remove any dead or dying matter that might take oxygen out of the water and so kill other creatures and plants. Siphon out and replenish some of the mud occasionally.

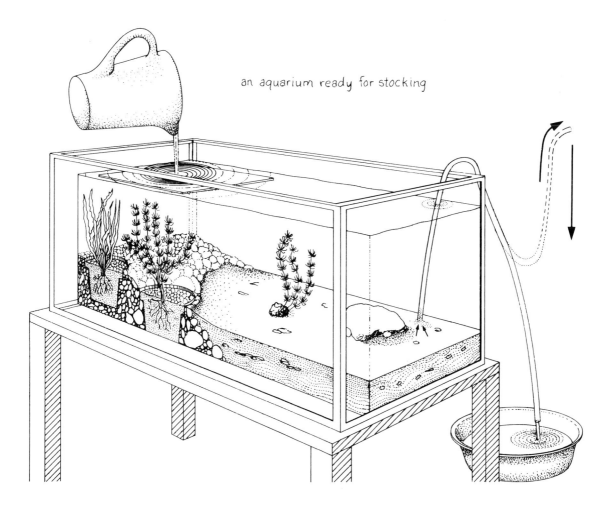

an aquarium ready for stocking

# REARING BUTTERFLIES, MOTHS AND GRASSHOPPERS

## CAGE REARING

Rearing butterflies and moths in captivity is not too difficult, but the beginner is advised to start with the easy species first. Emperor moths and small tortoiseshell butterflies are among the easiest to rear and their eggs and pupae can be obtained from stockists (see page 183). Grasshoppers and crickets are a little more difficult to rear and need a source of heat, usually provided by a light bulb which must be switched on for 14-16 hours a day.

Purpose-built rearing cages are available but a large plastic sweet jar or plastic aquarium tank are often just as good. Moderate levels of humidity are important to many species but condensation *must* be avoided. Gauze or muslin stretched over the top of the jar or tank and held firm by string or a rubber band will keep specimens in the cage while allowing a proper air flow. For species that pupate or lay eggs in soil fill the bottom of the cage with clean sand. Put a piece of wood or bark on one side of the cage for species that pupate above ground.

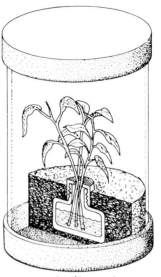

a purpose-built rearing cage with a water pot set in sand

Always remember these important points and you should be able to rear butterflies and moths very successfully:

- **Never** allow condensation to form within the rearing cage.
- **Always** be careful when handling caterpillars as they are easily killed. Use a soft paintbrush to move very young caterpillars.
- **Never** leave dead or decaying remains of plants or insects in the cage and do not be tempted to clutter the cage with greenery as this may cause fungal and bacterial disease.

## 'SLEEVE' REARING

If you find a colony of caterpillars on a bush or tree in your garden you can watch their progress by 'sleeving' them on the branch. Enclose the whole branch in muslin tied tight at both ends. Check the caterpillars frequently and move them to another branch once their food is exhausted.

a simple rearing cage made with wire, muslin and a large plant pot with a food plant growing in it

Plant food has to be kept fresh. Change it daily and keep it in a pot of water sunk into the sand. To prevent the caterpillars from falling into the water seal the pot with a cork and bore a hole in it to take the sprigs of grass or leaves. Caterpillars are very fussy about their food plant and must be given precisely the right species. Grasshoppers are happy to feed on any fresh, young grass.

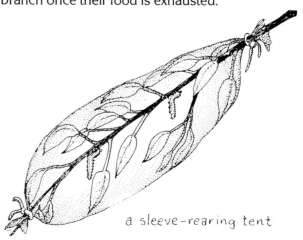

a sleeve-rearing tent

# AN ANT COLONY

Ants are social insects with fascinating life cycles. They build complicated nests which contain special chambers for the queens and rearing chambers for their eggs, larvae and pupae. Ants can be persuaded to take up residence in an artifical nest, usually known as a formicarium, without too much difficulty. The simple one described in this project can be installed on a window ledge or in a sunny place in a garden.

To build a formicarium you will need two sheets of clear, rigid plastic, four pieces of wood and some screw clamps. Make a frame from the wood and place it on a sheet of the plastic. Fill the frame with sifted soil or fine sand and clamp the whole thing together. Bore an access hole in one edge of the formicarium and a number of smaller holes (about 1mm in diameter) so that water can be added occasionally to moisten the soil or sand. It is important to keep the soil damp. So long as there is no more than 1cm (½in) between the plastic sheets and you keep the formicarium covered with a piece of wood or opaque plastic to keep out the light the ants will excavate their galleries and chambers against the glass. When the ants are established simply remove the cover now and again to see their chambers and tunnels.

## STOCKING THE ANT COLONY

For a successful colony you must have a queen and the colony must be stocked with one of the smaller ants which build small nests. Large ants such as wood ants cannot be kept in a small formicarium. You could go out into your garden and dig an ant nest from the lawn and take a queen and some workers but it is far better just to leave out your box, bait it with food and let the ants find it and establish a nest for themselves.

## FEEDING THE ANTS

Connect two jars to the nest with plastic tubing. Put cotton wool soaked in a dilute sugar or honey solution in one, and because ants also need some animal food, meat scraps, dead flies and insects in the other. The cotton wool is easily replaced when it becomes soiled.

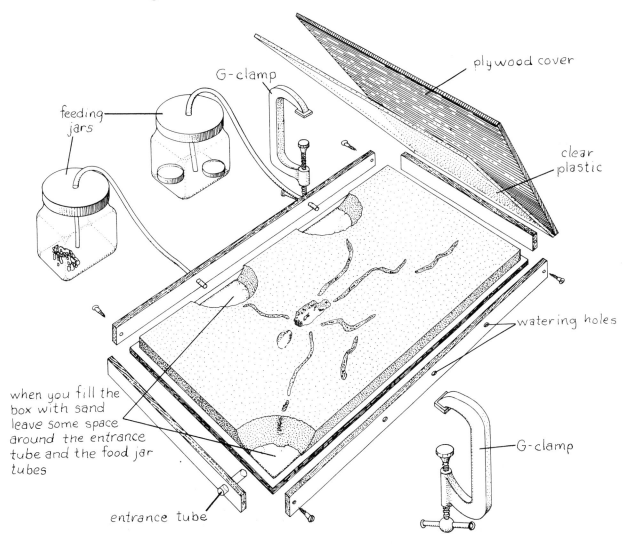

feeding jars

G-clamp

plywood cover

clear plastic

watering holes

when you fill the box with sand leave some space around the entrance tube and the food jar tubes

G-clamp

entrance tube

# MAKING A SPIDER WEB COLLECTION

Spiders' ability to weave intricate and beautiful webs has fascinated man for thousands of years. The webs are marvels of perfect engineering. When laden with dew in the early morning or with raindrops after a shower they sparkle like jewels. Different species of spider spin different kinds of webs and in spite of their very delicate construction it is quite easy to make a permanent collection of webs. To do this you will need a can of white spray paint, a piece of black or dark-coloured stiff paper or card and a can of clear spray varnish.

Find a web in good condition and with plenty of space for you to get behind it easily. Before you do anything else, persuade the spider to leave the web (tickle it gently with a blade of grass or gently tap the twigs or stems that support the web) as you are going to use spray paint and this would kill the spider if any landed on it. Now spray the web with the paint from about 25-30cm (10–12in) away then carefully and firmly bring the paper up from behind the web. The paint-covered web will stick to the paper and you can carefully lift it away from its moorings. This part will need a little practice until you can produce perfect specimens. Handle the wet web with great care and leave it to dry for a few days before giving it a final spray with clear varnish to protect it.

# ATTRACTING MOTHS AND OTHER INSECTS

## LIGHT TRAP

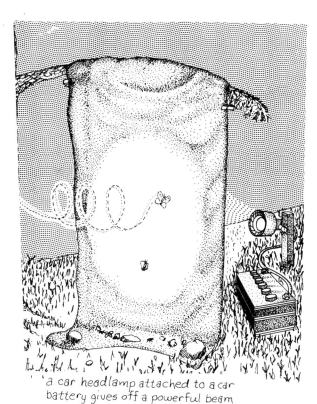
a car headlamp attached to a car battery gives off a powerful beam

If you leave a light on and the curtains open on a warm summer night you will find a lot of insects flying to the window, attracted by the light. If you open the window the insects will fly in and settle on the walls or fly round the lamp. This is the simplest of all insect traps! In the countryside you can use a similar trick to attract moths and other night-flying insects. A light shone on to a white sheet (any size will do but about 1m x 1m (3ft x 3ft) is the most convenient) will attract a large number of flying insects. Use a bright camping gas lamp to illuminate the sheet. Place the light behind the sheet with the bright expanse of the sheet facing upwind.

## SUGAR TRAP

Another old-fashioned but successful method of attracting insects is 'sugaring'. A thick sugar and treacle solution painted on to tree trunks, fences or walls attracts quite a number of insects. Sugar patches can be visited by day or night – at night examine them in the light of a torch – and the insects can be picked off quite easily for closer scrutiny.

### RECIPE FOR A SUGAR SOLUTION
500g (1lb) treacle or golden syrup
1kg (2lb) brown sugar
250ml (½ pint) beer
dash of rum

Boil the mixture in an old saucepan until it is sticky. Try different thickness of syrup and flavourings of spirits and see which produce the best results.

# FRUIT-FLY CULTURE

Fruit-flies are fascinating little insects which are extremely common but usually overlooked as most species are very tiny. They are attracted to over-ripe and rotting fruit where they sip the fermenting juice and lay their eggs. They are quite harmless and in a culture you can follow their life cycle.

Put out some jam jars one-third filled with bait in a sunny part of the garden. Banana is a favourite bait but try other types of fruit to see if different species are attracted. First of all try three banana bait jars: in one put mashed banana on its own, in the second mashed banana mixed with cut-up banana skin and in the third mashed banana mixed with a little fresh yeast. Leave the jars for about five days and then bring them inside and cover the open tops of the jars with muslin fastened with a rubber band. Keep the jars in a warm place, but out of direct sunlight, and things will soon begin to happen. Keep notes of when the first maggots appear, when the first flies hatch and which bait produces the most flies.

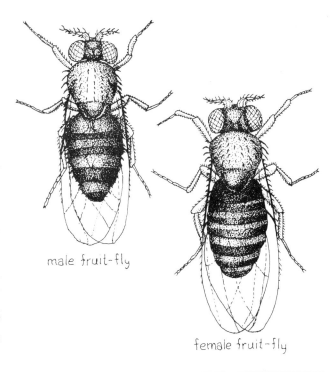

male fruit-fly

female fruit-fly

# GROWING WILD FLOWERS, TREES AND SHRUBS

Many wild plants are relatively easy to grow and a number of wild flowers can now be bought as seeds or potted plants from garden centres. Seeds can be sprinkled in rows in the garden or in a seedbox and planted out once they have germinated. Follow the directions on the seed packet carefully as many wild seeds need special treatment before they are sown. Some wild plants are very difficult to grow. Wild orchids, for example, with their complicated life cycles, are almost impossible for professionals to grow, so attempts by the amateur hobbyist are very likely to fail. Even the common hawthorn needs special attention for successful germination.

Seeds of oak, field maple and horse chestnut can be planted directly into soil-filled plant pots where they will germinate the following spring. Keep them in the pots, remembering to water them, for the first year and plant them out the second year. Most other trees and bushes need to be 'stratified'. This can be done in a biscuit tin or cocoa tin. Pierce holes in the bottom and sides of the tin and add a layer of gravel about 1cm (½in) deep. Mix the seeds thinly in moist sand and put them in the tin, finally covering them with another 1cm (½in) of gravel. Cover the tin with wire netting to keep out mice and bury the tin almost up to the top in the garden. Keep the sand moist and check the tin occasionally to make sure that none of the seeds have sprouted. If they have, plant them immediately. Most of the seeds will germinate between fourteen and eighteen months after sowing, so they will generally be ready for planting out in the *second* spring after collection.

An easier but very messy way of getting seed ready for planting without such a long wait is to search for bird droppings. As the seeds pass through the birds' guts the digestive juices break the seeds' dormancy and they will then grow the following spring.

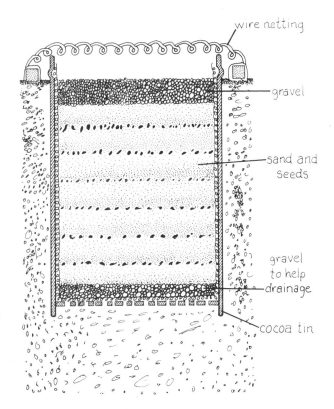

wire netting

gravel

sand and seeds

gravel to help drainage

cocoa tin

# SEED DISPERSAL

A seed is the source of a plant's next generation so the dispersal of seeds to places where they are likely to grow is of great importance to all plants. Plants with only short lives or plants which grow in disturbed ground and are soon squeezed out by more vigorous competitors have to produce lots of seed in a very short time. Their seeds also have to travel a very long way to find the often rare habitat that suits them. Large, long-lived plants, such as trees, dominate the plant community and generally have plenty of time to produce seed. There are always exceptions to these rules but the following simple experiment will show just how different and effective are plants' methods of dispersal.

To start with, collect the seeds of oak or horse chestnut, ash or sycamore, and thistle or dandelion. You can try other seeds later. Stand on a low wall, hold one of the seeds in your hand raised high over your head, let it go and measure how far each seed travels from where you are standing. Now repeat this with all the seeds you have collected. Try the experiment on a still day and again on a windy day and compare the results. As another experiment, cut off the wings of the ash or sycamore seeds and the 'down' of the thistle or dandelion and compare the results with those you got from the uncut seeds.

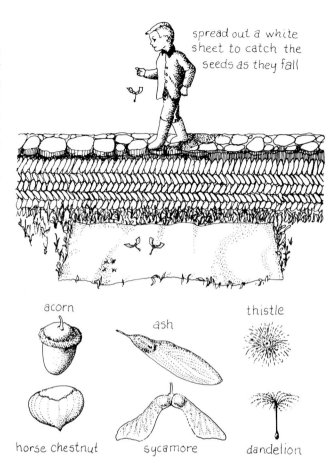

spread out a white sheet to catch the seeds as they fall

acorn
horse chestnut
ash
sycamore
thistle
dandelion

# MAKING A TREE TRANSECT

A transect is a strip of vegetation chosen for study. It is a very simple way of recording changes among plants and trees in woods, hedgerows and ditches.

A transect must be made in a straight line. Over short distances a long tape measure – 20m (60ft) if you can get one – can be used but over longer distances it is more difficult to keep the transect in a straight line. One simple way of getting over this problem is by the use of three white-painted poles (broomsticks or garden canes). Stick pole No. 1 in the ground at your chosen starting point then line up the other two poles behind the first about 20m (60ft) apart. Tie a string or tape between pole No. 1 and pole No. 2. Begin your study and when you reach pole No. 2 untie the tape or string from pole No. 1 and tie it round pole No. 3, at the same time moving pole No. 1 to a position 20m (60ft) beyond pole No. 3. In this way you will be able to keep a straight line for a surprisingly long way.

For a woodland transect measure the distance between trees or shrubs that touch your string or tape or lie within 2m (6ft) of the *right hand* side of it. At the same time measure the height and girth and note any other special features about the trees. Do the same transect again after a few years and you will be surprised at the changes.

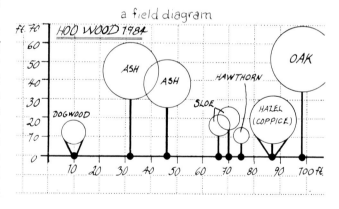

a field diagram

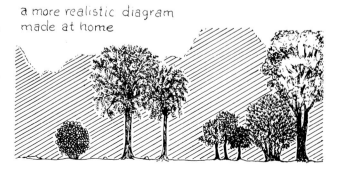

a more realistic diagram made at home

# MEASURING THE HEIGHT OF A TREE

To measure the height of a tree all you need is a ruler marked in inches with a deep notch at the 1-inch mark and a friend to help you. Hold the ruler upright in front of you with your arm outstretched and move backwards until you can line up the distant tree exactly between the '0' and '12' on the ruler. Get your friend to stand beside the tree and move his hand up the trunk. Guide him so that he marks the spot which exactly matches the notch on your ruler. Now measure the distance in inches from the ground below the tree to the mark your friend made on the tree. The number of inches measured will correspond exactly to the height of the tree in feet. For example, if the point your friend marked was 20 inches from the ground, that tree would be 20ft tall.

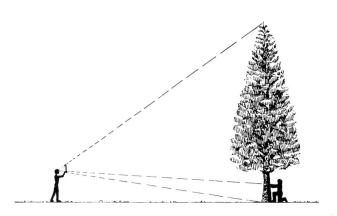

# HOW OLD IS THAT HEDGEROW?

Hedgerows were not planted very much in Britain until the seventeenth century when landowners enclosed land to make small fields on which to graze sheep. Most of our hedgerows then are no more than a few hundred years old, but some do date back to Saxon and Norman times when hedges were planted to mark parish boundaries and trackways. These hedgerows may be many hundreds of years old. It has been discovered that as a general rule a hedge will gain one species of tree, shrub or woody climber for each hundred years of its life, so finding out the age of a hedge is quite easy.

Measure out a 30-metre (100ft) stretch of hedgerow and count the number of species of trees and shrubs present – including bramble and dog-rose. If there are three species your hedge may be 300 years old; if there are seven it could be 700–800 years old. This method is not completely accurate because some new hedges were planted with lots of species. If you find what looks like a very old hedge go to your local library and look at old maps to see whether your hedge was on the map a hundred or more years ago.

# ADOPT-A-TREE

Trees are disappearing from our countryside at an alarming rate. Hedgerows with their occasional tall trees are being grubbed up to make bigger fields. The hedges that remain are often so closely trimmed that no young saplings are able to grow through to make the tall trees of the future. Dutch elm disease has killed elm trees and has changed the face of the countryside in many parts of Britain. Not all farmers and landowners are prepared to see our trees vanish forever though. Some would like your help to encourage young saplings to grow. This is a project that you or your school could do to help replace our lost trees.

If you live in the country contact a local farmer or explain your project to the National Farmers' Union and see if there is a farmer in your area prepared to help. You need a farmer who would be willing to leave some saplings when he trims his hedges. You will need to choose the young trees and mark them with brightly-coloured tape so that they can be easily identified. This will prevent their being cut down when the farmer trims the hedge each year. The saplings will need to be checked and new tape attached regularly until they are large enough not to be at risk of accidentally being cut down. Choose young, strong saplings which are rooted firmly in the bottom of the hedge and trim off any side shoots with secateurs. As the trees grow keep them free of choking weeds and climbing plants and measure them regularly to see how fast they grow in both height and girth around their trunks.

If you live in a city or town ask your local council to let trees grow on waste ground or get their permission to plant groups of trees yourself. If they are close to your home or school you can keep them watered in summer and make sure that they stay tied firmly to their supporting stakes until they are well established.

# MAKING A POND

Ponds are not only good for aquatic life, they also attract birds and sometimes mammals. They can easily be made in your own back garden or in your school grounds. It doesn't matter if the pond is rambling, overgrown and informal, or decorative, neat and formal – each type will contain a lot of wildlife, though an informal pond will usually harbour a greater variety of plants and animals. A pond can be large or small, but small ponds, while easier to make, are liable to freeze in the winter, possibly damaging the lining. In summer the water in small ponds becomes very warm, making it difficult for some creatures to survive. About 1.8m (6ft) across is the minimum practical size.

A good wildlife pond should have gently-sloping sides so that animals such as frogs, toads and newts can climb out without difficulty. It should also have a base of varying depth to suit the greatest range of plant and animal life. The pond should be sited away from trees as their shade can prevent many aquatic plants from growing and their leaves soon clog it up and cause it to become de-oxygenated.

## BUILDING THE POND

Ready-made fibreglass ponds in many different shapes and sizes can be bought from garden centres but if you want to design your own or to make it fit into a particular site then a plastic-lined pond is the simplest to make. The other alternative, a concrete pond, is very difficult and very expensive to build.

With a fibreglass pond all that needs to be done is to dig a hole the size and shape of the pond you have bought. Pack down the earth in the hole to prevent movement later and bed the pond on a layer of loose soil or sand. It is obviously very important to get the pond level.

A plastic-lined pond needs a little more work. With this type it is essential to level the ground around it. As with the fibreglass pond, dig out the shape of the pond but this time also remove any stones sticking out from the base or sides that might tear the plastic lining. Laying strips of carpet around the base of the hole helps prevent tears caused by stones working their way to the surface later. Spread the plastic sheet over the hole and fill it with water. This will form the plastic into the shape of your pond and it will also reveal any leaks and tears in the sheet which can be repaired before you go any further. Put stones or turf on the edge of the sheet to anchor it. Empty out the water – this will remove any toxic chemicals which might have been on the plastic sheet. Once empty, cover the base of the pond with a layer of fine soil and it is then ready to stock.

## STOCKING THE POND

Put aquatic plants into the pond before it is refilled with water. Most plants can be grown in baskets which also makes them easier to control and move around if necessary. Tie submerged aquatics in a bundle weighted with a stone. Most garden centres and often pet shops stock a range of suitable native plants.

Allow the pond to settle for a week or two before adding any pond animals. A pond will quickly colonise naturally but you can help things along by putting straw in the water or by adding buckets of mud from local ponds. Other special plants or animals can be added at any time when you find or capture them.

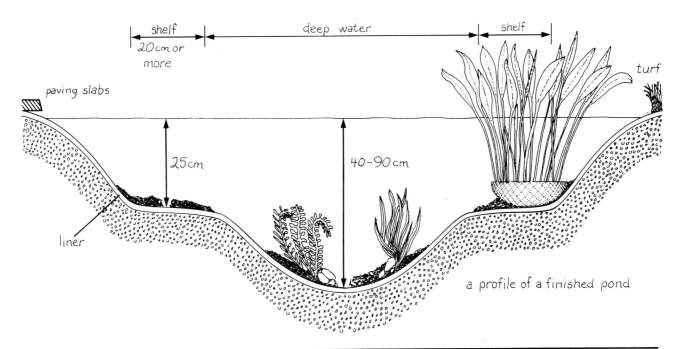

shelf
20cm or more

deep water

shelf

turf

paving slabs

25cm

40-90 cm

liner

a profile of a finished pond

---

# PLASTIC EMBEDDING

Plastic embedding is a craft process involving covering an object in liquid plastic and leaving it to harden. Almost anything can be embedded and the resulting 'casts' of plants, flowers, insects, shells or pebbles can be very attractive and informative. Once embedded, or cast, a specimen can be viewed from any angle through the clear plastic and the most delicate specimens are protected and will survive any amount of rough handling. Some disadvantages of the process are that care and skill are needed in the casting of biological specimens and it is difficult to cast very large objects, but these problems can be overcome with practice. As a craft, plastic embedding has gained in popularity in recent years and kits with full instructions are available from most craft shops.

Plastic embedding involves three basic steps:

## 1. PREPARATION OF THE SPECIMEN
All objects must be thoroughly cleaned and wiped over with a solvent to help the plastic stick to the surface. Plants and insects need a little more preparation. Plants must be dried out completely before embedding. Surround them with equal parts of silica gel and salt in a suitable container and seal it up. Leave it for a minimum of 24–48 hours. If the plant is fleshy drying may take up to a week. This technique also preserves the colour of flowers and leaves.

Insects need to be fixed in a natural position. Pin freshly-dead specimens on to a cork board until they harden. If the insect has already hardened in an unnatural position it can be 'relaxed' by brushing on some relaxing fluid (see page 183) before pinning it on to the board. Wash specimens in acetone before embedding to make the plastic stick.

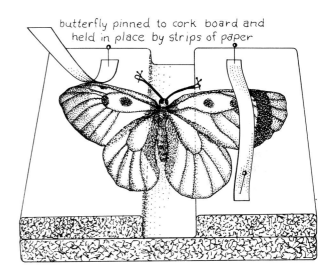

butterfly pinned to cork board and held in place by strips of paper

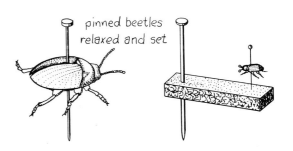

pinned beetles relaxed and set

## 2. SELECT A SUITABLE MOULD
Ceramic moulds can be obtained from craft shops, though aluminium tubes and pottery moulds can be used. Never use glass. Wipe the mould with wax before you begin.

### 3. MAKING THE CAST

Pour a thin layer of plastic into the mould and let it harden. Lay the specimen on this layer and then carefully pour on more plastic. If the object is large you may need to pour the plastic on in several layers to prevent distortion and to stop bubbles forming. If you pour the plastic gently down the stirring rod into the mould this will also help to eliminate bubbles.

Once your cast has hardened tap it out of its mould and polish it with a soft cloth. Casts of plants and insects make very attractive paper weights as well as providing a permanent record of your 'finds'.

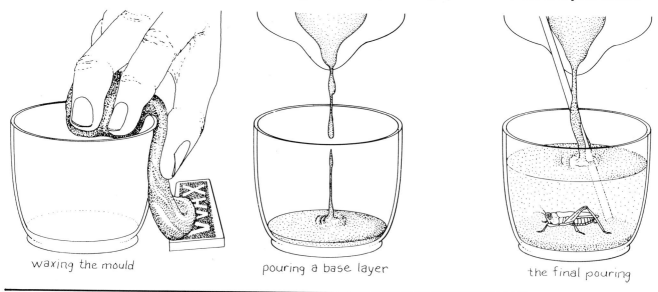

waxing the mould

pouring a base layer

the final pouring

# MAKING A DISTRIBUTION MAP

If you spend a lot of time in the countryside it is a good idea to keep a notebook or diary. List and describe the things you find and when and where you found them. It's surprising how much you can forget if you do not write it down. Note down sightings of plants and animals and eventually you might be able to make a map of their distribution in your area. Moles and rabbits are easy animals to start with.

Draw or trace a map of your area and draw a grid over it like that on an Ordnance Survey map. Mark your sightings with a dot. Then look at your notes and an Ordnance Survey map. Do all the sightings occur in woodland? Are they all in fields? Is there water nearby? You will soon discover all sorts of fascinating things about the plants and animals you record and where are the best places to find them.

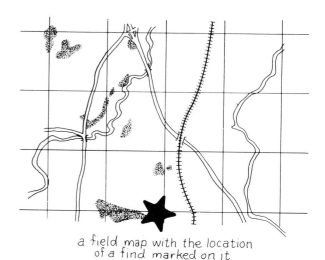

a field map with the location of a find marked on it

# SUPPLIERS

## INVERTEBRATE SUPPLIES

Butterfly Farm (Christchurch),
14 Grove Road East,
Christchurch,
Dorset BH23 2DQ
Butterfly and moth eggs and
pupae, and rearing cages.

E. W. Classy Ltd,
P.O. Box 93,
Faringdon,
Oxon SN7 7DR
New and second-hand natural
history books. Specialists in
insect and other invertebrate
books.

Hampshire Micro,
3 Southlea,
Cliddesden,
Basingstoke,
Hants RG25 2JN
Microscopes and accessories.

Watkins and Doncaster,
Four Throws,
Hawkhurst,
Kent TN18 5ED
Suppliers of microscopes, light
traps, nets, breeding cages,
relaxing fluid and accessories.

Worldwide Butterflies Ltd,
Compton House,
Sherborne,
Dorset.
Suppliers of butterfly and moth
eggs and pupae. Also free-flying,
walk-through butterfly cases and
a silk farm.

## MAMMAL SUPPLIES

J. Barbour and Son Ltd,
Simonside,
South Shields,
Tyne and Wear NE34 9PD
Suppliers of robust all-weather
clothing.

Longworth Scientific
   Instruments,
Radley Road,
Abingdon,
Berks.
Suppliers of Longworth small
mammal live-traps.

The Mammal Society,
Harvest House,
62 London Road,
Reading,
Berks RG1 5AS
Membership is open to anyone
interested in the study of
mammals. Suppliers of a wide
range of advisory and
informative literature on
mammals.

Watkins and Doncaster,
Four Throws,
Hawkhurst,
Kent TN18 5ED
Suppliers of Longworth small
mammal live-traps and
taxidermy equipment.

# WILDLIFE and THE LAW

The Wildlife and Countryside Act 1981* has brought together all the previous laws and Acts of Parliament concerning wildlife into one comprehensive document. Anyone who spends any time in the countryside ought to be aware of the law and anyone intending to collect specimens MUST be aware of the law. Under the new Act many species have been given total protection and apparently innocent actions could result in prosecution.

## ACCESS TO THE COUNTRYSIDE

There is no general right of access to the countryside. With few exceptions all land in Britain has an owner and unless the owner gives permission you have no right of entry. Even in the National Parks access has, in many places, had to have been sanctioned by the landowner. Even so, large areas may be closed to the public from time to time, as in the case of grouse moors during the shooting season.

However, there are two peculiarly British institutions that do give us access to the countryside: footpaths and commons. Footpaths give everyone the right to traverse a stretch of land *on foot* without obstruction or hindrance. The law requires a landowner with a footpath crossing his land to maintain stiles and gates along the footpath and prevent any obstruction of the path. Once you are on a footpath you must stick to it, even if it means trampling through a field of crops. Unless you have been given permission to do so by the owner, skirting round the edge of the field to avoid damaging the crop is actually an act of trespass. If on your rambles you discover a footpath has been blocked off or obstructed do check with you local council offices that it hasn't been deregistered before you charge on to the land to claim your 'rights'.

The law concerning access to common land is very complicated but be sure of one thing – the word 'common' does not mean you have the right to do what you like on common land. On most commons there are restrictions on access by motor vehicles, the use of guns, the extent of grazing and a prohibition on camping. On many commons the public have an unrestricted right of access on foot but there are also commons where public access is denied altogether.

* An explanatory booklet about the Wildlife and Countryside Act can be obtained from Interpretative Branch, Nature Conservancy Council, Attingham Park, Shrewsbury SY4 4TW.

## DOGS IN THE COUNTRYSIDE

The Wildlife and Countryside Act has considerably toughened up the laws concerning dogs and livestock. It is now an offence to allow a dog to enter a field containing sheep unless it is on a lead. If a dog is not on a lead and roaming among sheep then it can be shot by the owner of the sheep *whether or not it is worrying the sheep*. The situation on commons and public open spaces where sheep graze is a little more confusing but generally in these places a dog need not be on a lead but must be under control. That is, it must be kept at heel or called in when sheep are about. If it worries the sheep then it can be shot.

## GUNS IN THE COUNTRYSIDE

It is against the law to carry a gun, loaded or unloaded, on private land without permission, or to carry an uncovered gun in a public place without permission. Where permission is given you cannot shoot within 15m (50ft) of a public highway, road, public park or public open space.

It is against the law to receive or possess an air gun if you are under 14 years of age or to carry an uncovered gun in a public place if you are under 17 years old. You must have a Shot Gun Certificate obtained from the police before you can own, buy or sell a shotgun.

It is against the law to shoot any protected bird or other animal or to shoot any unprotected bird or animal without permission from the landowner.

## WILD FLOWERS AND FRUIT

It is not an offence to pick wild flowers unless they are on the protected list of the Wildlife and Countryside Act BUT it *is* an offence to enter private land to pick wild flowers without permission of the landowner. It is also an offence to dig up or remove *any* wild plant without the landowner's permission and this includes plants on roadside verges. The picking or removal of fruit without the landowner's consent is also an offence but there is no restriction on gathering fruit from roadside verges.

## BATS

*All* British bats are now protected. The alarming drop in their numbers has been attributed to the now widespread practice of treating roof timbers with insecticides and preservatives. If you need to carry out work in your loft, or discover bats roosting in a tree you wish to fell then you *must* immediately contact your local Nature Conservancy Council office who will advise you on what action to take.

## BIRDS

Except for game birds and certain species of birds described as 'pests' under the Wildlife and Countryside Act, all birds, their nests and eggs are protected by law. It is an offence to take a bird's egg from a nest or even to take an egg from a deserted nest. It is also an offence to own, buy, sell or exchange birds' eggs unless you have a licence from the Nature Conservancy Council.

Keeping wild birds in captivity is illegal but it is permissible to keep and care for an injured wild bird so long as it is returned to the wild as soon as it can fend for itself.

## PHOTOGRAPHY OF BIRDS

It is now an offence to disturb by photography, on or near the nest, any birds specially listed in the Wildlife and Countryside Act unless you have a licence from the Nature Conservancy Council. Unlisted birds may be photographed at the nest but be fair to the bird and cause as little disturbance as possible.

# THE COUNTRY CODE

When in the country always follow these rules
- Guard against fires
- Fasten all gates
- Keep dogs under proper control
- Keep to footpaths
- Avoid damaging fences, hedges and walls
- Leave no litter
- Safeguard water supplies
- Protect wildlife
- Take care on country roads
- Respect the life of the countryside

# GLOSSARY

**ARABLE** (LAND)  Land that is ploughed.

**ARACHNID**  An arthropod, such as a spider or scorpion, with four pairs of legs.

**ARTHROPOD**  A creature with an exoskeleton, segmented body and jointed legs.

**ARID**  Dry and barren.

**BACTERIA**  Microscopic one-celled plants.

**BARBEL**  A projecting feeler on the jaws of certain fishes.

**BIVALVE**  An animal with a hinged double shell.

**BROADLEAVED**  A general term used to describe trees such as oak, ash, etc., to distinguish them from the narrow-leaved conifers.

**BRACKISH** (WATER)  A mixture of fresh and salt water.

**BRASSICA**  A plant of the cabbage family.

**CANOPY**  The leafy top of a tree.

**CARNIVORE**  A creature that eats meat, for example a lion.

**CARR**  A waterlogged woodland at the edge of a body of fresh water.

**CELLULOSE**  The structural material of the cell walls in plants.

**CONIFEROUS**  A general term used to describe trees with sharp, narrow leaves, which are usually evergreen. Their seeds are carried in cones.

**COPPICE**  A group of trees cut down to ground level at regular intervals and left to resprout. This is called coppicing.

**COPSE**  A small wood or coppice.

**CRUSTACEAN**  A creature, such as a crab or shrimp, which has a hard crust or shell. They are generally sea-dwellers.

**CULL**  To selectively kill animals, for example deer and seals, to reduce their numbers.

**DECIDUOUS**  A term describing trees or shrubs which shed their leaves annually at the end of the growing season.

**DEFOLIATE**  To strip of leaves.

**DESICCATE**  To dry out.

**DORSAL**  Of the back (for example, the dorsal fin of fishes is along the back).

**DREY**  The nest of a squirrel.

**EPIPHYTE**  A plant attached to another plant.

**EXOSKELETON**  A skeleton covering the outside of the body, or situated in the skin.

**FAECES**  Waste products of digestion expelled from the body.

**FOETUS**  The young of a mammal developing in the womb.

**FOSSIL**  The remains of a plant or animal from the distant past which has been preserved in rock.

**GIZZARD**  A bird's second stomach, where food is ground up.

**HAEMOGLOBIN**  A substance containing iron, which is found in red blood cells.

**HERBIVORE**  A plant eater, for example a cow.

**HONEYDEW**  A sugary secretion given off by aphids (greenfly or blackfly).

**HYBRID**  An offspring resulting from cross-breeding of two different species.

**INSECTIVORE**  A mammal that eats insects, for example a shrew.

**LARVA**  The immature state of many insects, seen as caterpillars, grubs, etc. (Plural LARVAE.)

**LICHEN**  A plant found on rocks or trees which is a combination of an alga and a fungus.

**MOLLUSC**  An invertebrate with a muscular foot and often a shell (snails, slugs, etc. are molluscs).

**MYXOMATOSIS**  A serious virus infection of rabbits.

**OMNIVOROUS**  Able to eat all kinds of food. Man is omnivorous.

**OXIDATION**  Combining of oxygen with another chemical element.

**PARASITE**  A creature or plant living in or on another and taking nourishment from its host.

**PASSERINE**  Generally, one of a group of small perching birds which includes sparrows.

**PELVIC**  Relating to the pelvis, the girdle of bone in vertebrates to which the legs are attached. Also refers to the fins of fishes which are under the body.

**PERMEABLE**  Having the ability to allow substances (such as air or water) to pass through.

**POLYGAMOUS**  Having more than one mate at the same time.

**PROBOSCIS**  The long mouth part of some insects, used for probing deep into flowers to reach the nectar.

**PUPA**  The stage between the larva and the adult insect when the larva is enclosed in a hard shell. (Plural PUPAE.)

**QUARTER** (verb)  To range in all directions.

**RAPTOR**  A bird of prey such as an eagle, kestrel, etc.

**RECURVED**  Bent backwards.

**REGURGITATE**  To bring back what has been swallowed.

**SCAVENGER**  A creature which feeds on dead organic material.

**SCRAPE** (noun)  A small hollow in the ground.

**SEDENTARY**  Remaining in the same place, not active.

**SPAWN**  The mass of eggs deposited by fish, amphibians, etc.

**STAGNANT**  Describing a body of still water, which is often foul.

**STAND**  A group of plants growing together.

**STEPPES**  The vast, treeless plains in Asia and south-eastern Europe.

**SUCCULENT**  Full of juice or sap; plants with thick, fleshy leaves or stems.

**SWARD**  An expanse of land covered in short-cropped grass.

**TORPOR**  A dormant, sluggish state.

# INDEX

*Page numbers in italic indicate an illustration.*

# INDEX